Portrait of a Profession

PORTRAIT OF A PROFESSION
Teaching and Teachers in the 21st Century

Edited by David M. Moss,
Wendy J. Glenn and Richard L. Schwab

Educate US
David Gerwin and Terry A. Osborn, Series Editors

Westport, Connecticut
London

Library of Congress Cataloging-in-Publication Data

Portrait of a profession : teaching and teachers in the 21st century / edited by David M. Moss, Wendy J. Glenn, and Richard L. Schwab.
     p. cm.—(Educate US; ISSN 1551-0425)
    Includes bibliographical references and index.
    ISBN 0-275-98218-1 (alk. paper)
    1. Teaching—United States—Philosophy. 2. Education—Aims and objectives—United States. 3. School improvement programs—United States. I. Moss, David M. II. Glenn, Wendy J., 1970– III. Schwab, Richard Lewis. IV. Title.
    LB1025.3.P68 2005
    371.1—dc22   2004017674

British Library Cataloguing in Publication Data is available.

Library of Congress Catalog Card Number: 2004017674
ISBN: 0-275-98218-1
ISSN: 1551-0425

First published in 2005

Praeger Publishers, 88 Post Road West, Westport, CT 06881
An imprint of Greenwood Publishing Group, Inc.
www.praeger.com

Printed in the United States of America

The paper used in this book complies with the Permanent Paper Standard issued by the National Information Standards Organization (Z39.48-1984).

10 9 8 7 6 5 4 3 2 1

Dedicated to

My wife, Korina, whose love and support have made all the difference—D.M.

Martin, Miranda, and Shelby Glenn whose laughter and zest for life sustain me each day—W.G.

My family that supports a very busy husband and dad: my wife, Kristin, and my children, Garrett and Emily—R.S.

Contents

Illustrations

Figures

Tables

Series Foreword

It is a rare week in which an issue in education fails to make headlines in the United States. Parents, policymakers, educators, and taxpayers have a stake in the developments regarding schools and schooling. Though the public is increasingly sophisticated in its understanding of certain aspects of education, popular media venues offer little opportunity for an in-depth treatment of the relevant points related to the vital decisions that are made in boardrooms, classrooms, homes, and voting booths. *Educate US* is a series presenting a comprehensive discussion of issues in a forum that minimizes technical jargon as it explores the various facets of the problems and potential in U.S. education. The authors and contributors to this series are those whose concerns about the health and welfare of education in the United States are translated into activism. Scholarship is not merely about the gaining of expertise; it includes an inherent component of advocacy. The nature of education in a democracy requires one to take a well-advised position and then let one's voice be heard. This activity is at least as important as—in many ways so much more vital than—the technical aspects of the scholar's craft.

Scholars have dedicated their lives, often, to the study of a field in what is mistakenly referred to as the "life of the mind." Though intellectual work certainly requires much mental preparation and discipline, its effects are rarely limited to the realm of thought. Perhaps this is never truer than in the field of teacher education. Professors D. M. Moss, W. J. Glenn, and R. L. Schwab bring to the series a fitting genesis in their scholarly conversations presented in this text about preparing the next generation of teachers. They set the stage in terms of historical and cultural contexts within which we endeavor in contemporary practice and explore some of the pressing issues of today. They show us that teaching is much more complex than a sound bite can depict and, in many ways, is much less transparent than we may believe. In short, the editors provide us with an insider's look at some of those less visible aspects.

The editors and contributors fulfill the more ambitious goals of the series, expanding the dialogue to include all of us who, as participants in a democracy, must make reasoned choices when we elect officials, support causes, and together shape the future of public education. Make no mistake, the world of public schooling, as is true for our democracy, is not a fait accompli. We make and remake our future collectively every day.

To participate in a meaningful and beneficial way, therefore, we all must recognize that, deeper than questions of election year politics and slogans, many decisions regarding education are essentially moral in nature. Choices that seem expedient or fit ideologically charged models designed to appeal to the masses may nevertheless be harmful to our society and, ultimately, our children. If *Educate US* convinces series readers to weigh choices in that vein, it will have achieved its purpose. Living in a time of daily concerns related to homeland security and numerous wars, we would do well to remember the words of Mark Twain, "It is curious—curious that physical courage should be so common in the world, and moral courage so rare." Curious, indeed.

Professor Terry A. Osborn, Series Editor

Acknowledgments

We are grateful to many who contributed ideas and advice as we formulated this book. Our colleagues and friends in the Neag School comprise a wonderful and supportive group of scholars with whom it is an honor to serve and teach. In particular, we acknowledge the support of Professors Casey Cobb, Millie Goil, Doug Kaufman, and Terry Osborn. In addition, our teacher education partners in our Professional Development Schools have provided us with enthusiasm for this project. Marie Ellen Larcada, Elizabeth Potenza, and all of the professionals at Greenwood Press have been helpful in navigating the particulars of this publication. Finally, we wish to thank all of our great teachers over the years—there are too many to name, yet all have served as countless sources of inspiration.

Introduction

The complexity of teaching, including the perception of conflicting academic and moral dimensions, is the basis for widespread disagreement concerning the responsibilities of teachers. As such, teachers are often marginalized as mere technicians and offered little autonomy or respect. The reconceptualization of teaching as a true profession is a fundamental precursor for educational reform. There is no single element of schooling as important as teachers. All children in America's classrooms deserve nothing less than a well-prepared and caring professional who has the knowledge base and power to ensure that they reach their full potential. The contributors to this book are pro-teacher, pro-student, and pro-reform and, thus, unwavering in their support of public education.

Our agenda is explicit, and we make no pretense regarding the urgent need to translate ideas into action. Acknowledging the inadequacies and achievements of the previous century with regard to how teachers were prepared and supported, this book provides a timely portrait of the profession. Although the calendar connotes that we are in the inaugural years of a new millennium, the dawning of a new era for education will materialize only if the numerous stakeholders of education identify education as vital to the very notion of a free and open society. As seen in this book, we have made progress toward this aim, yet there is much work to be done.

In our Chapter 1, "In Search of a Profession: A History of American Teachers," Kate Rousmaniere debunks the notion of a golden age of education and paints a portrait of teaching in America as one riddled with political, social, and philosophical strife. Making use of primary source material, yet writing through a lens of today, she frames her discussion around four time periods: The Colonial and Revolutionary period (1600–1800), the Common School Era (1800–1880), the Progressive Era (1880–1930), and the Modern Era (1930–present). She concludes that, historically, teachers have been entrusted not only with the academic education of American youth, but with great social and moral responsibility as well. This tension persists today.

In Chapter 2, "Teacher Preparation—Transition and Turmoil," Michael Andrew examines an often overlooked dimension to teaching—the evolution of teacher preparation in the United States. Building upon the history of American teachers discussed in the first chapter, his focus is on the search for an elusive knowledge base necessary to advance teaching as a profession. Incorporating a strong research-based perspective, he concludes that teacher education is in turmoil and that radical changes are needed to move beyond the mediocrity common to many programs in existence today. Specific recommendations are made for the reform of teacher preparation in hopes of closing the door to the profession to those who are unprepared for the classroom.

Building upon the first two chapters, Chapter 3, "Teachers as Leaders, Teachers as Researchers, Teachers Who Care: The University of Connecticut's Journey," by Wendy Glenn, David Moss, Douglas Kaufman, Kay Norlander-Case, Charles Case, and Robert Lonning, chronicles the development of a nationally recognized teacher education program. Known for not only preparing excellent teachers, but also having those teachers remain in the profession, this innovative program is underpinned by key tenets such as a strong liberal arts background, a common core of learning and subject-specific pedagogy, varied and long-term work in schools, and a commitment to inquiry and reflection. This chapter offers a year-by-year insiders' look at this model of teacher preparation and chronicles what it takes to become a caring and competent educator.

A glimpse into the daily realities of three professional teachers is offered in Chapter 4, "Walk a Mile in Their Shoes: A Day in the Life of Professional Educators," by David Moss with Shirley Reilly, Christopher Burdman, and Sayward Parsons. These teachers share brief narratives that both discuss their work over the course a school day and provide insight into their thinking through reflective commentary. Common themes, such as professional autonomy and time, meeting the needs of diverse learners, professional development, and the hidden responsibilities of teaching, are embedded within each of the elementary, middle, and high school vignettes. The knowledge base and emotional toll required of great teachers become readily apparent as readers look in on their everyday work.

In Chapter 5, "Key Challenges for Teachers: Windows into the Complexity of American Classrooms," John Settlage and Karl Wheatley make use of various perspectives, including the practical, political, and personal as windows into the complexities of the profession. Their in-depth discussion of six challenges of teaching, including the challenges of teaching anyone anything, deciding what to teach, teaching what you decide to teach, teaching each and every student, doing "unnatural" things, and teaching day after day, builds upon the glimpse into the profession provided in the previous chapter. They conclude that helping all children reach their greatest potential is of primary import and that such a vital aim can be realized only if the general public is aware of the nuances and intricacies of teaching and is willing to support the profession and its professionals.

Focusing on two key challenges to the profession, Allen Glenn authors Chapter 6, "Technology and Professional Development." The notions of technology and professional development are portrayed as inexorably linked and fundamental to the reform of the profession. In today's classrooms, both teacher and student must *learn to use* new technologies and also *use them to learn*. The latter poses significant challenges that may require a rethinking of how technologies and schools interface. New technologies will enhance learning opportunities and enrich learning experiences for students only if sustained, meaningful professional development is available and offered in innovative ways that meet the needs of the professional.

Chapter 7, " 'Highly Qualified' " Teachers and the Teaching Profession: Policy Lessons from the Field," authored by Barnett Berry, Mandy Hoke, and Eric Hirsch, explores the impact of policy making on teachers and the teaching profession. Noting that teachers themselves are key to fostering student achievement, the reality that educational reform remains driven by curriculum mandates and high-stakes testing is brought into question. The authors conclude that the impetus needed to improve the teaching profession will not stem from current federal legislation and that the real, and substantially more complex, definition of a "highly qualified" teacher extends well beyond the federal definition. Without adequate resources, ensuring a caring, competent, and qualified teacher for each child will remain an elusive goal.

In Chapter 8, "What's Next? Challenges and Opportunities Facing Teachers and the Teaching Profession," David Moss and Wendy Glenn respond to two timely and critical questions designed to give each author an opportunity to offer further perspectives on the future of education: What forces will shape the teaching profession over the next decade? What qualities will teachers need to possess to meet the demands of the profession in the twenty-first century? The heart-felt, and sometimes controversial, responses offer a summative dimension by reinforcing the common themes found throughout the book.

Together, these chapters offer a portrait of a profession with great promise not yet realized. There exist today discrete pockets of reform-minded, dedicated individuals working tirelessly toward change. The welfare of each and every child, and, collectively, our society, serves as their motivation. By and large, however, much of the day-to-day happenings in education, for better or worse, remain invisible to most citizens. Perhaps this lack of awareness is merely the result of a preponderance of benign neglect. Regardless, the time is long past due for education to be considered *the* top priority of our nation. It is public education that has the single utmost potential to serve as a catalyst for change that will result in equitable and prosperous opportunities for all.

Professor David M. Moss, Editor

In Search of a Profession: A History of American Teachers

Kate Rousmaniere

Americans like to hold a vision of a "golden age" of education, when teaching was a noble and valued profession, children were well behaved and attentive, and educational objectives were clear and simple. Such a golden age never existed, as any study of the history of education immediately shows. The history of teaching in America is a history rife with political dynamics, social drama, and philosophical debate. It is also a history of a class of workers struggling with economic insecurity and social ambiguity while at the same time striving for their own understanding of professional excellence. Teaching is a unique occupation that encompasses a range of dichotomies: Teaching is highly regulated, even as teachers work under fairly autonomous working conditions; teachers hold social prestige even as they have little cultural authority and reap few economic rewards; teaching is based on a select body of professional knowledge, yet teachers are subject to the control of citizens who have none of that expertise; and teachers are idealized as the social caretakers of children and simultaneously denunciated for being anti-intellectual. All of these tensions have roots in the historical origins of the profession.

One theme encapsulates the complex history of the work of public school teachers in the United States. As public education developed and expanded, increased expectations were placed on teachers at the same time that the economic insecurity and ambiguous professional identity of teachers remained static.

Historians generally divide their study of American education into four time periods: The Colonial and Revolutionary period (1600–1800), the Common School Era (1800–1880), the Progressive Era (1880–1930) and the Modern Era (1930–present). Such a structure is useful for a study of American teachers as well, since the development of teaching as an occupation is interwoven with the historical development of American schooling at large.

It is instructive to note that the written history of education has generally excluded the history of classroom teachers. Historians of education have tended to focus on the institutional development of American education systems and on shifts in educational philosophy, curriculum, and policy, rather than on the day-to-day experiences of children and teachers in the past or on the development of teaching as an occupation. The exclusion of teachers from these narratives speaks to the ambiguous condition of teaching as an occupation both in the past and in the present. As school reformers and policy makers have designed American education, they have generally ignored the effect of their proposals on classroom teachers' work in schools. Visions of educational excellence have been spun without much regard to the way in which such visions might materialize in the classroom, and teachers have traditionally been left facing the burden of implementing such expectations. A history of teaching offers a view of how schools have actually worked in the past (as opposed to how reformers *hoped* they would work) and highlights the gaps or fissures between educational expectations and educational reality. In this section, I offer a broad survey of the institutional context of teachers' work in four historical periods, drawing on illustrative examples of teachers' practices and lives.

THE COLONIAL AND REVOLUTIONARY PERIOD (1600–1800)

From the moment Europeans first settled in the new world, they focused on methods of affirming and replicating their own cultural values. Education was introduced across the colonies as a deliberate attempt to transplant European customs and institutions among settlers in the New World. In New England, the antecedent to formal schooling was first established with the schooling law of 1642. Puritan settlers were particularly concerned about how illiteracy would allow "that olde deluder Satan" to take over the hearts and minds of colonial children. The instruction of religious and cultural values was thus a core purpose of early schooling.

In spite of such concerns, colonial schooling remained a largely unregulated and eclectic operation, available only to young white children and older white boys. Schooling was largely a private operation and took the form of church schools, private academies, tutoring, and informal homeschooling. Dame schools—which were small home-based academies for young children staffed by mothers and widows—offered the only teaching opportunities for women, whose own educational and professional aspirations were sharply circumscribed.

Well through the American Revolution, there was no formal academic preparation for teaching, and teachers were chosen not for any instructional skills, but for their religious background, moral character, and political affinity with the family or community that hired them. Outside of the dame schools, the typical teacher was a young, single, itinerant male who taught for about two years before he moved into a more stable career of ministry or law.

Although state school laws of the late seventeenth century, particularly in New England, provided a financial structure for what became known as district schools, colonial teachers' wages and working conditions were haphazard. Teachers usually boarded with families, thereby cutting the community's costs. Payment was based on what the community could afford, and rural teachers were often paid in vegetables, firewood, or livestock. There were no regular hours of employment and no uniform curriculum or duties, and student attendance varied according to weather, labor demands of the family, and ability to pay tuition. Teaching children was often only one of many duties facing the teacher, who might also be called upon to work in the church or for town fathers. Some teachers regularly kept other means of employment, working as farmers, innkeepers, or craftsmen.

Teaching itself took place in a one-room schoolhouse, if the community had erected one, or in private homes. Because there were no common textbooks, teachers relied on the materials that pupils brought to school with them, such as alphabet hornbooks or religious pamphlets. Teachers taught multiaged classrooms, basing their instruction on drilling and recitation with the goals of basic literacy and understanding arithmetic figures. Pedagogical methods were authoritarian, and disciplinary methods were severe (Altenbaugh, 2003).

Teaching was in no way a prestigious or easy job. Teachers had no contract and so could be summarily expelled from their post by a dissatisfied parent or board member, or their employment could be swiftly cut short when the town ran out of money. Personal accounts of teaching in this period are universally dark reports of a thankless and stressful occupation. Soon after the Revolution, Philip Freneau wrote of his experience as a private tutor as a "wretched state of meanness and servility" (Freneau in Cohen & Scheer, 1997, p. 24). Other teachers recounted how their originally inspired plans of intellectual enlightenment collapsed when they faced recalcitrant students, decrepit classrooms, contemptuous employers, and social isolation. Hiram Orcutt, who taught in Vermont and boarded with students' parents, complained about the lack of privacy and the ongoing criticism of "ignorant and meddlesome fathers and mothers" (Orcutt, 1898, pp. 49–50). John Trumbell reiterated this frustration when he described how itinerant teachers were treated at the whim of parents who annually seek "to keep [a teacher] just as good, and just as cheap" (Trumbell in Cohen & Scheer, 1997, p. 21).

If the working conditions facing teachers were difficult, the public portrayal of teachers was no more appealing. In popular culture, colonial teachers were often mocked as pathetic, unmanly creatures that did not have the physicality for farming or the gumption for the legal profession. Ultimately, they stood alone in their classroom in a strange community, and, on a number of recorded occasions, were attacked and chased out of their posts by rebellious students. Washington Irving describes the iconographic teacher in his portrayal of Ichabod Crane, the effete, gangly, and sadistic teacher who carves a living out of teaching in rural communities. Ichabod Crane is the caricature of the mean spirited teacher who ruled his classroom with corporal punishment and dulled his students with tedious recitations, while trying to worm his way into the parlors of local ladies (Cohen & Scheer, 1997). Other teachers were commonly described as social incompetents who seemed to deserve the horrible state of their employment. Concluded Freneau, there is "no animal more worthy of pity" (Freneau in Cohen & Scheer, 1997, p. 24).

The experience of colonial teachers introduces two recurring patterns in the history of teaching. First, while Americans articulated a great faith in education to help them create and maintain their culture, they developed no concomitant support of teachers. Colonialists held great expectations that formal schooling would create an orderly and godly society, even as they allowed schooling to be irregular, unavailable to the poorest children, to girls, or to children of color. For all their reliance on education to maintain godly habits, they offered few guidelines or supports for teachers. In addition, although they valued education, they were less likely to value the educator, treating teachers as strange outsiders who were worthy of neither friendship nor authority. Secondly, the colonial experience offers an early example of American faith in community-supported schooling, with a parallel movement to cut the costs of those same supports. New England laws set the precedence for publicly funded schooling for all children, but already colonialists displayed a parsimonious attitude toward their public school teachers, providing meager housing and minimal pay. Teaching in America, then, started off in an ambiguous cultural position.

THE COMMON SCHOOL ERA (1800–1880)

In the early nineteenth century, social reformers expanded the breadth and scope of American education, while developing an infrastructure for educational delivery in what was called the "common school." To a great extent, the Common School movement described an ideological crusade as much as specific institutional developments. Common schools generally meant local, tax-supported schools for young children. Unique to the vision of common schools was the systematic reliance on local support—usually property taxes—to create a civic relationship between communities and their educational services. Also unique was the accessibility of common schools to most children regardless of their class background, although children from African American and minority ethnic and religious backgrounds were not welcome. The Common School movement proposed an efficient method of school governance and management, thereby setting the stage for the universal education of young Americans in a common culture.

The organization of a formal schooling structure became a priority with the founders of the new republic in the years after the American Revolution. The same intellectual ideas from the European Enlightenment that had inspired the Revolution led early American leaders to think about the cultural necessity of influencing young children to become good citizens. Educational and political theory merged in an understanding that a strong and democratic nation could only grow with a well-educated citizenry and that the state needed to take up the responsibility for such education. A number of the nation's first leaders proposed systems of public education: Thomas Jefferson's education bill of 1779 advocated an educational system, extending from primary to higher education, that was based on public support; Benjamin Rush proposed a general tax for the support of public schooling for all children; and Noah Webster advocated an American curriculum with a common language that he laid out in his dictionary and spellers. Education advocates argued various rationales for publicly funded education. Some argued that it would allow for liberty and equity among citizens; others argued that education would impose cultural order and religious piety among citizens. It remained debatable, then, whether education provided freedom or control, and whether the purpose of education was to teach individuality or conformity. All of these visions remained limited by the focus on white male Americans, although some educators established private academies for girls, arguing that future mothers needed an equally strong education to support their role as cultural transmitters to young Americans (Urban & Wagoner, 2004).

Common School reformers often had the passion of religious missionaries, and no preacher of the new educational gospel was more persuasive than Horace Mann. As Secretary of the Massachusetts Board of Public Schools in the 1830s and 1840s, Mann wrote his annual reports to the board as treatises about the need for public education, arguing that wealthy citizens and business owners would do well to support the education of the poor because, in so doing, they would help create a docile and stable workforce. To poor citizens, he argued that education offered social advancement and equality. To all, he argued that public support for schooling was a community responsibility. He proposed a nonsectarian Protestant curriculum, thereby minimizing conflicts between Protestant groups, although continuing to exclude non-Protestants. After studying new educational ideas in Europe, Mann promoted a child-centered vision of education that rejected corporal punishment and emphasized a humane and nurturing learning process. He also advocated teacher education to help professionalize teaching, and he supervised the establishment of the first teacher training schools in Massachusetts. His effect extended outside of the state, leading to the development of compulsory education laws and the expansion of public schooling for white boys and girls across the new nation. Because of the scope of his vision and the impact of his ideas, Horace Mann is commonly, and justifiably, referred to as the "father of the common school" (Urban & Wagoner, 2004, p. 99).

The centerpiece to Mann's common school was the professional teacher who was prepared in new teacher education schools. Called "normal schools" from the French name for their education of teachers in general or "normal" fields of study, the first state-supported normal school opened in Lexington, Massachusetts, in 1839. By 1870, forty state normal schools existed across the country. Normal school advocates described teaching as grounded in a systematic body of knowledge, not merely the individual acts of adults in a room with children, and argued that teachers needed specific training in curriculum and pedagogy. In spite of teacher educators' attempts to make teaching a profession based on select scientific knowledge, normal schools remained informal, often nondegree granting, institutions through much of the nineteenth century, as the hiring of teachers in school districts remained an eclectic practice. Only in the early twentieth century would common education requirements and certification processes be established for American schools. Indeed, through the nineteenth century, elementary teachers in most states needed little more than a high school education to obtain a teaching position. Such practices frustrated many educational reformers' dreams that teaching would become a highly competitive profession (Herbst, 1989).

The Common School movement spurred other developments in educational thought. Through the nineteenth century, American educators adopted from Europe new learning theories that enlivened classroom practice. By the Civil War, common school reformers advocated the radical notion of teaching to the child's interest and not to the prescribed subject; proposed a revised plan for teaching reading through study of the whole word, not simply memorization and phonics; and advocated for the abolition of corporal punishment. Other educational advances included the publication of popular readers, such as the McGuffey readers, that offered common readings for students and the development of administrative, financial, legal, and architectural policies for schools (Altenbaugh, 2003).

Yet the most significant reform had less to do with school organization or curriculum and more to do with Horace Mann's advocacy of the hiring of women to teach in the new common schools. The genius behind identifying women to staff the nation's schools was based on a number of interlocking factors. First and foremost, women were a readily available and cheap labor force. Educated in the new common schools and freed from the most primitive demands of the household by modernization, young white women provided an ideal employee pool for low-pay work. Women, too, fulfilled Mann's vision of education as humane and caring, since women, it was believed, had a "natural" affinity for children. Caring and cost were happily linked in the eyes of frugal school administrators. As Mann argued, the fully mature woman had such "a preponderance of affection over intellect" that she would not search for a teaching post for the money or the fame (Mann in Altenbaugh, 2003, p. 113). In 1841, the Boston Board of Education agreed when it described women as "incomparably better teachers for young children than males," because:

> [T]heir manners are more mild and gentle, and hence more in consonance with the tenderness of childhood. They are endowed by nature

> *with stronger parental impulses, and this makes the society of children delightful, and turns duty into pleasure . . . They are also of purer morals. (Altenbaugh, 2003, p. 113)*

Educated middle-class women were hardly in a position to critique this portrait because teaching in local village schools offered one of the few paid employments available to them. In addition, church missionaries and educational reformers recruited thousands of teachers to start schools in isolated communities in the expanding western frontier. By the Civil War, women constituted 40 percent of the nation's teaching force. By 1900, 70 percent, and, by 1920, 85 percent (Newman, 2002, p. 186). Almost all of these women were unmarried, following legal and cultural proscriptions against working women having "two masters"—a husband and an employer.

In addition to the new coeducational state normal schools that offered women their first opportunities in higher education, a number of educators opened schools for women. Mary Lyon, Catherine Beecher, and Emma Willard established prominent female academies in the northeast and midwest in which they advocated for advanced education for women to prepare them to be servants of humanity in the classroom. Mary Lyon's Mount Holyoke Female Seminary, for example, was founded in Massachusetts in 1837 to "raise among the female part of the community a higher standard of science and literature, of economy and of refinement, of benevolence and religion" (Lyon in Shmurak, 1998, p. 254). Teaching was women's best avenue for exuding such influence, according to Lyon, who believed that "the teaching of children decides the destiny of the nation." Through the nineteenth century, well over three-quarters of Mount Holyoke's graduates taught for at least six years (Shmurak, 1998, pp. 254–255). As advocates for women teachers, these educators simultaneously advanced the educational and occupational opportunities for women while furthering the popular notion that, for women, teaching was more of a natural mission than a profession. The ideal teacher, said Catherine Beecher, worked "not for money, not for influence, nor for honour, nor for ease, but with the simple, single purpose of doing good" (Beecher in Hoffman, 1981, p. 10).

The feminization of the teaching force would profoundly shape the nature of the occupation. Like other feminized occupations, such as nursing and secretarial work, the low social status of women allowed male administrators to control and underpay women educators, arguing that teaching was "women's work" that young women took on for only a few years until they married and, therefore, was not a "real" profession. In fact, women had little choice in this matter since marriage laws in many communities required them to leave teaching after they married whether they wanted to or not. The feminization of education also furthered the analogy of teaching as missionary work rather than as a profession, thereby setting the expectations that teachers would accept even the most difficult school work and the least pay. This missionary ideology colored teaching with an occupational passivity that belied attempts to create a more assertive professional status.

The feminization of teaching also continued the trend of expanding the purpose of education from instruction in academic skills to the inculcation of social and cultural norms. To church missionaries and educational leaders alike, white women teachers embodied the type of middle-class, Anglo-Protestant identity that educators hoped would "civilize" African American, ethnic immigrant, and native children, and their task as educators was explicitly linked to nationalist visions of cultural uniformity. Schooling for children of color, immigrant, and native families was explicitly designed to disconnect children from their cultural communities and assimilate them into dominant Anglo-American culture. The agent of this cultural education was often a white woman who taught both literacy and Americanization. Most teachers uncritically embraced their role, believing that they were doing good by teaching children to adopt to the dominant culture. The social and cultural role of education was not secondary to their position as teachers; rather, it was their main responsibility.

For some teachers, this cultural role positioned them to be progressive activists. African American women teachers in the post–Civil War south were seen by community members as nothing less than agents of cultural and political liberation. When white southerners continued to deny freed African American slaves the right to education after the Civil War, African American families resisted by establishing, and funding, their own schools and hiring their own women teachers (Anderson, 1988). African American women teachers from both the north and south provided inspiration and resources, as well as academic skills, to impoverished African American communities. For these women, the missionary role of teaching took a radical turn as they extended their educational work outside of the schoolhouse into other avenues of social improvement and racial uplift. Pauli Murray's description of her work in an African American community in late nineteenth-century rural North Carolina shows the extent to which her school-based work blended with community work:

> *Up at five every morning and usually at school before seven-thirty. Got*
> *home late in the afternoon, prepared supper, and then returned to night*
> *school to conduct literacy classes for the hardworking parents and*
> *grandparents of her day school pupils. If a child was absent, she visited*
> *the child's home after school to discover the reason. She was expected*
> *to attend all community gatherings in addition to teachers' meetings*
> *and parents' meetings. On Sundays she usually went to church twice:*
> *morning service at her own St. Titus Episcopal Church and evening*
> *service at the neighborhood Second Baptist Church, which many of her*
> *students' parents attended. (Murray in Littlefield, 1999, pp. 152–153)*

For some white women teachers, too, teaching in poor and marginalized communities was a liberating experience. More than 7,000 white northern women took jobs as teachers for newly freed slaves in the south in the decade after the Civil War. Deeply moved by their students' commitment to education and appalled by southern racism, many of these women developed activist components to their work. Laura Towne, a white woman from the north, lived and taught on the South Caroline Sea Islands for over thirty years. She saw her work as that of a social missionary as much as an academic instructor. "We have come to do anti-slavery work, and we think it noble work, and we mean to do it earnestly," she wrote upon her arrival in her new community in 1862 (Towne in Hoffman, 1981, pp. 94–95). Over ten years later, she committed to spending the remainder of her life with her community, asserting her activist purpose: "I want to agitate, even as I am agitated" (Towne in Hoffman, 1981, p. 106).

Other white women teachers merged their classroom practice with Christian missionary vision. When Ellen Lee moved from her home state of Massachusetts to Indiana in 1852, her Baptist faith was reinforced by preparation as a teacher by the Board of National Popular Education—an agency founded by Catherine Beecher and based in Hartford, Connecticut, that trained women to become Christian teachers for the frontier. Lee believed that she was able to control her school of young country boys by her sheer moral force. She reported: "I gave them only one rule, that was—Do right. And by awakening their consciences to a sense of right and wrong, and other similar influences, I have succeeded much better than I expected, and have had to use no other influences than kindness" (Lee in Hoffman, 1981, p. 60). Some teachers who worked in ethnic minority communities found that the expectation to convert students to Anglo ways conflicted with their own understanding of effective instruction; in response, teachers learned about and adopted part of the local culture into their educational framework (Yohn, 1991). Some frontier teachers developed progressive curricula simply by drawing on the resources of the local community. Sarah Huftalen, a teacher in rural Iowa at the turn of the century, had her students work on learning projects with resources drawn from the nearby college, magazines, and specimens of local nature. Some projects involved improving the building and environs of the tiny one-room schoolhouse, and some included the parents and community. Huftalen described her school as "a team in every project and endeavor. Harmony reigned over the hill" (Huftalen in Cordier, 1992, p. 223). In individual actions within the classroom and the communities in which they lived, many women teachers on the frontier supported the growth of local culture, industry, and individual initiative.

For all women teachers in the tiny district school of the pioneer west or the rural south, the physical conditions of teaching were little improved from that of their colonial predecessors. Schoolhouses were little more than crude shacks, and teachers faced all children, from infants to adolescents, in one large room. Unlike their male predecessors, women teachers could not marry, and they were subject to the Victorian social regulations of their communities, leaving many teachers desperately alone. Ellen Lee, who was so successful as a teacher in Indiana, still suffered the isolation of her placement: "In my school I am content, and happy for I hope I am doing good, but I am entirely deprived of sympathy, and good society. I have no human being here, in whom I can confide, or who possesses kindred feelings with mine" (Lee in Hoffman, 1981, p. 60). Martha Barratt, a teacher in rural Massachusetts in the mid-nineteenth century, expressed her frustrations more desperately: "My school seems more troublesome than ever before and I feel almost discouraged. I wish I was never obliged to leave my home and friends" (Barratt in Rousmaniere, 1997a, pp. 123–124).

Teachers in city schools in the mid-nineteenth century faced challenges of a different sort, as they led huge, multiaged classrooms with hundreds of students following the monitorial system of a regimented school day and course of study. In each large classroom, students sat in rows on long benches, grouped roughly by age and ability, and responded en masse to drills. The system was both economically and socially efficient; large numbers of students were taught collectively in a common curriculum that taught specific skills and obedience. Student work was performed only in group recitations and dictations, and rigid discipline was enforced with a system of rewards and punishments. The goal of the entire operation was system and order, which appealed to some educators in increasingly disordered American cities (Kaestle, 1983). Opponents of the model were sharply critical of the authoritarian position that teachers were required to take. As one observer to a New York City monitorial school in 1868 observed:

> *To manage successfully a hundred children, or even half that number, the teacher must reduce them as near as possible to a unit. Nothing must be done that all can not do at the same time. Everything must be sacrificed to regularity, everything like spontaneity repressed. The children must be made like so many pins—so much alike that all undergo the same processes in exactly the same way. (Finkelstein, 1989, p. 319)*

Teachers' work consisted of drilling students on the required assignments and leading group recitations. Lessons were impersonal, highly structured, and noisy as students dictated their responses. Commented an observer at a Cincinnati monitorial school in 1893, the group recitations were a type of instruction that is "preeminently fitted to deaden the soul and convert human beings into automatons" (Finkelstein, 1989, p. 324). Teachers, as well as students, were expected to be part of that automatic machine.

The Common School reform movement introduced preliminary structure to public schooling, and it advanced the position of teachers by offering some occupational structures and improvements in working conditions. But the feminization of teaching furthered American ambivalence about the "professional" status of teaching. Because of the low social status of women, the assignment of teachers' work to them undermined any attempt by school reformers to make teaching a high paying, high prestige occupation. Simultaneously, school reformers, policy makers, and the common citizen embraced the ideology that teachers should have an expansive role as academic instructor, cultural and civic authority, social and moral influence, community mentor, and exemplar of American values, while still requiring only minimal training and offering only minimal pay. As more students flocked to schools in the late nineteenth century, teachers were barely prepared to handle the onslaught.

THE PROGRESSIVE ERA (1880–1930)

Historians have identified the period from roughly 1880 to 1930 as the "Progressive Era," describing a wave of multilayered social and economic reform movements that addressed the broad social changes of modernization. Educators played a major role in Progressive reform by expanding their vision of the purpose of American schooling. Some of these developments were the result of the work of the earlier generation of school reformers. Common School reformers, for example, advocated compulsory schooling laws for primary school–aged children, passing the first laws in the 1850s. By 1900, thirty states had compulsory schooling laws, and, by 1918, every state did (Newman, 2002, p. 190). Combined with Progressive Era laws that restricted child labor, the effect was an explosion in student enrollment, particularly in the elementary schools. Compulsory schooling laws also diversified the types of students in schools, requiring the attendance of girls, students of color, and poor and immigrant students, thereby increasing the diversity of students' backgrounds and experiences in the classroom. Reformers also extended the required amount of schooling. While in 1900 barely 6 percent of American seventeen-year-olds graduated from high school; by 1930, 30 percent of that age group earned a high school diploma (Angus & Mirel, 1999, p. 293). Progressive school reformers also advocated for kindergartens, special needs classrooms, and vocational education, thus broadening the age and abilities of enrolled students. Growing school systems struggled to accommodate the increased number of students and to address increasingly complex issues of classroom instruction, social relations, and appropriate curriculum content. The Progressive movement in education addressed these changes in two parallel reform initiatives, the first in administrative development and the second in classroom organization and educational offerings. Both reform initiatives had a significant impact on the work of American teachers.

The first reform wing of Progressive educators believed that greater organization and systemization would lead to improved social order. Historians have called these reformers administrative progressives because they believed that improved administrative structure would improve educational practice (Tyack, 1974). These school reformers looked to advancements in the business world as models for advancing education, particularly in the rapidly growing city school districts. They promoted a centralized administrative structure, whereby all decisions about schooling would be addressed not by local parents, teachers, and community members who were often ill-informed of new educational ideas, but by professional school administrators well versed in educational theory, law, finance, scientific methods of instruction, and measurement and assessment of academic performance. Modern school policies introduced the separation of children by age into different graded classrooms, a standardized and sequenced curriculum, and regular testing—all of which promised uniformity, predictability, and cost efficiency in the total school operation.

The growth in school administration radically changed the working dynamics of the teacher's classroom, particularly in large, urban school districts. Where, previously, teachers may have felt unprepared and isolated, they now perhaps felt suffocated by bureaucratic demands. Where the school principal had previously been little more than a lead teacher in a building who instructed classroom teachers in the wishes of the school board, there was now a whole constellation of administrative positions, including a superintendent, assistant superintendents, curriculum directors, and specialists in school law, finance, facilities, and personnel. Between 1890 and 1920, the number of such "supervisory officers" increased dramatically in major urban districts: in Baltimore, the number jumped from 9 to 144, in Boston from 7 to 159, in Cleveland from 10 to 159 (Tyack, 1974, p. 185). The administrator's dream was that, with increases in specialized personnel, school districts would become well-oiled, hierarchical organizations that would result in expert decisions emanating from professional offices. Such a structure, reformers believed, would educate all children equitably.

The second wing of Progressive education reformers, termed "pedagogical progressives," centered their attention on the classroom and curriculum. Some of these reformers expanded the child-centered theories first studied by Horace Mann and further developed by the new field of psychology. Educational reformers such as theorist John Dewey, Progressive school founder Lucy Sprague Mitchell, and kindergarten advocate Susan Blow developed far-reaching educational philosophies about child learning and teacher practice, promoting a flexible, child-centered curriculum that was based on students' needs and interests. Central to their ideas was positioning the child at the center of the classroom and designing curriculum around the child's developmental needs. Not surprisingly, their ideas often clashed with the more rigid structural notions of the administrative progressives who promoted standardized curriculum and testing (Kliebard, 1987; Sadovnik & Semel, 2002).

Another emphasis of pedagogical progressives was to expand the offerings of the school from the traditional academic subjects to more socially oriented learning in such classes as physical education, home economics, vocational education, the arts, and after-school clubs and activities. A more diversified curriculum, these reformers argued, would provide more variety for students of different needs and interests, including the increasing number of girls, working-class and immigrant students, and students of color entering schools. This was often achieved by segregating those groups into specially tracked programs that would guide these students into their special place in society (Franklin, 1986).

The effect of these changes on teachers was both positive and negative. On the positive side, the development of large school administrative structures made teachers' work more orderly, offering more regular services such as teacher preparation programs, certification and hiring procedures, benefits and salary scales, and providing healthier working conditions and standard curriculum and expectations. In rural communities, the consolidation of schools led to the replacement of isolated and antiquated rural schoolhouses with larger, better-equipped buildings. These efforts made teaching one of the best paid and most stable jobs available to women in the 1920s, offering employment in a civil service system with a tenure policy, a pension to support them in old age, and a regular salary. The diversification of American schools also opened up teaching to African American and immigrant teachers, if only to segregate them into special schools. By 1930, school laws protected many public school teachers from the hiring and firing whims of disagreeable parents and school board members, and teachers were able to rely on a regular school schedule with a standard administrative structure and curriculum format (Rousmaniere, 1997b).

There was, however, a dark side to these reforms. The same administrative structures that offered teachers protections also limited their freedoms and individuality on the job, leading many critics to argue that the new American school had become "factoryized" and that teachers' work was now as monotonous as work on an assembly line, as they closely followed set curriculum and heeded domineering administrators. The new centralized school system was guided by an emphasis on economic efficiency and standards imposed from above, forcing teachers to consider the cost-accounting aspects of their work more than intellectual or creative aspects. Teachers were increasingly frustrated with increased paperwork, tests, reports, and other requirements delivered from above. Paradoxically, such rigidity was accompanied by the expanded expectations of teachers' work into social and cultural education, as pedagogical progressives had zealously advocated. In 1918, Isabel Ennis, a teacher with twenty-three years experience in Brooklyn elementary schools, expressed her frustration about the seemingly endless demands on teachers:

> *We are expected to be an arithmetician, a historian, a grammarian, a disciplinarian, a librarian, a sociologist, a penman, an artist, a musi-*

cian, a model, a moralist, an attendance officer, a clerk, a nurse, a
banker, an athlete, a dancer, a supervisor of play and recreation, an en-
gineer, a community-center worker, a farmer, a housekeeper, a medical
and sanitary inspector, a host or a hostess. We are expected to discover
the morally deficient, the deaf, the feeble-minded, the exceptional and
a few more just such. Besides the three R's we are expected to teach
thrift, self-government [and] sex hygiene ... We must be resourceful,
display initiative, have confidence in ourselves, make our teaching at-
tractive ... In fact the demand is so great, teachers hardly know what
to slur or what to stress. (Ennis, 1918, p. 13)

A junior high school teacher in Memphis in the 1930s penned a satirical poem in which a teacher was so harassed by interruptions to her planned curriculum that she broke down and was carted off to an insane asylum. The poet concluded with her fantasy:

Place me on Sunium's marbled steep
Surround me with the ocean deep;
Put a class within my reach,
And then, good Lord, just let me teach! (Owen, 1931, p. 3)

Furthering the tension of the increased demands on teachers were the gender dynamics of school management. As school systems developed complicated bureaucratic structures to address their expanding role, men educators took on high-paid administration positions, relegating women to low-pay classroom work. In 1930, well over 25 percent of local school superintendents were women. As those positions consolidated and became more prestigious and high paying, they were awarded to more men so that, in 1960, only 3 percent of school leaders were women (Blount, 1998, pp. 171–201). The school system thus became a highly gender-segregated occupation, with powerful men administrators at the top and women teachers subject to them. Teachers reported on the double pressure of increased regulation over their work enforced by male administrators with arrogant and oppressive attitudes toward women teachers. As one New York City teacher reported in 1922:

You feel a depression in the air from the moment you begin to teach in
some schools. It's as though someone at the top were pushing down hard
and the rest kept pushing until it reached you. Suddenly from out of
the blue the principal or assistant swoops upon you almost breathless
and asks for a lot of detail that you didn't think was expected. You catch
the panicky feeling and rush around madly, letting the teaching slide.
(Armstrong, 1922, p. 11)

Furthermore, teachers remained subject to the close personal scrutiny of their employers. The marriage bar remained in small cities and rural communities well through the middle of the twentieth century, and teachers in small districts were often subject to specific personal behavior in their employment contract, such as a promise to abstain from "dancing, immodest dressing and other conduct unbecoming a teacher and a lady," smoking, any private meetings with men, and a promise "to sleep at least eight hours each night, to eat carefully, [and] to keep every precaution to keep in the best of health and spirits" (Altenbaugh, 2003, pp. 217–218). In teacher education schools across the nation, teachers were instructed in proper dress, decorum, beliefs, and social behaviors as part of their "qualifications" to become a teacher. The teaching force was publicly criticized because it had too few men teachers, which, it was feared, would lead to the feminization of young boys, and because it had too many teachers from immigrant backgrounds and holding radical political beliefs who, it was feared, would not teach appropriate American values. Teachers' qualifications had as much to do with their social and cultural characteristics as with their skills as an instructor (Rousmaniere, 1997b).

Even as teachers' job descriptions and qualifications expanded during the Progressive Era, they experienced no comparative rise in pay or social status as a result of these changes. Growing divisions within the teaching occupation shrouded some of these trends. Public secondary education, which represented only a tiny minority of educational offerings in the nineteenth century, grew in the early twentieth century as compulsory schooling laws required older children to attend school. The growth of high schools rearranged the composition of teaching; the more prestigious academic high schools attracted men teachers, who, in turn, demanded higher pay. By the first World War, teaching was essentially a bifurcated occupation with the small numbers of men high school teachers earning up to twice that of their more numerous female sisters in the elementary schools. By World War II, members of the predominantly female elementary teaching force were among the lowest paid of white collar workers (Altenbaugh, 2003).

Increased pressures and stagnant remuneration led some teachers to organize into teachers' associations and unions to fight for their participation in school decision making, occupational autonomy, and improved working conditions. Ironically, their only political option to fight for professional status was in workers' unions, which characteristically denoted nonprofessional laborers. Margaret Haley, a former elementary teacher who led thousands of women elementary teachers in the Chicago's Teachers Federation through the early twentieth century, argued that teachers needed to fight not just for improved salaries, but also for a more democratically run school system and increased resources to all schools. Haley argued that the problems facing schools were the result of educators adopting "the ideal of the industrial factory system, which made the man at the top the only person with power, and the thousands below him there mere tools to carry out his directions" (Haley in Reid, 1982, p. 86). The result, she claimed, was the "factoryization" of schools in which the teacher became "an automaton, a mere factory hand, whose duty it is to carry out mechanically and unquestioningly the ideas and orders of those clothed with the authority of position and who may or may not know the needs of the children or how to minister to them" (Haley, 1904, p. 148).

Early twentieth-century teachers also organized in other movements for social change. Like many of their predecessors, they expanded the social role of the teacher outside the confines of the classroom into broad social and political reform movements, not always representing the type of social role that was expected of them. Women teachers took on leadership roles in the women's suffrage movement, professional women's clubs, peace and temperance movements, and social settlement work with the poor (Carter, 2002). Within education, women teachers organized in local and national associations in battles to equalize pay for men and women teachers and to end the hiring prohibitions for married women teachers and for women teachers with children. They encouraged and supported women going into school administration. So active were women teachers in movements to improve schools that Ella Flagg Young, the first woman school superintendent of Chicago and one of the few women superintendents in any large city, prophesied in 1901 that "Women are destined to rule the schools of every city" (Young in Blount, 1998, p. 1). These women teachers took advantage of the feminization of teaching to unite as women, and they realigned the traditional dictum that women teachers be positive moral influences on students to a more activist model of progressive social change agent.

By the beginning of World War II, American schooling held many of the characteristics of modern mass public schooling, and the occupation of teaching held many of its modern complicated ambiguities. The expansion of schooling during the Progressive Era offered many improvements to teachers, but the changes also increased teachers' work loads. Teachers gained a basic guarantee of civil service rights and protections, but they remained economically marginalized. As a feminized workforce, teachers were subject to persistent gender inequality and low occupational status, and they found themselves locked at the bottom of the system. Public opinion exacerbated employment issues by reinforcing idealized images of the self-sacrificing lady teacher who devoted her life to nurturing loyal citizens. Teachers who argued to improve their working conditions through teacher unions were criticized as being unladylike and selfish, even as male administrators reaped economic rewards and social prestige for their work outside of the classroom. The growing pains of the profession left teachers in a deep conundrum.

THE MODERN ERA (1930–PRESENT)

The Cold War that defined American politics for half a century after World War II had a deep impact on American education. The competition between the United States and the Soviet Union raised a profound national panic about American competencies that intensified scrutiny on American schools. A core of the debate centered on educational philosophy and curriculum. A critique of American schooling that began soon after the war was that the child-centered, pedagogically progressive educational ideas of earlier generations had made American students intellectually flabby and had focused on life skills such as home economics and human relations and not on hard science. Lost on most critics was the fact that, by the 1950s, more Americans were going to school than ever before, and, in that respect, American academic achievement was at an all-time high. Also ignored was the continued low pay and status of teachers and the underfunding of poor schools.

One response to the criticism of American schools was the growth of the federal role in elementary and secondary education. The Soviet Union's successful launching of their satellite Sputnik into space in October 1957 intensified American fears about a communist threat, and, as a result, the development of advanced science and technology education became a matter of national security. The 1958 National Defense Education Act provided federal dollars for improvements in elementary and secondary science classrooms and initiated a series of federal supports for education (Rudolph, 2002). President Lyndon Johnson's Great Society program of the mid-1960s further enhanced the federal role in education. In particular, the Elementary and Secondary Education Act of 1965 targeted the educational disadvantages facing American children in poverty and provided funding for cultural and social enrichment activities; curricular and pedagogical innovations; and parent, community, nutritional, and medical programs in schools. Of equal significance were the federal mandates to reconstruct racially segregated schools as a result of the 1954 *Brown v. Board of Education* Supreme Court decision. Through the 1960s and 1970s, federal courts issued orders to substantially reshape the racial character of American schools through policies such as bussing, magnet schools, and redistricting. Civil rights legislation in schools expanded through the 1970s in judicial decisions and federal legislation regarding bilingual education, special education, gender equity in educational offerings, and preschool education. The federal government's share of education spending in local schools peaked at 9 percent in the 1970s (Newman, 2002, pp. 211–212).

The effect of these reforms on teachers mirrored that of the Progressive Era. When the educational vision expanded and became more inclusive, classrooms became increasingly complicated sites where the public expected teachers to attend to students' vastly diverse social, intellectual, linguistic, cultural, and physical interests and abilities. Educational research explored many of these topics, thus expanding the body of knowledge available to teachers but rarely affecting the actual structure of schooling or teachers' working conditions. As education had become more complex, it had also become inextricably political, and school boards and politicians struggled to articulate their own popular vision of education, often overlooking the increasing demands made on teachers without concomitant support or remuneration.

Teachers organized to try to improve these working conditions through two different avenues—professional associations and teacher unions. The largest and most significant of teachers' professional associations was the National Education Association (NEA), originally founded in the mid-nineteenth century as a forum for "school men" to discuss educational issues. The NEA later developed into a powerful political lobby for school administrators. Classroom teachers, and particularly the growing body of women elementary teachers, were excluded from participating in NEA governance, and teachers' concerns about salary, working conditions, and their absence from decision making in schools were largely ignored. In response, teachers founded their own organizations to address their immediate concerns. Following the lead of Margaret Haley's Chicago Teachers' Federation, which affiliated with organized labor in 1903, many urban teachers organized into unions that focused specifically on working conditions. In 1916, a number of these groups organized into the American Federation of Teachers (AFT). During the political and economic crises surrounding World War I, more than one hundred teacher unions were organized across the country. For decades, these organizations remained relatively powerless, as the unions had no legal recognition, and their members were persecuted for promoting radical ideas. In the 1920s, the NEA attracted more members than the AFT by reshaping its mission to be a more proactive agency advocating for improved teachers' working conditions, more equitable school financing, and federal support in education (Urban, 2000; Murphy, 1990).

By the 1950s, teacher activists reinvigorated their unions by taking advantage of new collective bargaining laws for public sector workers. After organizing a series of significant urban teacher strikes in the 1960s and 1970s, the AFT became the first national teachers' union of significance. Following that lead, the NEA moved away from its traditional identity as a professional lobbying group and developed union methods to help organize thousands of teachers. Today, 25 percent of American teachers is represented by the AFT and 60 percent by the NEA (Newman, 2002, p. 115).

The rise of teacher unionism in the 1960s furthered the age-old debate about the extent to which teaching is a profession. If it is a profession, why did teachers resort to the tactics of industrial, blue collar unions? Defenders of teachers' unions argue that such strategies as collective bargaining are instrumental in creating the conditions for a profession—improved economic security and working conditions, particularly, and broad advocacy for students, teachers, and public education generally (Urban & Wagoner, 2004, p. 307). From a historical perspective, teachers' unions take on much of the work of school reformers of the past, from Thomas Jefferson to Horace Mann to John Dewey to Margaret Haley, who each advocated for an improved and solidly financed system of education in which teachers can best perform their obligations to children. But teachers' unions remain embroiled in the contradictory identity of teaching that has long historical roots. The public expects teachers to accomplish an ever increasing array of academic and social tasks but resists the full recognition of and compensation for that work.

In 1983, the release of President Ronald Reagan's report, *A Nation at Risk*, shifted the previously progressive impetus of federal support for civil rights to a more focused role of monitoring academic performance and educational budgets. The report introduced a wave of reforms, continued through President George W. Bush's 2002 No Child Left Behind Act, which established federal and state accountability measures of individual school and teacher performance, high-stakes testing, and restricted funding. Simultaneously, the federal government began to authorize competing systems of education, such as school choice and school vouchers, that encourage the funneling of school funds into separate educational ventures, including for-profit and church-supported schooling. Teacher preparation requirements and licensure standards under these new reforms are contradictory. Assessment policies require most public school teachers to complete licensure requirements, while, under voucher and charter school plans, teachers in private and Catholic schools who are not formally licensed can receive publicly funded salaries. In addition, while alternative funding schemes such as vouchers and charters allow for more local control of schools, most public school teachers are required to follow national and state curriculum mandates and to teach to standardized tests without additional resources.

Amidst the vast confusion of educational policy reforms of the last three decades, perhaps the most significant effect on teachers has been the financial drain on public schools and the ever increasing role of the public school as a social service agency for high poverty, socially marginalized, and academically underprepared students. Since the 1970s, school funding issues have constituted the prominent civil rights issue in education. High courts in more than thirty states have issued decisions in school finance cases, focusing on the constitutionality of state funding formulas that rely on local property taxes. On a national average, local property taxes provide 44 percent of all school funding, leaving vast differences between wealthy and poor tax-based communities. But, much like the desegregation court cases in earlier years, court rulings have not been able to force state and local legislatures to enact change, and teachers in poor school districts continue to work with thousands of dollars less per student than their peers in wealthier districts in the same state (Karp, 2003).

Theodore Sizer has aptly described the multiplicity of challenges facing modern teachers in his composite portrait of a fictional American high school teacher, Horace Smith, whose first name is intentionally the same as the "father" of American public schools, Horace Mann. In his trilogy study, Sizer describes how Horace consistently compromises his vision of education as he struggles with too many students, class periods that are too short, a curriculum that requires too much to concentrate on any single subject, and a job that demands too much of his abilities. Like Isabel Ennis one hundred years before, Horace wishes that schools would simply give him the opportunity to teach. Sizer's proposed solution to Horace's crisis is for a clarified curriculum, smaller and more cohesive groups of students, more cooperation across classrooms, and more autonomy for teachers to educate students in depth (Newman, 2002). Other reformers, notably Deborah Meier, advocate a similar reform platform of small schools that allow for academic rigor, engaged curriculum and pedagogy, cultural validation and support of all students with all abilities and from all backgrounds, and an understanding of education that goes beyond performance on tests to full comprehension of academic work, civic responsibility, and personal growth (Hall, 2002). These visions of contemporary school reform harken back to Horace Mann's vision of public schools funded collectively for the purpose of providing equal opportunities for all children and, ultimately, for the nation. It was Mann who wrote in 1848 that education, "beyond all other devices of human origin, is the great equalizer of the conditions of men—the balance-wheel of the social machinery" (Altenbaugh, 2003, p. 81). The teacher activist Margaret Haley positioned teachers at the center of that "balance-wheel," asserting that "If our democracy is to continue, the teachers of this nation must teach the children of the nation the obligations of citizenship in a true democracy" (Haley in Reid, 1982, p. 271).

CONCLUDING REMARKS

In this chapter, I have argued that the history of teaching in America is rich with political dynamics, economic crises, and social tensions. Part of the complexity of teaching is that Americans imbue the work with many expectations and moral assumptions, holding great hopes and many anxieties. This is not surprising, given that teachers have been entrusted not only with the academic education of American youth, but with great social, moral, and national expectations as well.

In any survey of the history of teaching, it would be wrong to ignore the kernel of what the act of teaching is about and to overlook the reasons why so many thousands of men and women have stepped to the front of the classroom. For all the challenges and stresses of the job, teaching is ultimately driven by human passions and interests that can be so personal that we are accustomed to calling a person a "born teacher," thereby echoing Horace Mann's belief that some people had natural instincts and abilities for the job. Many teachers through history have testified to this sense of a personal mission that supercedes their concerns about working conditions, pedagogy, or school organization.

Ezekial Cheever, for example, was the ideal colonial schoolteacher, earning cultural authority and great academic respect from his peers and students. A teacher for over sixty years in eighteenth-century New England, young men flocked to his school for advanced scholars to learn from the master who was known for his knowledge of subject matter, deep religious devotion, patience toward students, and restraint in discipline. By promoting social good and religious devotion through teaching, Cheever prepared students to be leaders in a new civic society. As one observer wrote of Cheever's teaching:

> *He has labored in that calling skillfully, diligently, constantly, religiously, seventy years . . . a rare instance of Piety, Health, Strength, and Serviceableness. The wealth of Providence was much upon his spirit. (Preston, 2003, p. 354)*

Harriet Cook, who taught in rural Vermont in the early nineteenth century, also took on her life's work of teaching with almost spiritual reverence. She turned down other employment opportunities because she felt she was destined for the life of a teacher:

> *My mind had become more and more impressed with the belief that it was my duty to teach, and as circumstances all seemed to point to this as my future employment, most willingly, though with much fear and trembling, I assumed new responsibilities, and . . . commenced a school. (Cook in Biklin, 1995, p. 56)*

Septima Clark, who, like many other women, credited teaching with the source of her later activism in the civil rights movement of the mid-twentieth century, reflected that teaching offered her both independence and connection to her African American community:

> *From my early childhood I wanted to be a schoolteacher. That desire grew and strengthened through the year. And I believe it was born and nourished out of both my heredity and my environment. (Clark in Biklin, 1995, p. 91)*

The passion for teaching continues in today's most challenging schools. In her diary of her first year teaching in a Chicago elementary public school, Esme Raji Codell describes the profound intersection of the personal and professional—an attribute that furthers both the contradictory status, and the social power, of teachers' work:

> *[N]ow I experience a teacher's great euphoria, the knowledge like a drug that will keep me: thirty-one children. Thirty-one chances. Thirty-one futures, our futures. It's almost a psychotic feeling, believing that part*

of their lives belong to me. Everything they become, I also become. And everything about me, they helped to create. (Codell, 2001, p. 194)

BIBLIOGRAPHY

Altenbaugh, R. J. (2003). *The American people and their education: A social history.* Columbus, OH: Merrill Prentice Hall.

Anderson, J. D. (1988). *The education of blacks in the south, 1860–1935.* Chapel Hill: University of North Carolina Press.

Angus, D. L., & Mirel, J. E. (1999). *The failed promise of the American high school, 1890–1995.* New York: Teachers College Press.

Armstrong, M. G. (1922, January 21). Why aren't more teachers really happy? *New York Evening Post,* 11.

Biklin, S. K. (1995). *School work: Gender and cultural construction of teaching.* New York: Teachers College Press.

Blount, J. M. (1998). *Destined to rule the schools: Women and the superintendency, 1873–1995.* Albany: State University of New York Press.

Carter, P. A. (2002). *'Everybody's paid but the teacher:' The teaching profession and the women's movement.* New York: Teachers College Press.

Codell, E. R. (2001). *Educating Esme: Diary of a teacher's first year.* Chapel Hill, NC: Algonquin Books.

Cohen, R. M., & Scheer, S. (Eds.). (1997). *The work of teachers in America: A social history through stories.* Mahwah, NJ: Lawrence Erlbaum.

Cordier, M. H. (1992). *Schoolwomen of the prairies and plains.* Albuquerque: University of New Mexico Press.

Ennis, I. (1918). What the public owes the teacher. *Forty-fourth annual report of the Brooklyn Teachers' Association,* 13–18.

Finkelstein, B. (1989). *Governing the young: Teacher behavior in popular primary schools in nineteenth-century United States.* New York: Falmer Press.

Franklin, B. F. (1986). *Building the American community: The school curriculum and the search for social control.* Philadelphia: Falmer.

Haley, M. (1904). Why teachers should organize. *Journal of the addresses and proceedings of the National Education Association,* 145–152.

Hall, J. (2002). From Susan Isaacs to Lillian Weber to Deborah Meier: A progressive legacy in England and the United States. In A. R. Sadovnik & S. F. Semel (Eds.), *Founding mothers and others: Women educational leaders during the Progressive era* (pp. 237–252). New York: Palgrave.

Herbst, J. (1989). *And sadly teach: Teacher education and professionalization in American culture.* Madison: University of Wisconsin Press.

Hoffman, N. (1981). *Women's "true" profession: Voices from the history of teaching.* New York: The Feminist Press.

Kaestle, C. F. (1983). *Pillars of the republic: Common schools and American society, 1780–1860.* New York: Hill and Wang.

Karp, S. (2003). Money, Schools, and Justice. *Rethinking Schools, 18*(1), 26–30.

Kliebard, H. M. (1987). *The struggle for the American curriculum, 1893–1958*. New York: Routledge and Kegan Paul.

Littlefield, V. (1999). An open-ended education: Problems in reconstructing the history of an African-American classroom. In I. Grosvenor, M. Lawn, & K. Rousmaniere (Eds.), *Silences and images: The social history of the classroom* (pp. 145–161). New York: Peter Lang.

Murphy, M. (1990). *Blackboard unions: The AFT and the NEA, 1900–1980*. Ithaca, NY: Cornell University Press.

National Commission on Excellence in Education. (1983). *A nation at risk: The imperative for educational reform*. Washington, DC: U.S. Government Printing Office.

Newman, J. W. (2002). *America's teachers: An introduction to education*. Boston: Allyn and Bacon.

No Child Left Behind Act, H.R. 1 (2002) (enacted).

Orcutt, H. (1898). *Reminiscences of school life: an autobiography*. Cambridge, MA.

Owen, N. (1931). Just another day. *The Teachers' Forum 1*. Memphis Teachers' Association.

Preston, J. (2003). "He lives as a *Master*": Seventeenth-Century masculinity, gendered teaching, and careers of New England schoolmasters. *History of Education Quarterly, 43*(1), 350–371.

Reid, R. L. (1982). *Battleground: The autobiography of Margaret A. Haley*. Urbana: University of Illinois Press.

Rousmaniere, K. (1997a). Good teachers are born, not made: Self-Regulation in the work of nineteenth-century American women teachers. In K. Rousmaniere, K. Dehli, & N. de Coninck-Smith (Eds.), *Discipline, Moral Regulation and Schooling: A Social History* (pp. 117–133). New York: Garland Press.

Rousmaniere, K. (1997b). *City teachers: Teaching and school reform in historical perspective*. New York: Teachers College Press.

Rudolph, J. L. (2002). *Scientists in the classroom: The Cold War reconstruction of American science education*. New York: Palgrave.

Sadovnik, A. R., & Semel, S. F. (Eds.). (2002). *Founding mothers and others: Women educational leaders during the Progressive era*. New York: Palgrave.

Shmurak, C. B. (1998). Mary Lyon. In L. Eisenmann (Ed.), *Historical dictionary of women's education in the United States*. Westport, CT: Greenwood Press, 253–255.

Tyack, D. B. (1974). *The one best system: A history of American urban education*. Cambridge: Harvard University Press.

Urban, W. J. (2000). *Gender, race, and the National Education Association: Professionalism and its limitations*. New York: Routledge and Falmer.

Urban, W. J., & Wagoner, J. L., Jr. (2004). *American education: A history*. Boston: McGraw Hill.

Yohn, S. M. (1991). An education in the validity of pluralism: The meeting between Presbyterian mission teachers and Hispanic Catholics in New Mexico, 1870–1912. *History of Education Quarterly, 31*(3), 343–364.

Teacher Preparation—Transition and Turmoil

Michael D. Andrew

In this chapter, I will examine the evolution of teacher preparation in the United States, paying particular attention to attempts to extend teacher preparation and to identify an agreed-upon knowledge base. As Kate Rousmaniere describes in Chapter 1, "Well through the American Revolution, there was no formal academic preparation for teaching, and teachers were chosen not for any instructional skills, but for their religious background, moral character, and political affinity with the family or community which hired them." As we shall see in this chapter, vestiges of the eighteenth and nineteenth centuries remain—teacher preparation is in turmoil.

FOUR PATHS TO TEACHING

There have been four evolving paths for producing teachers in the United States.

1. The first path—the sanctioning of teachers with no prior professional training—has the oldest origins. This path has been kept alive by home-schooling, private schools, and state departments of education that allow "alternate," emergency, or critical shortage routes to public school teaching with no prior professional preparation.

For those pursuing this route, there are limited educational expectations;

teachers may be required to have only a high school education or a four-year college degree. Most states now require some form of teacher test to award a license for public school teaching. Some teachers along this path are required to have state or school district sponsored instruction and an on-the-job education plan. Most states allege to have district-supported mentoring, but, for many teachers in both public and private settings, success in teaching has been and continues to be "sink or swim." (See Chapter 7, this volume.) Quality of teaching or growth in teaching ability of those without professional training has gone almost unmeasured. Even the survival rate of beginning teachers from this route remains unresearched. More frequently than one might imagine, teachers with no professional preparation have been hired in public schools before official permission from the state has been given and fail out of teaching before their presence is officially counted. In many school districts, the number of "emergency" uncertified teachers far exceeds the official count kept by the states. In most states, there is no assessment or accreditation system in place to hold local districts, private schools, or state departments of education accountable for the quality of "programs" to assist teachers with no prior professional preparation. In some private schools, especially small religiously affiliated schools, there are several teachers teaching with only a high school diploma and little or no expertise in subjects they are asked to teach. This virtually unregulated path is free from any accountability. Surprisingly, it is this path that is growing at the fastest rate in the early part of the twenty-first century.

2. The second route—the direct entry route—is relatively recent and is, in some cases, a minor variant of the first. It consists of organized programs for teacher preparation that are not college or university based. These are usually short-term, intensive summer programs run by private businesses, school districts, nonprofit organizations, and state departments of education. Increasingly, these programs are encouraged and funded by the federal government (e.g., Troops for Teachers). A few of these programs include some college or university course work.

The term "alternative route" has been indiscriminately used to describe both the noncollege based routes and any college preparation programs which differ from the traditional four-year pattern. It is more helpful to use "alternative" to refer to noncollege based programs, but the variation in all types of programs is now so great that use of the term "alternative" may be more confusing than helpful.

3. The third path involves formal, college-based teacher preparation in schools where teacher training has been a primary mission. This route emerged as normal schools evolved to state teachers' colleges, then to state liberal arts colleges, to regional state colleges, and, eventually, to regional state universities. In some cases, the teacher training institutions have been private colleges. Teachers who travel this path complete four-year undergraduate degree programs in education. Goodlad (1990, 1994) and others point out that the evolution in state institutions has been more of a search for academic respectability than a push to professionalize teaching or radically reform teacher preparation. As the evolution has proceeded to state liberal arts colleges and regional state universities, the status of teacher preparation within the institutions has often declined. It is this path that has produced most of America's public school teachers over the past fifty years.

4. The fourth path involves the preparation of teachers at private liberal arts colleges and major research universities. These institutions have often grounded teacher preparation in subject field majors with various levels of pedagogical training. Most have focused on secondary school teaching. Many small liberal arts colleges have not offered enough professional course work to allow state credentialing. Since the beginning of the twentieth century, the largest of the research-oriented state universities and colleges have developed schools and colleges of education. These schools and colleges, in order to compete for resources and students, have often developed majors in education to parallel or replace subject matter majors. A few have chosen to operate solely at the graduate level and have taken prospective teachers who have completed a subject matter major, many of whom are career-changing adults.

The focus of this chapter is on teacher preparation programs at the nation's colleges and universities, the third and fourth paths described above. This may be akin to fiddling while Rome burns since the forces favoring sanctioning teachers without professional preparation are growing at a rapid rate and are now well established in federal policy making circles.

In the following pages, I will briefly review the development of professions other than teaching and provide a contrast to the evolution of the professional preparation of teachers.

THE EVOLUTION OF PREPARATION IN
OTHER PROFESSIONS

There are several well-supported criteria for defining professionals. (For example, see Darling-Hammond, 1992). The following list is typical:

- There is an accepted body of specialized knowledge necessary for good professional practice.
- Expert knowledge and professional skill require extensive specialized training.
- Admission to professional training is selective and based on academic aptitude and appropriate personal qualities.
- Professional work is complex, not standardized, and requires professional judgment.
- There are standards of practice to which professionals are expected to adhere.
- Standards are developed, transmitted, and enforced by professionals.
- Professionals are committed and obligated to act in the best interest of their clients.

Hatch (1988), writing about professions other than teaching, limits the criteria to three: (1) a definable body of organized knowledge and expertise that derives from extensive academic training, (2) a moral commitment of service to the public, and (3) relative independence and autonomy of professional life. Hatch maintains that professional training is "tightly linked in an institutional setting that certifies quality and competence"(1988, p. 2). Hatch's analysis, with chapters by noted historians, omits elementary or secondary teaching as a profession.

Writing on law, Maxwell H. Bloomfield notes that, by 1900, the law profession began to upgrade and standardize educational requirements. By the 1930s, states insisted on law school as the sole method to prepare for the bar. After World War II, states standardized legal education. Only professional schools approved by the American Bar Association (ABA) or Association of American Law Schools (AALS) could prepare lawyers (Hatch, 1988, Chapter 2).

In medicine, the American Medical Association began early in the twentieth century to control access to the profession and to standardize medical education and licensing. By 1930, the field of medicine uniformly required a baccalaureate degree and rigorous postbaccalaureate professional training (Hatch, 1988, Chapter 3). According to Ludmerer (1985), who provides a comprehensive history of medical education, the structural evolution was completed by the 1920s and called for active participation of students in labs and clinical work in addition to subject specific preparation.

TEACHING AS A SEMIPROFESSION

Amitar Etzioni describes teaching as one of several "semi-professions" in his edited book, *The Semi-Professions and Their Organization—Teachers, Nurses and Social Workers*. The semiprofessions, according to Etzioni, have several traits in common:

> *Their training is shorter, their status is less legitimate, their right to privileged communication less established, there is less of a specialized body of knowledge, and they have less autonomy from supervision or societal control than "the" professions. (Etzioni, 1969, p. v)*

In a chapter on elementary teaching, Dan Lortie comments that "there are few settled matters in pedagogy" (Etzioni, 1969, p. 9) and describes "the largely intuitive nature of teaching." Lortie sees few role changes since 1918 and limited evidence of evolution toward professional status among educators. Lortie, like most writers on professionalism, focuses heavily on the need for a specialized knowledge base, noting that preservice experiences neither provide prospective teachers what they need to know nor positively affect their work values in lasting fashion.

William Goode, who writes the summary chapter in Etzioni's book, distills professionalism down to: "(1) a body of specialized knowledge and (2) the ideal of service." He predicts that teaching will not become a profession and faults the knowledge base in pedagogy as "relatively small in amount and shallow intellectually" (Etzioni, 1969, p. 213).

THE CURRENT SCENE

Much has happened since Etzioni's description in 1969. The knowledge base on teaching has exploded but is still not organized, legitimated, or disseminated to schools of education in any systematic fashion. On the whole, the semiprofession of teaching has made little progress toward professionalism. Instead of reducing paths of entry to the profession, new and less regulated paths are proliferating. Alternative routes that require limited, if any, college or university study are being applauded. Entry by poorly mentored apprenticeship is widely accepted. Undergraduate preservice programs thrive while remaining little different from those of fifty years ago. Little progress is occurring to move teacher preparation beyond its niche in four-year baccalaureate programs. States shun the regulation of instructors for homeschoolers or private schools and welcome direct entry of unprepared individuals into public school classrooms. Federal policies support alternative, noncollege based entry into teaching and provide definitions of highly qualified teachers that exclude any professional preparation. Verbal ability and subject matter knowledge are seen by many, including United States Department of Education officials, as the only measurable criteria for teaching. College-based teacher education is increasingly seen as "hoops and hurdles" (U.S. Department of Education, 2002), and control over the preparation of teachers is shifting to outside entities. Teacher preparation is in turmoil.

THE EVOLUTION OF COLLEGE-BASED TEACHER PREPARATION

In the early nineteenth century, the establishment of "normal schools" paralleled the rise of common schools and provided a steady supply of teachers. Haberman (1986) alleges that the first normal school was initiated by Samuel Hall in Concord, Vermont, in 1823. According to Rousmaniere (Chapter 1, this volume), the first state-supported normal school began in 1839 in Lexington, Massachusetts. The normal schools provided training in basic subjects to be taught in schools and were mostly two-year programs. These early normal schools provided academic knowledge to would-be teachers, but it was well known that the standards of knowledge were considerably below those of the four-year universities and liberal arts colleges. Historians of education tell us that pedagogical studies began to be introduced after the Civil War. Haberman describes the early influences of Pestalozzi, Herbart, Froebel, and Spencer (Haberman, 1986).

From the early days, colleges and universities saw normal schools as second-rate institutions, and the pressure for respectability and a broader student base pushed normal schools to become four-year teachers' colleges and, more recently, state colleges or regional state universities. Historically, the more prestigious four-year colleges and universities produced secondary teachers and introduced studies of pedagogy. Haberman reminds us that the sources of the knowledge explosion in pedagogy "were not vacuous pedagogues from the normal schools but some of the most prestigious . . . , most highly honored scholars in our leading universities" (Haberman, 1986, p. 10).[1]

Once the normal schools of the 1800s began to morph into four-year teachers' colleges in the 1930s and 1940s, the dominant curriculum structure for the preparation of teachers became more or less static. Majors in education were filled with courses in pedagogy. For elementary teachers, there were generic methods courses and specialized curriculum and methods courses in each area of elementary instruction (language arts, mathematics, social studies, science, music, art, and physical education). "Foundations" courses evolved as courses in history, philosophy, and sociology of education. One or more courses were required in human learning and development. The culmination of the curriculum was a senior experience—student teaching—that varied in length from eight to sixteen weeks. The education major was embedded in a curriculum of general studies common to students of all majors. Secondary school candidates followed a similar program, but one with fewer methods courses and more emphasis on subject field background with a minor or perhaps a dual major in the subject to be taught. This pattern was cemented in place by regulatory agencies at the state level.

This curriculum structure has come to be known as "traditional" teacher preparation. According to Wong and Osguthorpe's 1993 survey, four-year baccalaureate programs still prevail. Ninety percent of institutions surveyed retain a four-year undergraduate program in elementary education, 89 percent in secondary education, and 67 percent in special education. Extended programs at the graduate level are generally reserved for students who decide to become teachers late in their educational experience or who are changing careers. This model reflects the dominant curriculum and structure for teacher preparation at state colleges and state universities where most of the nation's public school teachers are prepared. The most recent Directory of Schools (2004) that lists institutions that belong to the American Association of Colleges for Teacher Education (AACTE) reports that all 660 of its member institutions offer four-year teacher preparation programs. Seventy-eight offer five-year programs to prepare teachers.

The evolution from normal school to regional university has not been kind to teacher education. Professional educators have sought to distance themselves from the dirty work of teacher preparation, and professors have found ways to stay in "education" but not prepare teachers. A major contributor to this peculiar separation has been the organization of schools of education around "disciplines" such as educational psychology, measurement, special education, reading, and foundations instead of around programs of teacher preparation. This has legitimized research and courses for those studying for leadership positions in education. Meanwhile, programs preparing teachers have often existed separately, having to beg for staffing from among the supposedly more academic departments in their own fields of education.

The system of rewards in schools of education has been similarly structured to encourage grants, research, and publication, leaving the teaching of methods courses and clinical supervision of students as the least rewarded and most labor-intensive chores. Likewise, the task of administration of teacher preparation programs and coordination of field placements often goes begging or falls to junior faculty.

At the larger regional and state institutions, Ph.D. programs have emerged to siphon away more would-be teacher educators. These programs, with their small classes and research emphasis, are not only seen as high-status activities but activities which are much easier than teaching large undergraduate courses and completing time-consuming school supervision.

The end result has been that teacher education programs have been forced to use large numbers of part-time instructors and clinical professors and are thus staffed primarily with public school teachers and administrators. The size of teacher preparation programs has not diminished since student demand is high, and the tuition dollars fuel the small classes and research-oriented graduate programs. Through this devaluation of status, the curriculum and structure for teacher preparation have remained largely unchanged for the last eighty years.

A STATIC CURRICULUM AND STRUCTURE: WHY?

We can speculate on the endurance of the so-called traditional curriculum and structures for teacher education. While professional preparation evolved to postbaccalaureate professional schools in law and medicine, teacher education has remained largely embedded in four-year colleges. I give the reader eight theories to consider:

1. The four-year traditional curriculum hasn't changed because it is the best way to prepare teachers.

2. Because the prestige in schools of education lies in research and specialist programs, no one cares about changing teacher education.

3. Teacher education hasn't evolved beyond four years because teacher education should remain close to undergraduate subject acquisition. The challenge to this theory is that the study of pedagogy and the study of the disciplines have long histories of unhappy or distant relationships. The close working relationship between the liberal arts and professional education continues to be elusive, and the assumption of such a needed relationship is unproven.

4. The relatively low pay for teachers makes extended, postbaccalaureate training costs prohibitive.

5. The field of teacher preparation is heavily populated with conservative people who resist change. By conservative, I mean not prone to change or innovation but likely to do what is expected and to endure and embrace the routine. (The conservative tendencies of teachers was discussed many years ago by Durkheim [1956].)

6. There is a state and national regulatory structure surrounding teacher education that resists change and enforces conformity. State regulatory agencies are heavily populated with representatives of teacher education institutions, thus increasing the tendency to preserve and expand the status quo.

7. The traditional curriculum and structure make money for the colleges and universities and provide secure jobs for many professors. The traditional structure and curriculum fill as much of the undergraduate curriculum as they possibly can, are relatively cheap to operate, and draw a continual supply of students.

8. There is little accountability for the quality of the programs and, therefore, no pressure for change. If poor teachers are produced, faculty members still keep their jobs. There is no penalty for producing poor teachers, too many teachers, or too few teachers.

All eight of the theories outlined above probably contribute to the endurance of so-called traditional teacher preparation.

EFFORTS TO CHANGE THE TRADITIONAL PATTERN OF TEACHER PREPARATION

Calls for change in traditional teacher preparation have been continuous. They have come from inside and outside the profession. The outside critiques have often been merciless. Some have been vicious. James D. Koerner's book *The Miseducation of America's Teachers* (1963) attacked teacher education on all fronts. In 1991, Rita Kramer's *Education School Follies: The Miseducation of America's Teachers* mirrored Koerner's criticisms. These two critiques are precursors to current policy makers who wish to eliminate all required professional preparation for teachers.

More Subject Matter—Less Pedagogy

Most critics have called for more subject matter preparation for teachers and less pedagogy. Arthur Bestor (1953) roundly criticized teacher education for too many courses in pedagogy. James B. Conant, while president of Harvard University, wrote *The Education of American Teachers* (1963) in which he argued for more breadth and depth in subject matter preparation of America's teachers (for elementary teachers, twelve courses or thirty-six semester hours and for, secondary teachers, sixteen courses or forty-eight semester hours) and for some professional training. As Conant points out (as do others), "professors of education have not yet discovered or agreed upon a common body of knowledge that they all feel should be held by school teachers before the student takes his first full-time job" (1963, p. 141). Conant argues for colleges to have the freedom to develop their own programs and assume responsibility for the competence of their graduates.

Haberman points out that, from the earliest days of professional teacher preparation, "advocates of liberal studies criticized the professional educators as lacking substance, while the professional educators criticized the universities as unresponsive to life, to practice in the schools, and to their own new discoveries" (1986, p. 10). Hodenfield and Stinnett describe in detail the earlier battles between subject matter specialists in academic departments and teacher education in their book, *The Education of Teachers: Conflict and Consensus* (1961).

This split debate has continued to the present day and has moved outside the academy. The advocates of subject matter knowledge have never been more strident, more uncompromising, or more in control of federal policy initiatives than in the early part of the twenty-first century. The critics of pedagogical studies have moved out of the universities and into conservative policy making foundations and "think tanks."

The leap of subject matter knowledge proponents into the arena of federal policy making has had the effect of forcing the attention of teacher educators on more subject matter preparation. On the one hand, teachers must be taught the content found in state "curriculum frameworks" which supposedly provide the basis for the new high-stakes state tests, and, on the other hand, "highly qualified" teachers (No Child Left Behind terminology) must have subject area majors in the fields they teach.

Suggestions for Change from Within

While outside critics are bringing radical change to teacher education, calls from within the profession have taken four directions: (1) changing the current curriculum, (2) researching the components of traditional teacher preparation, (3) calling for structural change, and (4) organizing and disseminating the knowledge base required for effective teaching.

1. *Changing the Current Curriculum.* Many change efforts have sought to add the latest new knowledge to the teacher education curriculum. For example, in the 1960s and 1970s, teacher educators focused on individually guided education, behavioral objectives, mastery learning, activity-centered learning, discovery learning, and values clarification. In the 1980s and 1990s, behavioral objectives were renamed performance objectives and performance indicators, and attention shifted to whole language, rubrics, constructivism, multiple intelligences, heterogeneous grouping, cooperative learning, inclusion, and peer instruction. Since the 1990s, new computer technologies, brain-based learning, and balanced reading approaches illustrate the new curriculum additions. The list of new topics to be added to teacher education curriculum is long. Many of the new ideas suggested for addition to the curriculum have been worthy; some have been based on solid research, but many have not. Many have been short-term fads. This level of change involves simply adding and subtracting bits of content from existing course instruction.

2. *Researching the Components of Traditional Teacher Preparation.* Most investigations into the components of teacher preparation have been descriptive, correlational, or "process-product" research. Descriptive studies abound

with advocacy from a new approach that was tried at an institution. Evidence is mostly anecdotal.

In the 1990s, qualitative research methodologies ascended as a favored approach for studying the elements of teacher education and seeing the pieces as part of more holistic enterprises. These qualitative approaches provided rich descriptions of segments of teacher education. Methods of anthropology, ethnography, biography, and the storytelling became popular in schools of education. Use of some of these methods deepened and enriched our understanding of teaching, learning, and teacher education; others did not.

Correlational studies collected data from preservice teachers with different courses or experiences. Surveys provided frequencies and rating scale scores which were compared. Statistically significant correlations led to suggestions that one approach to preparing teachers was better than another. Process-product research usually focused on single interventions in courses offered for teachers. Control groups provided a quasi-experimental design, but random assignment to experimental and control groups was rare. Teacher educators have not, for the most part, applied the knowledge gained from these lines of research to improve teacher education programs. Teacher educators read about research on teacher education, hear about it at conferences, and then return to business as usual.

3. *Changing the Structure of Education.* Attempts to change the overall structure of teacher education were plentiful from 1980 to 2000. These attempts were often broad in scope and based on prescriptions by individuals with long careers in teacher preparation. John Goodlad in *Teachers for Our Nation's Schools* (1990), introduces nineteen postulates for changing teacher education based upon a study of twenty-nine different teacher education programs and a lifetime of experience as a teacher educator. Goodlad makes many recommendations regarding the institutional requirements for effective teacher preparation and suggestions for structural change in teacher preparation. In 1997, Alan Tom, a career teacher educator, in his book, *Redesigning Teacher Education*, offers eleven "principles" for redesign and claims that state and national regulation (including that of the National Council for the Accreditation of Teacher Education, or NCATE) constrains effective redesign (pp. 195–202). Other teacher educators have suggested changes that moved teacher preparation out of the traditional four-year mold. In the following section, I will suggest that program structure influences the outcomes of teacher preparation and will examine one call for structural change, that of extending teacher preparation beyond the four-year baccalaureate model.

THE CASE FOR CHANGE IN STRUCTURE

Kenneth M. Ludmerer, a noted scholar on the history of medical education, suggests that "Learning to heal, like every other type of learning, is profoundly influenced by the institutional framework in which instruction is carried out" (1985, p. 5). In *Learning to Heal: The Development of American Medical Education*, he describes the sea of change that reshaped medical education from 1885 to the 1920s. The process of preparing doctors shifted from short-term programs where students memorized facts to extended training with laboratories and carefully supervised internships. In Ludmerer's words, "The new goal of medical training was to foster critical thinking, not merely the memorization of facts" (1985, p. 5). According to Ludmerer, ideas of progressive education where the learner was actively engaged in the learning process began in medical education a generation before they appeared in elementary and secondary education. For the new educational ideals to be implemented, a structural revolution had to take place in medical education. The short-term "proprietary schools," small private schools for training doctors, were abandoned, and medical education was connected both to university professional schools and teaching hospitals. Prior to this shift, medical education was the brunt of enormous criticism. The medical profession was held in low esteem. Similar to what is happening in teacher education today, it was a short leap from criticizing physicians to criticizing medical education. The perceived decline in status of the profession was attributed to defective medical education (Ludmerer, 1985, p. 27).

In the early part of the twenty-first century, teacher educators are facing similar criticism. Instead of contemplating fundamental changes in structure, most are defending the status quo by arguing that teacher education matters and that there is a knowledge base that underlies successful classroom performance. Some teacher educators are seeking to further institutionalize traditional practices by adhering to a tighter regulatory structure, while others are welcoming "alternative" paths to teaching, which all but eliminate colleges and universities and treat teacher preparation as merely technical training. Still others are busy chasing federal dollars that tie teacher education and teaching to the narrow goal of student scores on standardized achievement tests.

A few attempts have sought to alter the traditional structure of teacher education. Examples include the addition of early experience courses, elimination of education majors, and creation of and collaboration with professional de-

velopment schools. These limited structural changes have seen some implementation. Another experiment has been to add a graduate or postbaccalaureate component to teacher education.

Extending Teacher Preparation

One of the more intriguing attempts to bring radical structural change to
teacher preparation has been to extend teacher preparation, either to five years
of integrated undergraduate-graduate education or to move preparation to the
graduate level. These attempts have been undertaken to increase subject field
preparation, encourage a liberal education, deepen clinical experiences in duration and/or frequency (including a year-long internship), and retain pedagogical training. The calls to extend programs fall into two categories: (1) calls
for postbaccalaureate programs, and (2) calls for extending preparation beyond four years through either a five-year baccalaureate or integrated
undergraduate-graduate programs. The latter are called "five-year" programs
or "fifth year" programs.

Postbaccalaureate programs were developed in many prestigious universities that adopted Master of Arts in Teaching programs in the 1950s and early
1960s. These programs sought to recruit academically able students who already held subject field degrees and to provide them with some professional
course work and (mostly) a year-long internship. Programs usually began
with an intense summer program addressing theory and practice and the internship complemented by course work in both subject matter and pedagogy.
Some programs required two summers and an academic year. In the post-
Sputnik era, National Science Foundation money lured math and science in-
terns into these programs, and school districts offered partial salary to allow
for the internship experience. These programs often lacked good communication between universities/colleges and cooperating schools, and supervision
during the internship was sometimes weak. The Master of Arts in Teaching
programs declined in number, although many have been re-created or still
exist in modified form. (The 2004 Directory of Members of AACTE, which
polled over half of the nation's 1,200 teacher education programs, found 163
Master of Arts in Teaching programs [AACTE, 2004].)

The calls for extending teacher preparation beyond four years but retaining
some professional preparation in the baccalaureate program sought to build
an integrated undergraduate-graduate experience for preservice teachers.
Harrison Gardiner describes how Brown University established a year-long
internship in 1909 for some of its education graduates. Similar internships

grew up in several cities and were built around principles established by the National Society of College Teachers of Education (1969, p. 42).

According to Gardiner, graduate internship programs grew in number, and most were based on the following six principles:

> *(1) Internship should be considered part of the basic preparation and training of the beginning teacher. (2) During the period of internship, the intern should engage in the large variety of activities in which a regular teacher engages. (3) The internship plan should include a cooperating teacher-training institution in which interns carry on correlated graduate work during their period of internship. (4) The internship should be at least a year in length. (5) Basic courses in professional education, including student teaching, should be completed prior to internship. (6) The internship should be in a school situation approximating as closely as possible that in which the intern will probably receive permanent appointment. (Gardiner, 1969, pp. 43–44)*

These undergraduate-graduate programs disappeared, and change in the structure of teacher education languished from the 1960s to the mid-1980s. Traditional four-year programs became further entrenched.

In 1974, the Association of Teacher Educators (ATE) published a fifty-seven-page monograph written by this author, *Teacher Leadership: A Model for Change*, that called for career ladders for teachers and a five-year program with a subject field major and a full year internship to prepare "teacher leaders" (Andrew, 1974). Teacher leaders were to take "a central role . . . in promoting change which improves the quality of education" (1974, p. 6). Teachers were to seek (1) continual self-improvement, (2) improvement of other teachers, and (3) initiation of curricular change (1974, p. 7). This monograph described the five-year program that was being implemented at the University of New Hampshire in 1973–1974.

Later, in the mid-1980s, a flurry of recommendations came from within the profession advocating extended programs of teacher education. The prescriptions from within the field included work by Howsam, Corrigan, and Denemark (*Educating a Profession*, 1985); the National Commission for Excellence in Teacher Education (1985); Lasley (1986); the Holmes Group (*Tomorrow's Teachers*, 1986); and Goodlad (*Teachers for our Nation's Schools*, 1990; and *Educational Renewal: Better Teachers, Better Schools*, 1994). AACTE formed a committee to study the idea of extended programs (AACTE, 1993; Monahan, 1983). Andrew (1983, 1984, 1986, 1989, 1990) continued to report on the "five-year" program at the University of New Hampshire. Baker (1984) reported on a similar program from Austin College in Texas. Saunders (1985), Smith (1984), and Scannell (1983) contributed. The critics marshalled rebuttals (Hawley, 1986; Howey & Zimpher, 1986; Tom, 1989, 1991).

The rationale for extended programs was two pronged:

1. The more highly regarded professions had evolved to require post-baccalaureate professional training. A few of the proponents (Howsam et al., 1985 and Andrew, 1974) pointed out the connection between extended preparation and professional status. None who voiced this opinion saw professionalism as the primary reason for extending programs. Increased professional status was simply a fortunate by-product.

2. Prospective teachers needed a strong liberal education, a subject field major, challenging professional course work, and clinical practice that went beyond the traditional eight to sixteen weeks. Most agreed that professional course work should be reduced from that which was common fare in education majors. Even so, calls for subject majors, year-long internships, liberal education, and professional preparation necessitated a repackaging of traditional preparation into other than a four-year framework.

Many advantages to the extended format were theorized. These include the following:

- More opportunity for a solid liberal/general education.
- Guarantee of a subject field major.
- Time for a longer internship preceded by phased practicum.
- More opportunity for performance-based screening (screening based on academic performance in subject field majors, early professional course work, and in early school practicum).
- A format to recruit both undergraduate and postbaccalaureate students. (A five-year sequence could be used for both, with career changers and college graduates coming in at the postbaccalaureate level.)
- Time for phased professional studies including the better integration of theory with practice.

- A longer supervised clinical experience to develop greater confidence and autonomy and stronger entry-level skills.
- Opportunity for more continuous and extended relationships with partner schools (early practicum and full-year internships).
- Opportunity to develop a master's degree as an incentive for the added time commitment.
- Incentive for students committed to subject field majors to also prepare to teach.
- Higher standards for graduate school entry as a means to attract stronger students.

Among the most vocal proponents of extended programs were the first two institutions to implement five-year integrated undergraduate-graduate programs: Austin College of Sherman, Texas, and the University of New Hampshire. Both had programs operating in 1973–1974. These two institutions were joined by the University of Florida at Gainesville and the University of Kansas. This foursome presented program descriptions, rationales, and data on admissions at annual meetings of AACTE and the American Educational Research Association (AERA) during the 1980s. Representatives of these institutions consulted with interested colleges and universities, and a small wave of proactive converts developed similar five-year programs (for example, the University of Connecticut, Truman State University, the University of Tennessee in Knoxville, and the University of Southern Maine).

In 1996, the National Commission on Teaching and America's Future (NCTAF) launched its first report, *What Matters Most: Teaching for America's Future*. The report's second major recommendation for improving teacher preparation was to develop extended teacher preparation programs that provide a yearlong internship in a professional development school (NCTAF, 1996, p. 77). This recommendation called for the most profound structural change in teacher education. The report offers four strong paragraphs of rationale for extended programs, and, unlike the Holmes and Carnegie reports that gave a relatively uncritical call for graduate-level teacher education, *What Matters Most* began to make important distinctions between integrated undergraduate-graduate programs, twelve-month graduate programs, and longer graduate programs. The authors identified the basic components necessary for such reform-minded structural changes. But there was little attempt in the report to deal with the confusion, fear, and misgivings that existed around this recommendation. What was made clear was the need for more space to adequately provide subject matter, pedagogical knowledge, and clinical practice. What was missing was the detailed discussion of variations in extended programs and the problems of implementing and sustaining good programs. The NCTAF placed its recommendation for extended programs on the back burner and focused its efforts on national accreditation, uniform state standards (in line with NCATE standards), rigorous state licensing, and advanced teacher certification through the National Board for Professional Teaching Standards (NBPTS). At the moment, NCTAF has shifted focus to teacher retention and the conditions of teaching.

While commissions, panels, and publications that advocated for extended programs—especially five-year programs—were supported or sponsored by the AACTE, the Association never took an official position supporting such programs. It would have been risky to take such a stand because the majority of the AACTE membership had four-year programs and might have withdrawn their financial support for AACTE. The same was true for NCATE.

In the late 1990s, teacher education's agenda could have been to unpack the recommendations for extended programs and develop a plan for change. This did not happen. There is still a long list of unexplained issues surrounding extended programs. The data available have either been ignored or angrily disputed by many teacher educators. The profession has successfully avoided the prescriptions for extended programs.

THE THREAT OF EXTENDED PROGRAMS

The extended program advocates in the late 1970s and 1980s were tolerated at national conferences. Dean Corrigan, Heinrich Gideonese, Richard Wisniewski, and Dale Scannell gave major speeches at AACTE advocating for extended programs. John Goodlad recommended extended programs, and a small group of extended program pioneers presented descriptions of five-year programs in operation. These presentations never reached center stage, however, and none of the proponents were ever invited to give keynote speeches or receive Major Forum status at the AACTE Annual Meetings. The advocates were either ignored or criticized. Why? Extended programs represented a potential threat to traditional four-year programs in that:

- Many of the 1,200-plus institutions preparing teachers were four-year colleges with no graduate programs. If they were forced to move to five-year or postbaccalaureate programs, it would take major college restructuring.

- Graduate-level education was more costly, and increased costs risked teacher education status as a cash cow. If teacher education programs didn't make money, they might not be tolerated.
- Teacher educators were convinced that extending programs would reduce the number of students in their programs. This would ultimately mean a loss of jobs.
- Moving to extended programs would require substantial program change.

Using a series of arguments, the supporters of traditional teacher preparation successfully put down most of the support for extended programs. The usual arguments were based on claims that students prefer four-year programs, there was a lack of evidence in support of five-year programs, five-year programs would not be cost-effective, giving graduate degrees for preservice preparation would cheapen the master's degree, and, most important, things were fine the way they were.

THE RESEARCH IN SUPPORT OF EXTENDED PROGRAMS

In 1986, this author did a study of ten years of graduates of teacher education programs at the University of New Hampshire (Andrew, 1990). These graduates represented students of similar academic characteristics who took most of the same core professional courses but were enrolled in three different types of programs: four-year traditional, five-year integrated undergraduate-graduate, and postbaccalaureate. Some surprising results came from this study.

1. 13 percent more students in the extended programs entered teaching.
2. 18 percent more of those entering were still teaching from five to ten years later.

This research raised a question. What was it about these programs that led to these differences? They were students at the same institution. They all took the same core courses.

Shortly after this, in the mid-1980s, a group of faculty at University of New

Hampshire met as the Teacher Education Research Group (TERG) and decided to take initiative to expand the follow-up studies to other institutions.
The group developed a student survey that looked primarily at teacher satisfaction, teacher performance, and teacher leadership and developed a survey
for school principals that paralleled the graduate survey. Instruments were
pilot tested. Ten other universities were invited to join. These institutions had
several things in common: similar academic characteristics of incoming students, desire to improve programs, recent or planned moves to extended five-
year programs, and a range of programs. The goal was to contrast programs
and see if there were any consistent differences that aligned with similar program structures. The project later became known as the Benchmark Study
(Andrew & Schwab, 1995). Graduates were studied at five-year intervals, thus
allowing for larger samples and several years for examination of performance,
entry, and retention.

The first five-year study on the graduates of eleven colleges and universities
assessed graduates from 1985 to 1990. The study was repeated with a slightly
different cluster of eleven colleges and universities in 1995.[2] The two Benchmark studies (graduates of 1985 to 1995) assessed a total of sixteen programs
across the country. The sample was comprised of 3,050 graduates and 770
principals. 24 percent of responding graduates were teaching in urban
schools, 30 percent in rural schools, and 46 percent in suburban schools. Of
the total sample, 50 percent were teaching in elementary schools, 26.1 percent in middle schools, and 23.8 percent in high schools. Eighteen percent of
the respondents reported teaching in schools with greater than 50 percent minority populations; 18.5 percent reported teaching in schools with 20 to 50
percent minority populations; and 46.4 percent reported teaching in schools
with less than 10 percent minorities. This distribution was roughly the same
for four-year, five-year, and postbaccalaureate programs. The study was repeated again in 2000 with just three institutions. Results included the following:

1. There are stronger and weaker programs of every type.

2. Good teachers come from all types of programs.

3. Graduates of extended programs generally excel. Although no one
   could claim that all graduates of all extended programs excel, there
   were consistent differences favoring extended programs. Graduates
   of extended programs, taken as a group, excelled over four-year pro-

TABLE 2.1: Percentages of graduates entering the teaching profession from four-year and extended teacher education programs.

	ENTERING TEACHING	
	1990–1995	1985–1990
Four year	80%	84%
Extended	91%	90%

gram graduates on every major variable examined in the studies. These differences remained consistent across three different studies. Some of the results will illustrate:

- *Entry.* Extended program graduates entered teaching at a higher rate than did graduates from four-year programs (see Table 2.1). (We defined *entry* as teaching for at least one year in the first five years since program completion.) An earlier study (graduates of 1976–1986) of four-year versus extended programs at the same institution (University of New Hampshire) showed 86 percent of four-year graduates entering teaching versus 93 percent for extended program graduates (Andrew, 1990).

- *Retention* (still teaching at time of survey and for two or more years). The comparison of ten years of University of New Hampshire graduates from four-year and from integrated undergraduate/graduate programs showed 74 percent of all extended program graduates still teaching (from two to ten years). This compared to 56 percent of four-year program graduates (see Table 2.2). These were percentages of all graduates, not just those who entered teaching[3] (Andrew, 1990). Results from the two Benchmark project surveys of graduates at sixteen colleges and universities had a 9 percent difference in retention rate.

- *On-the-Job Performance.* In the Benchmark Study (Andrew & Schwab, 1995), when principals rated graduates, the largest percentage of "top decile" performers was from integrated five-year programs. (Integrated five-year graduates 43%, postbaccalaureate and four-year graduates 37%).

TABLE 2.2: Percentages of retention in the teaching profession comparing four-year and extended teacher education programs.

NOW TEACHING*		
	1990–1995	1985–1990
Four year	80%	78%
Extended	89%	87%

Since many more extended graduates were still teaching, the mean numbers of years taught was significantly greater for extended program graduates.

Principals placed somewhat more individuals from extended programs in the top two deciles of performance than they did four-year graduates (70% vs. 67%).

Principals rated extended program graduates slightly higher on all measures (instructional items, interpersonal/professional items, and leadership items).

- *Overall Rating of Effectiveness of Teacher Preparation Program.* Extended program graduates consistently gave higher ratings to their teacher preparation programs.

There was great variation among programs of all types with many good and great teachers coming from every type of program, but, given similar institutional settings and even at the same institutions, results favored extended programs (both postbaccalaureate entry and five-year). The extended programs had several features in common:

- Most of the extended programs studied had internships longer than one semester. Those with the highest retention rate had the longest clinical experience. Those with the highest scores in most performance-related items had the longest clinical experience. It appears that a sustained, well-supervised internship is important to launch a confident and competent beginning teacher. Confident, competent beginning teachers are more likely to take jobs and stay in them.
- The requirements of a longer than normal program and entry to graduate school were strong self-screens which favored students with

very strong commitment to teaching and strong academic skills and records. Many of those without strong commitment undoubtedly chose not to enter extended programs, and graduate school academic standards screened out those students with weaker academic skills.

While there is much variation among extended programs, these two factors appear to be common in all programs: (1) there is time for a subject major, general education, pedagogical studies, *and* an extended clinical experience; and (2) extended programs act as effective screens for commitment and academic ability. Certain structural factors, then, appear to favor extended programs.

THE BURIAL OF THE EXTENDED PROGRAM MOVEMENT

Since 1996, when the NCTAF report, *What Matters Most: Teaching for America's Future*, advocated extended programs with year-long internships in professional development schools, there has been relative silence on the topic of extended programs. In a *Journal of Teacher Education* (2001) article, Ken Zeichner of the University of Wisconsin-Madison and Ann K. Shulte of California State University, Chico, are critical of the work on the structure of teacher education programs:

> Although claims have been made about the superiority of particular structural models of teacher education such as the 5-year extended program (e.g., Gideonse, 1982; National Commission on Teaching and America's Future, 1996; Scannell, 1999), the empirical evidence about the effects of different models is scarce and problematic. For example, most of the empirically based claims about the value of the 5-year extended program are based on the studies of one 5-year program at the University of New Hampshire (e.g., Andrew, 1990) and cannot necessarily be generalized to the rest of the country. In the one study that is frequently cited in support of the 5-year model that uses a sample beyond New Hampshire (Andrew & Schwab, 1995), it was concluded that there is a higher retention rate for teachers who participated in the extended programs in the 11-program sample. It was also reported that there is no difference in the teaching effectiveness of the graduates from the different programs as assessed by principals. No information was given, however, about the schools in which the teacher education graduates taught. In an earlier study of the research on graduate teacher education programs including master of

*arts in teaching programs (Zeichner, 1989), it was concluded that al-
though there is some evidence regarding the positive teaching evaluations and high retention rates of teachers who participated in graduate
teacher education programs in the 1950s through the 1980s, very few
of these graduates taught in schools in high poverty urban and rural
areas where they were most needed but opted for teaching in already
advantaged suburban schools (see also Coley & Thorpe, 1986). Positive teaching evaluations and higher retention rates mean little by
themselves without knowing the kind of schools where teachers work.
(Zeichner & Schulte, 2001, p. 271)*

These authors conclude:

*One reasonable direction to take in the future is to move away from the
nonproductive course of trying to determine which particular structural
model of teacher education is superior to others and recognize that all
of these various models will include a wide range of quality in programs
and courses. (p. 279)*

*If we continue to seek evidence that any one structural model of teacher
education is superior to others and to ignore the wide range of quality
that exists within all models, we will continue to be disappointed in the
results. (p. 280)*

The final nails in the coffin of the extended program movement will likely
be found in the forthcoming report of the AERA Panel on Research and
Teacher Education edited by Marilyn Cochran-Smith and Ken Zeichner. The
authors have voiced their intention to dismiss the research that compares
structural alternatives in teacher education programs and to label this arena
for research as unproductive. For the moment, it appears that the discussion
of the best models of teacher preparation and the effectiveness of extended
programs of teacher preparation is closed.

4. *Searching for a Knowledge Base.* One of the baseline criteria for status as a
profession is the existence of a specific knowledge base. It is assumed that
members of a profession should share some core understandings and that
having these understandings is important to effective functioning as a professional. This does not mean that a particular individual could not function effectively in the profession without this knowledge, but it does imply that any
individual would be better able to function with the knowledge. And, therefore, the knowledge should be required. Neither does it imply that all those

with the shared knowledge base are effective professionals. Surely some in every profession are not.

The problem with making this argument for teachers is that for years we have let individuals teach without this knowledge, we call anyone with responsibility for a classroom a teacher regardless of competence, and we have no good system of identifying differences in the quality of teachers. Thus, it is easy to say that someone could teach without the specialized knowledge of the profession because many so-called teachers do function with no professional preparation, and, presumably, a fair number with the professional knowledge function poorly. There is a growing research base demonstrating that certified teachers are more effective than uncertified, and this bolsters the argument for the importance of shared professional knowledge, but it is a difficult argument to make.

There have been several attempts by key educational organizations (NCATE, AACTE, and AERA, for example) to describe a teacher knowledge base in their publications and reports. However, because there is no one group or agency that codifies, legitimizes, or disseminates knowledge for the profession, the information fails to reach the teacher educators for whom it is aimed. In contrast, the standards developed for teacher education by the NBPTS, the Interstate New Teacher Assessment and Support Consortium (INTASC), and NCATE in the 1990s have had a substantial impact on the profession in terms of the knowledge base since they have been implemented through state and national accrediting agencies and thus have forced some compliance and curriculum modification on the profession. Yet, however forceful the standards have been, they have served only to focus curriculum on certain areas of concern and have not generated or imposed much new knowledge. The standards are simply statements of areas in which teachers must be competent, e.g., "Teachers should know their subjects and how to teach them." This focusing of efforts in teacher education is probably useful since the field of teacher education, although traditional in nature, has had little control over the content of curriculum, and the curriculum of many institutions has been driven as much by fad as by tradition. The result has been curriculum anarchy with no good mechanism for the introduction of well-researched or agreed-upon knowledge.

In 2000, a new effort was initiated to provide the basic knowledge that teachers need to have. This project is sponsored by the National Academy of Education (NAE), a self-appointed group of educators who invite participation of educators of their choice. They appointed a committee on teacher education chaired by John Bransford and Linda Darling-Hammond. The twenty-seven-member committee includes some well-known faculty in education, some lesser known, two teachers, and representatives from the American Federation of Teachers, the National Center for Education Information, the College Board, and the Carnegie Foundation for the Advancement of Teaching. In 2004, this group is still working on a twelve-chapter volume reportedly based on consensus of the committee. The goal is to identify the major content and ideas important for effective teaching. Chapters cover learning theories and their relationship to teaching, development, developing language, educational goals and purposes, content knowledge and pedagogy, teaching diverse learners, assessment, classroom management, teacher learning and development, curriculum design, pedagogy and assessment, and implementing curriculum renewal in teacher education. This project is aimed squarely at defining a knowledge base for teacher education.

Each of the attempts at laying out the knowledge base for teachers is laudable. The most recent, The National Academy's Committee on Teacher Education, is heroic in its attempt to achieve some consensus on a knowledge base for teacher educators based upon the views of the best-known scholars in the field. Unfortunately, few practitioners in the field read these reports, and there is no mechanism or agency to enforce that the knowledge put forth by any of the three groups gets translated into the curriculum of the 1,200-plus departments, schools, and colleges of education across the country.

The United States Department of Education has perhaps been most effective in its approach to defining a knowledge base in that it has broken down the knowledge base and tackled one piece at a time. A good example is the work sponsored by the National Academy Press that published *How People Learn: Brain, Mind, Experience, and School* (Bransford, Brown, & Cocking, 1999). Like all other attempts, a committee of experts (fifteen) was assembled and, after two years, produced a readable 240-page summary of research based on the past thirty years.

In 2002, the federal government has further impacted the knowledge base in the determination of what kind of research would be supported with federal funds. (Experimental and quasi-experimental research is favored.) The United States Department of Education in 1999 nominated a National Reading Panel to decide which knowledge about reading was to be sanctioned. The panel focused on reading achievement as the outcome measure, chose the topics it considered important, and looked for knowledge supported by experimental and quasi-experimental research. Qualitative, descriptive, and correlational studies were not given credibility.

THE CHALLENGE FOR GENERATING A KNOWLEDGE BASE FOR TEACHER EDUCATION

The search for a knowledge base for teacher education is confounded by three important considerations:

1. The business of teaching is heavily normative; it is intrinsically tied to appraisals and ethical and value considerations.

2. The business of teaching is heavily political. The codification of knowledge cannot be determined by the profession itself (which is political enough), but by the public, represented by local, state, and federal governments that have an inordinate interest in what teachers do.

3. A knowledge base can only affect practice if there is a system to legitimize, organize, update, disseminate, and encourage its use.

The Normative Nature of Teaching. The work of teachers is heavily dependent on appraisals. Appraisals are value judgments that require criteria for establishing good practice. In the area of classroom discipline, for instance, some might consider silence unless called upon, order, and obedience to be the criteria for good discipline. Others might conclude that happy, engaged, and productive children are the criteria for good discipline. The business of teaching is fraught with areas where appraisals are called for. These appraisals are tied to personal value systems and beliefs as well as documented knowledge.

Ethical and value considerations are at the heart of teaching. They frame the answers to essential questions about education such as: What are the purposes of education in a twenty-first-century democracy? To what extent is the school's role to care for children? The answers to these questions can be drawn from different philosophical frameworks. Recurrent and enduring philosophies of education weave alternative tapestries through the history of education. Fundamental differences about the purposes of education produce different versions of knowledge, of what to teach in the classroom, of how to teach effectively, and of how to assess learning. "Scientific" evidence can be mounted for competing theories.

Even the most credible research in education brings us to a conundrum. There is often no one right answer. Teaching is a disjunctive pursuit! For example, in the field of learning, we find that different learners learn the same things in different ways, and the same learner learns different things in different ways. What works, while sometimes generalizable, is often context specific and inexorably tied to appraisals and moral and ethical considerations.

To take into account the normative and value driven nature of teaching, a knowledge base would need a comprehensive view that would propose educating teachers in alternative perspectives with alternative knowledge constructs that could accommodate a reasonable range of important viewpoints on curriculum, teaching, and learning.

The Political Nature of Teaching. No other profession is so open to public scrutiny and public regulation. School boards sometimes determine curriculum and even teaching methods. States dictate curriculum frameworks, state tests, and state accreditation of teacher education. The federal government seeks more and more to determine curriculum, define qualified teachers, impose testing, set forth the outcomes and implications of test results, and codify what knowledge is to be considered legitimate. Any system for setting up a knowledge base for teacher education must account for the inputs and constraints of political entities.

A System to Organize, Legitimize, Update, Disseminate, and Encourage the Use of a Knowledge Base. There is an enormous gap between proclamation of a knowledge base and implementation of that knowledge into the business of preparing teachers. To date, the incredible investment of time, energy, and talent in setting out the various versions of a knowledge base for teacher education has had little impact on the field. There has been no recognized agency with the license to define, disseminate, or enforce a knowledge base. At the moment, we have a shouting match among panels of the AACTE, the National Research Council, the various AERA panels, and agencies of the United States Department of Education, all of them yelling without much of an audience. The only one with any power is the United States Department of Education, which can use federal grant dollars to encourage, if not coerce, compliance.

The comprehensive compendia of research and knowledge on teacher education, often in the range of 1,000 pages, have not reached the practitioners of teacher education. On the other hand, subject specific updates of knowledge—such as the National Research Council's 1999 publication, *How People Learn—Brain, Mind, Experience, and School*, or the National Council of Teachers of Mathematics Curriculum Guidelines—are quite widely read by practitioners in educational psychology and mathematics education. Efforts similar to this in each subfield of education provide a means of updating and disseminating knowledge in the field.

The Search for a Knowledge Base—An Illusion?

There is no lack of well-researched and documented knowledge in education. There is a need for more effective mechanisms to update, organize, and put well-researched knowledge in the hands of practitioners. However, it is an illusion to believe that one compendium, written by a panel of experts, can be accepted as *the* knowledge base for teacher education. To think there can be such a single framework is to hold a naïve epistemology that does not account for the normative and political nature of education. Even in the hard sciences, in medicine, or in any of the major disciplines, there is no uncontested version of a knowledge base, even for an instant. In education, we are faced with knowledge claims bound to varying ideologies and to school cultures and classrooms that vary in the most fundamental ways.

How, then, can we bring order to curriculum anarchy in teacher education? The recent standards movement, especially the core principles of the NBPTS and the general INTASC standards, has served the useful function of focusing the profession of teacher education on common areas of content. We can only hope for better dissemination and discourse of new knowledge. We will continue to argue over research methods. We will continue to argue for differing philosophical positions and corresponding knowledge interpretations. This is the nature of the field of education. Teacher education should not shrink into compliance to politically motivated federal or state versions of knowledge or effective practice. Teacher educators must act like members of a profession and find better ways to research, to debate, and to disseminate new versions of knowledge.

SUMMARY

The condition of teacher education continues to be a barrier to the advancement of teaching as a profession. Considerable changes must be made in teacher education to improve the status of teaching and the quality of teachers. At the moment, teacher education is in turmoil. Control over the profession is shifting to the federal and state governments. Short-term, noncollege based alternatives are proliferating with support and sanctioning by states and the United States Department of Education. There is no effective system for defining and disseminating an evolving knowledge base. Teacher educators have done little to help schools make quality distinctions among teachers or prepare teachers for differentiated leadership roles. College-based teacher educators have balked against radical structural change in programs. The response to demands for greater subject field competency has been inadequate, and research on teacher education has lacked direction.

To reverse the slide of teaching from semiprofession to a technician's trade, teacher educators must unite in the following actions:

- Develop and examine structural changes in teacher education, promoting an extended and carefully guided internship. This change will produce long-term partnerships with public school systems and force reorganization of patterns of teacher education.

- Create a system to update, organize, consolidate, and better disseminate a knowledge base for teacher preparation. This system must take into account the normative and contextual nature of much of our knowledge about teaching, learning, and scholarship.

- Pay greater attention to the characteristics and dispositions that are prerequisite to good teaching. Teacher education programs must be more selective and base their selection on the special qualities and dispositions needed for good teaching.

- Work to close the door to teaching for those who are unprepared and who lack the prerequisites for good teaching. Too many teacher educators have done little to discourage or challenge noncollege based routes to teaching. Indeed, many are supporting easy entry paths to teaching.

- Require subject matter majors for all teachers. New interdisciplinary majors may be needed for primary grade teachers.

- Work with schools to make quality distinctions among teachers and develop career ladders to differentiate roles. This will require comprehensive systems to assess teacher effectiveness. This effort can complement the work of NBPTS in certifying superior teachers.

- Set forth and act on a research agenda of essential issues in teacher education. This agenda must call for the highest standards of research but not be limited to single research paradigms. This agenda should welcome qualitative and quantitative studies and encourage nonempirical research that builds theory. Nothing is more needed in teacher education than new theoretical constructs and critical analyses that help to clarify our language and ideas. Much of the research in teacher education is flawed as much by imprecise definitions of research questions, and the wanton invention of new labels for old concepts, as it is by unsound methodology. While teacher educators should encourage state and federal funding for the research agenda, outside funding should neither determine nor deter the agenda.

The leadership for action in these recommended areas must be unified. A multitude of independent panels, commissions, and self-appointed experts has not been able to bring unified efforts toward a common agenda in teacher education. The AACTE is the most likely source of this leadership since it represents over half of the nation's colleges, schools, and departments of education and has the organization and resources to mount concerted actions. To date, AACTE, despite efforts to lead, has not been able to carry out this role. Instead, AACTE, and nearly all college-based teacher education, has retreated to a reactive posture, defending the status quo while trying to appease the political forces which seek to deprofessionalize teaching. The next twenty years will determine whether or not public school teaching advances as a profession or sinks to the role of a technical trade. The actions or lack of action of teacher educators will shape that outcome and determine the survival of college- and university-based professional teacher education.

NOTES

1. There are a number of accounts of history of teacher education that describe in detail the evolution of teacher education. John Goodlad (1990) ably describes the recent evolution of teacher education in *Teachers For Our Nation's Schools.* Christopher Lucas (1999) provides a thorough analysis in Part I of *Teacher Education in America.* Hodenfield and Stinnett (1961) provide a good description of the battle between subject field academics and teacher educators in *The Education of Teachers.*

2. Sixteen universities and colleges were involved with the research in 1990 and 1995. These include: Austin College, Sherman, TX; Drake University, Des Moines, IA; Idaho State University, Pocatello, ID; Louisiana State University, Baton Rouge, LA; Truman State University, Kirksville, MO; the University of Arkansas, Fayetteville, AR; the University of Florida, Gainesville, FL; the University of Kansas, Lawrence, KS; the University of New Hampshire, Durham, NH; the University of Tennessee, Knoxville, TN; the University of Virginia, Charlottesville, VA; the University of Rhode Island, Kingston, RI; Texas A&M University, College Station, TX; Trinity University, San Antonio, TX; the University of Nebraska, Lincoln, NE; and the University of Vermont, Burlington, VT.

3. $[x^2(1, n + 303) = 9.712, p < 01]$

BIBLIOGRAPHY

American Association of Colleges for Teacher Education. (1993). *Educating a profession: Extended programs for teacher education.* (Report No. SP 023 182). Washington, DC: AACTE. (ERIC Document Reproduction Service No. ED 236139)

American Association of Colleges for Teacher Education. (2004). *AACTE Directory of Members.* Washington, DC: AACTE.

Andrew, M. D. (1974). *Teacher leadership: A model for change.* Washington, DC: Association of Teacher Educators.

Andrew, M. D. (1983). The characteristics of students in a five year teacher education program. *Journal of Teacher Education, 34(1),* 20–23.

Andrew, M. D. (1984). Restructuring teacher education: The University of New Hampshire's five year program. Washington, DC: Educational Resources Information Center. (ERIC Document Reproduction Service No. ED 250310)

Andrew, M. D. (1986). Restructuring teacher education: The University of New Hampshire's five year program. In T. J. Lasley (Ed.), *The dynamics of change in education,* Vol. I. Washington, DC: AACTE.

Andrew, M. D. (1989). Subject-field depth and professional preparation: New Hampshire's teacher education program. In J. L. DeVitis & P. A. Sola (Eds.). *Building bridges for educational reform: New approaches to teacher education* (pp. 44–62). Ames: Iowa State University Press.

Andrew, M. D. (1990). Differences between graduates of 4-year and 5-year teacher preparation program. *Journal of Teacher Education, 41(2),* 45–51.

Andrew, M. D., & Schwab, R. L. (1993). Outcome-centered accreditation: Is teacher education ready? *Journal of Teacher Education, 44(3),* 176–182.

Andrew, M. D., & Schwab, R. L. (1995). Has reform in teacher education influcnced teacher performance? An outcome assessment of graduates of an eleven-university consortium. *Action in Teacher Education, 17(3),* 43–53.

Baker, T. E. (1984). *Extended teacher education programs: A survey of attitudes in Texas.* (Report No. SP 024133). Sherman, TX: Austin College. (ERIC Document Reproduction Service No. ED 242714)

Bestor, A. E. (1953). *Educational wastelands: The retreat from learning in our public schools.* Urbana: University of Illinois Press.

Bloomfield, M. H. (1988). Law: The development of a profession. In N. O. Hatch (Ed.), *The professions in American history* (pp. 33–50). Notre Dame, IN: University of Notre Dame Press.

Bransford, J. D., Brown, A. L., & Cocking, R. R. (Eds.). (1999). *How people learn: Brain, mind, experience, and school.* Washington, DC: National Academy Press.

Carnegie Forum on Education and the Economy. (1986). *A nation prepared: Teachers for the 21st century.* New York: Carnegie Corporation.

Conant, J. B. (1963). *The education of American teachers.* New York: McGraw Hill.

Darling-Hammond, L. (1992). *Perestroika and professionalsim: The case for restructuring teacher preparation.* Washington, DC: National Education Association.

Darling-Hammond, L., & Sykes, G. (2003, September 17). Wanted: A national teacher supply policy for education, The right way to meet the "highly qualified teacher" challenge. *Education Policy Analysis Archives, 11*(33). Retrieved September 1, 2004, from http://epaa.asu.edu/epaa/vlln33/

Dill, D. D. (1990). *What teachers need to know—the knowledge, skills, and values essential for good teaching.* San Francisco: Jossey Bass.

Durkheim, E. (1956). *Education and Sociology.* New York: Free Press.

Etzioni, A. (Ed.). (1969). *The Semi-professions and their organizations: Teachers, nurses, social workers.* New York: The Free Press.

Gardiner, H. (1969). Internship in historical perspective. *Educational Digest, 34*(7), 42–45.

Goode, W. J. (1969). The theoretical limits of professionalization. In A. Etzioni (Ed.), *The semi-professions and their organizations: Teachers, nurses, social workers* (pp. 266–313). New York: The Free Press.

Goodlad, J. (1990). *Teachers for our nation's schools.* San Francisco: Jossey-Bass.

Goodlad, J. (1994). *Educational renewal: Better teachers, better schools.* San Francisco: Jossey-Bass.

Haberman, M. (1986). An evaluation of the rationale for required teacher education: Beginning teachers with and without teacher preparation. In T. J. Lasley (Ed.), *Issues on teacher education, Volume II: Background paper from the National Commission for Excellence in Teacher Education* (pp. 7–54). Washington, DC: American Association of Colleges for Teacher Education.

Hatch, N. A. (Ed.). (1988). *The professions in American history.* Notre Dame, IN: University of Notre Dame Press.

Hawley, W. D. (1986). The risks and inadequacies of extended programs. *New Directions for teaching and learning, 27.* (ERIC Document Reproduction Service No. ED 340191)

Hodenfield, G. K., & Stinnett, T. M. (1961). *The education of teachers: Conflict and consensus.* Englewood Cliffs, NJ: Prentice-Hall.

Holmes Group. (1986). *Tomorrow's teachers: Report of the Holmes Group.* East Lansing, MI: The Holmes Group.

Howey, K. R., & Zimpher, N. L. (1986). The debate on teacher preparation. *Journal of Teacher Education, 37*(5), 41–49.

Howsam, R. B., Corrigan, D. C., & Denemark, G. W. (1985). *Educating a profession.* Washington, DC: American Association of Colleges for Teacher Education.

Hrock, M. C. (Ed.). (1986). *Handbook of research in teaching* (3rd ed.). New York: Simon and Schuster/Macmillan.

Koerner, J. D. (1963). *The miseducation of America's teachers.* Boston: Houghton Mifflin.

Kramer, R. (1991). *Education school follies: The miseducation of America's teachers.* New York: Free Press.

Lasley, T. (Ed.). (1986). *The dynamics of change in teacher education,* Vol. I. Washington, DC: American Association of Colleges for Teacher Education.

Lucas, C. (1999). *Teacher education in America: Reform agendas for the twenty-first century.* New York: St. Martin's Press.

Ludmerer, K. M. (1985). *Learning to heal: The development of American medical education*. New York: Basic Books.

Monahan, W. B. (1983). *Extended programs: Reactions from member institutions and from established programs. Final report of the AACTE Task Force on Extended Programs*. (Report No. SP 028 058). Washington, DC: AACTE. (ERIC Reproduction Service No. ED 247233)

Murray, F. (1996). *Teacher education's handbook: Building a knowledge base for the preparation of teachers*. Washington, DC: AACTE.

National Commission for Excellence in Teacher Education. (1985). *A call for change in teacher education*. Washington, DC: American Association of Colleges for Teacher Education.

National Commission on Teaching and America's Future. (1996). *What matters most: Teaching for America's future*. New York: National Commission on Teaching and America's Future.

Numbers, R. L. (1988). The fall and rise of the American medical profession. In N. O. Hatch (Ed.), *The professions in American history* (pp. 51–72). Notre Dame, IN: University of Notre Dame Press.

Reynolds, M. C. (Ed.). (1989). *Knowledge base for the beginning teacher*. Washington, DC: AACTE.

Richardson, V. (Ed.). (2001). *Handbook of research in teaching* (4th ed.). Washington, DC: American Educational Research Association.

Saunders, R. L. (1985). *Memphis State University's new five-year program for the initial preparation of teachers*. (Report No. SP 026 660). Memphis, TN: College of Education at Memphis State University. (ERIC Reproduction Service Document No. ED 264182)

Scannell, D. (1983). *Educating a profession: Profile of a beginning teacher*. Washington, DC: AACTE.

Sikula, J. (Ed.). (1996). *Handbook of research on teacher education* (2nd edition). New York: Prentice Hall International.

Smith, D. C. (Ed.). (1983). *Essential knowledge for beginning educators*. Washington, DC: American Association of Colleges for Teacher Education.

Smith, D. C. (1984). *PROTEACH: An extended preservice teacher preparation program*. (Report No. SP 025 595). Washington, DC: National Commission on Excellence in Teacher Education. (ERIC Reproduction Service Document No. ED 250317)

Tom, A. R. (1989). Critique of the new rationale for extended teacher preparation. In L. Weis, P. B. Altbach, G. P. Kelly, H. G. Petrie, & S. Slaughter (Eds.), *Crisis in teaching* (pp. 55–82). Albany: State University of New York Press.

Tom, A. R. (1991). *Stirring the embers: Reconsidering the structure of teacher education programs*. Tucson: University of Arizona.

Tom, A. R. (1997). *Redesigning teacher education*. Albany: State University of New York Press.

United States Department of Education. (2002). *Meeting the highly qualified teachers challenge*. (The Secretary's Annual report on Teacher Quality). Washington, DC: U.S. Department of Education.

Wang, M. C., & Walberg, H. J. (Eds.). (2001). *Tomorrow's teachers*. Richmond, CA: Mc-Cutchan Publishing Corporation.

Wong, M. J., & Osguthorpe, R. T. (1993). The continuing domination of the four-year teacher education program: A national survey. *Journal of Teacher Education, 44*(1), 64–70.

Zeichner, K., & Shulte, A. K. (2001). What we know and don't know from peer-reviewed research about alternative teacher certification programs. *Journal of Teacher Education, 52*(4), 266–282.

Teachers as Leaders, Teachers as Researchers, Teachers Who Care: The University of Connecticut's Journey

Wendy J. Glenn, David M. Moss, Douglas Kaufman, Kay Norlander-Case, Charles W. Case, and Robert A. Lonning

To foster real and lasting change in the lives of children enrolled in our public schools, we must question what exists, imagine what could be, and create a form of education in which young people are provided equal access and nurturing care. To this end, we must prepare educators who possess professional knowledge and skills, behave as reflective practitioners capable of using inquiry to elicit change, and believe that enabling children to become successful citizens in a democracy is a moral imperative. Over a decade ago, educators came together with a mission to create a renewed teacher education program where issues of quality education for all were central. The result of their work was the Integrated Bachelor's/Master's (IB/M) teacher preparation program in the Neag School of Education at the University of Connecticut. This program is grounded in a vision of teachers as professionals who are both broadly and deeply educated; have the propensity for questioning, reflection and leadership; and possess the capacity to meet the academic and social needs of the young people with whom they work.

WHY THE UNIVERSITY OF CONNECTICUT?

Although there are other quality institutions that prepare teacher candidates in the United States, we have chosen to focus our attention on the teacher preparation program at the University of Connecticut (UConn) due to its high caliber of admitted students, innovative design, faculty philosophy of mentoring and modeling, and high retention rate for teachers once they leave the university and begin work in their own classrooms. We recognize that other institutions may share some of these features but argue that our program, housed in a public land-grant university, works as an integrative whole. We not only provide well-qualified and committed teachers for the nation, but also offer an approach to teacher education that may inform programs across the country. Teaching, research, and service are widely recognized as the core principles of higher education, and our program embodies aspects of each. We are not in a special circumstance, but we have created a distinctive program that reflects our reform-minded attempt to address issues of professionalism; we embrace, rather than deny, the complexities inherent in teaching.

The IB/M program is driven by a student-centered philosophy that supports smaller classes, integration among courses and educational experiences, and a commitment to teacher leadership. The model demands from its students not only expertise in terms of content knowledge, but also significant experience in classroom settings and extensive reflection upon that experience. Our program insists that teaching requires more than the accumulation of subject and pedagogical knowledge and skills. It demands both passion and compassion and the willingness to care. Teaching is personal, difficult, and normative in nature. As Professor Mike Andrew notes in the previous chapter of this volume, ethical considerations are at the heart of teaching.

These programmatic components compel full-time faculty to interact closely with students. This interaction is defined by the long-term mentoring of students through all aspects of the program and the conscious, public modeling of professional attitudes, activities, and relationships that serve as exemplars of expert teaching for our students. Faculty serve as much more than information resources for students. They also identify themselves as multifaceted professionals who create trusting relationships with students and operate as living models for them, publicly living the professional and academic lives we expect they will live upon entering the profession. Our theoretical understandings— which guide our practice—move us to model those activities and methods that we believe are educationally effective, using our own teaching, advising, research, and learning as crucial components of the curriculum.

Ours is a research-based program in which a process of ongoing and thorough reflection, evaluation, and revision drives changes. Through the support from the Teachers for a New Era project, funded by the Carnegie, Ford, and

Annenberg foundations, we are currently working to improve our performance assessment of our graduates during their first two years of teaching as a means to help them transition into life as teacher leaders. The provision of such support, even after students leave our program, attests to our desire to prepare teachers who remain teachers. The current national retention rate of teachers five years into the field hovers around 50 percent. In marked contrast, 90 percent of UConn program graduates remain in the classroom after the same period. Many work in hard-to-staff schools characterized by low test scores and high poverty rates. This impressive accomplishment led UConn to be featured as an exemplary program by the National Commission on Teaching and America's Future (NCTAF), based upon the following criteria:

> *When teacher preparation programs are focused on a coherent approach to rigorous knowledge and teaching skill development, when they include extensive clinical practice designed to meet the needs of the schools and students they will serve, and when they provide early teaching support to their graduates, the rates of beginning teacher attrition are almost half the level found in beginning teachers who have not had this kind of preparation. Well-prepared graduates are more likely to stick with teaching and contribute to the development of a strong professional learning community in the schools they serve. (NCTAF, 2003)*

Our program supplies our nation with teachers who maintain a lasting commitment to the profession.

CONSTRUCTING A PROGRAM OF PROFESSIONAL PREPARATION: HISTORY AND PHILOSOPHICAL UNDERPINNINGS

The teacher education program in the Neag School of Education represents a redesign of the way classroom teachers have traditionally been prepared. Underlying our reform process was a rejection of the apprenticeship model on which most teacher education programs have been based. Prior to this reform, our program looked similar to many traditional programs. Seven departments and separate subprograms of preparation in elementary, secondary, music, and special education provided disparate experiences for students. We had only a superficial relationship with the College of Liberal

Arts and Sciences, and many School of Education faculty were not involved directly in the preparation of teachers. Teacher education was not a schoolwide endeavor. Field experiences took place at various unconnected sites throughout the state, and schools benefited little from serving as hosts to our students.

As we moved toward reform, we focused our attention on the concept of teachers as professional educators, paying special attention to the roles that reflection, curiosity, and altruism play in the promotion of professional practice (Case, Lanier, & Miskel, 1986; Strike, 1990). Program redesign was strongly influenced by the work of Dewey, the writings and deliberations of the Holmes Group (now the Holmes Partnership, 1986, 1990, 1996), and the life-long work of John Goodlad at the National Network for Educational Renewal (see Goodlad, 1990a, 1990b, 1994).

In the course of the reform process, five broad tenets of professional preparation provided the structure around which the specifics of the program were built:

1. Every student's course of study would include a broad liberal arts background in a specific subject area major.

2. The program would include a common core of pedagogical knowledge for all students and specific pedagogical preparation in the area or areas of elected certification.

3. Every student would engage in a series of six progressively challenging clinical experiences in professional development schools (including a mandatory urban placement and experiences with special needs students) that would span the grade levels.

4. Teaching competence would be built across the six clinical experiences, which are tied closely to the seminar and pedagogical courses.

5. Analysis of and reflection upon classroom practice, as well as the building of school and community relations, would play important roles in educating the future teachers to become effective decision makers and contributors to the growth of knowledge. IB/M program graduates would become teacher leaders and teacher researchers.

The Importance of a Liberal Education

A liberal education promotes tolerance, welcomes diversity, celebrates human ingenuity, encourages critical thinking, provides knowledge, fosters creativity, and builds a sense of community. It helps students place themselves in a context, to see what has come before and, most importantly, what might emerge in the future. Teachers who lack a strong liberal arts background and a firm grasp on what they teach all too often find themselves trapped by the standard curriculum—unable to use their own knowledge to expand upon and enrich the experiences of students. They teach what they are told to teach, unable or unwilling to advocate for changes that better serve their students.

A Common Core for All Educators

Core coursework represents the educational content that faculty members collaboratively determined to be essential for all students, regardless of certification area and consistent with state and national teacher education standards. This knowledge includes issues of learning, assessment of learning, the multicultural nature of schools and society, the acceptance and accommodation of individual differences, access to and teaching of new technologies, the limitations and consequences of technology as a learning tool, and action research that promotes teacher leadership and stewardship of our nation's schools.

Subject-Specific Pedagogy

Although a common core of learning is essential to a coherent program of teacher education, a body of knowledge and competence within each of the teaching disciplines is equally important. Students must be aware of specific beliefs and practices unique to their chosen disciplines. An understanding of the nature of science is necessary in the context of science education, just as an awareness of the competing theories and techniques underlying writing instruction is imperative for the informed and effective teaching of English.

Clinic Placements

Clinic refers to the carefully designed sequence of fieldwork experiences during which students view, practice, and analyze the content of the core courses. Regardless of intended area of certification, a student's clinic experiences span the grades and disciplines. They include placements in urban settings and with students who have special education needs. A planned sequence of clinical experiences prepares well-rounded educators who are not solely "second-grade teachers" or "high school social studies teachers." Effective teachers are aware of what goes on at every educational level; they understand a student's prior experiences and support the student's previous teachers. We believe that, as a teaching community, we are all accountable for the success of the children in our schools.

Seminar

Seminar bridges the gap between theoretical content (core) and practice (clinic). In seminar, students meet weekly to reflect upon, analyze, and discuss what they are learning in classes and in schools. The seminar provides a forum for focused conversation and reflection. It nurtures knowledgeable and serious students dedicated to a quest of common interests and provides an opportunity for students and teachers to explore together the many facets of those common interests. It is, ideally, a collegium, promoting shared authority and responsibility among peers.

Inquiry and Reflection

Our ongoing commitment to educational renewal concerns itself with promoting reflective practice, both in our students and in ourselves. In order to improve our work as educators, we must look honestly at our own practices, acknowledge our deficiencies, and work diligently to better ourselves through reform-minded modifications. We understand that teaching decisions require careful consideration of both the issues underlying the choices we make and the implications of those choices.

IDEAS INTO ACTION: THE CURRENT PROGRAM YEAR BY YEAR

Pre-Education

Prior to admission into the IB/M teacher preparation program at the University of Connecticut, prospective freshman and sophomore students are generally classified as pre-education students. During these first two years of university study, students benefit from the Neag School of Education's strong partnership with the College of Liberal Arts and Sciences and its concurrent commitment to a strong liberal arts education. In addition to working to fulfill the university's general education requirements, each student selects a subject area major in his/her desired teaching field, usually exceeding course credit requirements of students earning a liberal arts degree outside the Neag School of Education. Elementary education students select a content area major in science, mathematics, English, or social studies and complete twenty-four credit hours in that area along with twelve hours of additional subject area coursework in a related area. Given that elementary school teachers typically work in self-contained classrooms and are responsible for teaching many subjects, our program seeks a balance between breadth and depth of coursework. Secondary education students select a subject area major and, by completion of the undergraduate degree, complete thirty-six hours of coursework in that area. Pre-education advisors who are familiar with the IB/M program requirements guide prospective IB/M students during these first two years.

Admissions

The admissions process begins in the spring semester of a student's sophomore year with accepted students beginning the program the following fall. Admission to the IB/M program is highly competitive. Over each of the past four years, we have received an average of one hundred applications for forty positions in the elementary education program. For the secondary and special education programs, the number of applicants varies by discipline, with social studies and English generally receiving considerably more applications than available spaces, and mathematics and science receiving applications nearly equal to or slightly below the number of available positions. More recently, however, the critical shortage of math and science teachers in the state and nation has contributed to higher numbers of applicants in these areas, as well. The secondary program admits no more than fifteen students in each content area. The emphasis we place on close professional relationships with our students necessitates the relatively small size of the admitted cohort groups. Maintaining smaller class sizes, particularly in courses taken during the last two years of our program, is a primary goal and essential for the creation of the mentoring and modeling paradigm noted earlier.

The admissions process is in keeping with the program goals of preparing educators to be decision makers, leaders, and innovators for the twenty-first century. Members of the Admissions Committee, composed of a small group of IB/M faculty, initially review application materials, evaluating each candidate based upon his/her GPA, writing sample, letters of recommendation, and descriptions of prior extracurricular experiences related to teaching. Using various assessment tools, they come to consensus about how well the candidate's potential contributions align with program goals. As a result of this initial screening, a percentage of applicants identified as competitive is invited for interviews. These applicants are then assigned to groups of three and interviewed by two members of the Admissions Committee. Interviews last approximately forty-five minutes and are evaluated using a rubric that assesses interpersonal skills, language/articulation, and evidence of reflection.

Following the interviews, the committee reevaluates each candidate based on five criteria: GPA; written expression; teaching-related experience; letters of recommendation; and the interview. It is obvious that we take the admissions process very seriously; we willingly commit significant time to ensure that accepted candidates are among the most talented academically and are most committed to the profession. A comparison of the admissions procedures utilized by our peer institutions reveals the thorough and unique nature of our process.

Profile of a Typical Student Accepted into the Program

Student demographic data for the class admitted for the fall of 2003 reflect the nature of the current student population in the Neag School of Education. One hundred eleven students were admitted to the program in elementary, secondary, and special education. The average GPA for the class was 3.67, and the average combined SAT I score was 1165. Thirteen percent of the students were members of groups typically underrepresented in teaching. Eighty-two percent of the students came from sixty-two towns across Connecticut, while the remaining students came from nine other states. The state of Connecticut uses a system of grouping towns, called Educational Reference Groups (ERG), based on a variety of demographic data, including, median family income, percentage of families with a college-educated parent, percentage of single-parent families, etc. The nine ERG's range in median family income from ERG A at $98,495 to ERG I at $24,349. Sixty-four percent of the class admitted for the fall of 2003 came from ERG's A through D. Prior to applying to the program, students engaged in wide variety of teaching-related activities during high school and their first two years of college. These activities included teaching in preschools, volunteering in after-school programs in public schools, tutoring, camp counseling, and coaching various sports.

The Professional Program

Upon admission into the program, students become members of cohort groups. We encourage them to form strong peer relationships as they grapple with the ever-increasing rigor of their core and subject area pedagogy courses, clinic experiences in the schools, and professional seminars. The program is organized around three themes—student as learner, student as teacher, teacher as leader—that require progressively more complex and demanding ways of thinking about teaching as students move from issues of learning and assessment to more philosophical questions of what it means to be a professional educator.

The following section serves as a guide to the experiences of two typical students admitted into our professional program. Maya is a secondary English student, and Franklin is an elementary student with an emphasis in science.

THE JUNIOR YEAR (STUDENT AS LEARNER)

Advisement. Maya and Franklin develop their course schedules under the guidance of their academic advisors, IB/M faculty members who work with them throughout the course of their studies in the program. During a visit early in the year, Maya and Franklin discuss with their respective advisors the courses they completed prior to admission. Together, student and advisor determine the remaining two years of coursework that will define the undergraduate program of study. Advisors also serve as mentors in the students' development as reflective practitioners. Maya and Franklin will experience an almost continuous cycle of reflection and evaluation during their three years of the program. Beginning in the junior year, they start to develop an electronic developmental portfolio that documents their thinking, learning, and growth over time. Portfolio development continues through the remaining years of the program, and the portfolio evolves as Maya and Franklin undergo new academic and field experiences. During their first year, the students include artifacts that describe their philosophy of education, demonstrate their ability to enhance lesson plans through the use of technology, and document an understanding of various learning theories.

Coursework. In the first year of the program, Maya and Franklin enroll in the same core courses. Although they are working toward certification in two different grade and subject areas, they travel together in a cohort group and are able to share ideas, compare experiences, and build relationships over the duration of the program. Core courses include those listed below:

Fall

Introduction to Teaching introduces the IB/M program. Course content includes discussions of the program's philosophical and theoretical foundations, its structure and components, the nature and purposes of schooling, the relationship between school and society, recent educational reform movements, and the nature and purposes of reflective practice for those engaged in professional education.

Learning I and *Learning II* expose students to various theories of learning, from behaviorism to constructivism, and discuss the implications of each in terms of professional practice.

Technology in Education explores the use of educational technology in the context of schooling, paying particular attention to available computer technology, software evaluation, and instructional techniques that draw upon technology as a means to enhance student learning.

Seminar integrates the broader concepts of the program's framework and guiding philosophy, learning, and technology with clinic experiences.

Spring

Sociolinguistic Diversity and the Classroom examines the role of language in the educational process and the educational implications of language diversity, as one component of multicultural diversity, in the classroom. The course emphasizes the nature and elements of human language, prescriptive and descriptive approaches to language study, first and second language acquisition, language variation and its social and educational implications, the relationship between language and culture, and bilingual and English-as-a-Second-Language (ESL) programs.

Social and Community Issues in Education examines a wide variety of topics, including the effects of alcohol, drugs, and tobacco, that teachers in contemporary society must address.

Exceptionality I examines the characteristics of students with exceptionalities and special needs and addresses techniques and strategies that best support them.

Seminar integrates the broader concepts of linguistic diversity, social and community issues, and exceptionality, bridging coursework with clinic experiences.

As a secondary English student, Maya rounds out her course schedule with classes offered in her subject area major, working toward the previously noted thirty-six hour English course requirement. While Maya took several English classes in the two years prior to her admission to the program, during her junior year, her English courses might include the following:

The English Language provides a descriptive study of modern American English with attention given to such concepts as constituent sounds (phonology), structure of words (morphology), and syntax, with some discussion of lexicography and usage.

Shakespeare examines the author's romantic comedies and principal tragedies.

American Literature to 1880 exposes students to the broad range of American authors from the Puritans through the Realists. Authors whose works are studied include, but are not limited to, Poe, Emerson, Thoreau, Hawthorne, Melville, Whitman, Douglass, Stowe, Dickinson, and Twain.

American Literature since 1880 focuses on modern and contemporary American literature and includes the study of such authors as James, Wharton, Dreiser, Cather, Frost, Hemingway, Fitzgerald, Faulkner, and Morrison.

Poetry immerses students in the study of the techniques and conventions of the chief forms and traditions of poetry, including the ode, sonnet, free verse forms, and others.

Literature and Culture of the Third World provides an examination of social and cultural aspects of printed literature and its relationship to other media. Topics vary each semester but may include, for example, the exploration of Caribbean or African literature.

Studies in Literature allows students to pursue advanced explorations of various, more limited, topics such as a particular literary theme, form, or movement.

Advanced Composition for Prospective Teachers provides instruction in the teaching of writing, examining both the theoretical underpinnings that guide effective practices and the means to implement those practices in the classroom setting. Particular attention is paid to the workshop method advocated by Murray, Graves, Atwell, and others.

As an elementary education major with an emphasis in science, Franklin's remaining courses, many with labs, during this year may include:

Chemistry for an Informed Electorate covers the basic concepts and applications of chemistry, explores the contributions of chemistry to our everyday lives, and addresses societal issues and problems related to chemicals.

Climate and Weather analyzes the dynamic and integrated atmospheric processes that give rise to weather systems and climate patterns.

Oceanography examines the processes governing the geology, circulation, chemistry, and biological productivity of the world's oceans, emphasizing the variability of the marine environment.

Physics of the Environment covers concepts of physics applied to current problems of the physical environment such as energy, transportation, and pollution.

Astronomy is a survey course that describes the principles of celestial coordinate systems and telescope design; applications of fundamental physical laws to the sun, planets, stars, and galaxies; evolution of stars and the universe; recent space probe results; and astrobiology.

The Nature of Scientific Thought explores the underlying assumptions and aims of scientific knowledge and the current theories in the biological and physical sciences.

Fundamentals of Nutrition introduces the concepts of nutrition, emphasizing the nature and function of carbohydrates, fats, proteins, minerals, and vitamins and their application to the human organism.

Introduction to Botany examines the structure, physiology, and reproduction of seed plants as a basis for understanding the broader principles of biology and the relation of plants to human life.

Clinic Placement. During the clinic experience, Maya and Franklin spend four hours each week in one of our partner schools. During these early experiences, the students assume primarily the role of careful observer, taking note of what is occurring in the classroom in terms of student-teacher inter-actions, curriculum implementation, etc. During the fall semester, Maya is placed in a self-contained special education classroom in an urban middle school. She reads and analyzes students' Individual Education Plans (IEPs), observes modifications implemented by the classroom teacher to meet these individual needs, and talks at length with the classroom paraprofessional to learn his role in the classroom. During the spring semester, Maya finds her-self in an urban, second-grade classroom. The veteran clinic teacher, Mrs. Johnson, not only models strategies for effective classroom management, parental involvement, and lesson design, she also encourages Maya to de-velop a rapport with students by working with them during cooperative ac-tivities and providing one-on-one support for those in need of additional guidance. Franklin experiences challenging out-of-certification-area place-ments, as well. In the fall, he works in a high school social studies environ-ment, immersing himself in a class that uses primary source documents to facilitate historical understanding. He begins to see similarities between what historians and scientists do in terms of inquiry. In the spring, he works in a middle school mathematics enrichment cluster. There he contributes to a gifted and talented program that matches students with community-based mentors who facilitate project-based work. These out-of-grade-level/subject area experiences allow Maya and Franklin to experience the broad range of schooling, thus promoting their understanding of the articulations between grade levels and among subject areas.

Seminar. Maya and Franklin's seminar course includes all of the junior year students within the same partner district/school where they are conducting their clinic work. This seminar bridges the gap between theory and practice by encouraging discussion of the relationship between their experiences in their clinic classrooms and what they have learned in their university courses. For example, when Maya becomes troubled by the apparent lack of parental support she witnesses in her ethnically diverse second-grade classroom, she brings her concerns to her classmates. She expresses her disappointment that many parents did not attend the school's open house. As a result of a thought-ful discussion with her peers and instructor, which draws upon material dis-cussed in the "Sociolinguistic Diversity and the Classroom" course, she comes away with a clearer understanding of the obstacles faced by parents who may be intimidated by or uncomfortable in the school setting due to their own neg-ative experiences. Franklin loves the notion of a project-based curriculum, and many of his peers are curious about this innovative means to facilitate learning. The seminar leader capitalizes on this interest and provides resources for all students to explore further this student-centered approach. Although the students express surprise that the origins of project-based classrooms in this country go back over a century, they come away with a deeper understanding of why such an approach may be valuable.

THE SENIOR YEAR (STUDENT AS TEACHER)

Advisement. Maya and Franklin have met informally with their advisors many times during the past year. At the beginning of their senior year, they meet formally to prepare a final plan of study, which often mirrors their preliminary plan of study but also accounts for any changes in coursework that they have agreed upon during the junior year. Maya and Franklin continue to develop their portfolios. Their advisors encourage them to reflect upon the artifacts that they included during the junior year, exploring and documenting their growth as students and as educators. The students now add an IEP and sociocultural case study.

Coursework. Maya and Franklin enroll in several of the same core courses during the senior year. These include the following during the fall semester:

> *Exceptionality II* builds upon student understanding of pupils with special needs and discusses specific educational programming for exceptional learners.
>
> *Assessment of Learning I* and *Assessment of Learning II* address various theories of learning, assessment, and the practices and implications associated with each.
>
> *Seminar* integrates broader concepts of learning assessment and exceptionality with area-specific methods.

To complete requirements unique to the secondary English program, Maya also enrolls in several subject-specific pedagogy courses during the fall semester:

> *Teaching of Reading in Middle and High Schools* provides methods of teaching reading with particular emphasis on understanding differentiated instructional methods designed to meet the needs of diverse readers.

Methods of Teaching English explores several theories and models of curriculum and instruction in language, writing, and literature.

Literature for High School Students provides an introduction to literature written for a young adult audience.

During the first two weeks of the spring semester (just prior to student teaching), secondary education students enroll in an additional class, *Teaching Reading and Writing in the Content Areas*. This course addresses strategies and approaches designed to help pupils succeed as readers in each discipline. Students evaluate textbooks and other materials and develop practices that meaningfully integrate reading and writing into the various content areas.

As an elementary education candidate, Franklin also takes course work in subject-specific teaching methods during the fall semester:

Teaching Reading and Writing in the Elementary School immerses students in current approaches to fostering literacy by introducing theories, philosophies, methods, and practices of teaching and learning literacy in the elementary school. It also emphasizes the use of new technologies.

Teaching Mathematics in the Elementary School introduces current approaches to learning and teaching of math, including the use of hands-on manipulatives to foster a conceptual understanding of mathematical process as opposed to the rote memorization of numbers.

Teaching Science in the Elementary School explores science through a hands-on and minds-on approach. Instructors facilitate an understanding of the nature of science via inquiry into the life, physical, and earth sciences.

Teaching Social Studies in the Elementary School emphasizes history, geography, and the social sciences as a foundation for building an understanding of a sense of self and place. Students explore notions of community, citizenship, and democracy, avoiding the mere memorization of places and dates.

During the first two weeks of the spring semester, elementary education students enroll in *Teaching Language Arts in the Elementary School*. This course extends the study of current theories and practices of effective language arts instruction by connecting speaking, listening, reading, and writing and by integrating children's literature and content learning.

Clinic Placement. During the fall of the senior year, the emphases of Maya and Franklin's clinic experiences change in terms of time commitment and focus. Maya works in a secondary English classroom. Because she has already experienced out-of-grade-level special education and urban settings, she spends this semester in a suburban high school. Franklin is placed in a self-contained elementary school classroom. Both students are now required to be in their school placement for a minimum of six hours each week, and they must do much more than observe. Clinic teachers encourage them to become active participants in the classroom setting and provide them with guidance and practice in planning and implementing lessons, evaluating student work, communicating with parents and other school staff members, working with students with diverse or special needs, etc., thus reinforcing what Maya and Franklin are learning in their pedagogy courses.

In the spring semester, Maya and Franklin's clinic experiences take the form of full-time student teaching, the logical extension of their experiences thus far. Maya teaches in the classroom of an English teacher who has undergone extensive training in preparation for her mentor role. Franklin works closely with his own mentor (referred to as his "cooperating teacher"). To ensure an appropriate amount of formative feedback, University of Connecticut faculty or staff conduct a minimum of six formal observations during the semester. As student teachers, Maya and Franklin are expected to assume the comprehensive roles of classroom teachers. They are responsible for planning and implementing lessons, assessing student work, organizing a classroom, managing behavior, attending parent-student conferences, and much more, knowing, of course, that they can, and should, depend upon the support network provided by the cooperating teacher, university supervisor, and faculty advisor.

Seminar. The seminar focus continues to connect theory and practice, but with their increased time in the classroom, Maya and Franklin now have additional contexts upon which to draw as they explore educational issues. The seminar also provides a forum where students work through problems or issues that they inevitably face during student teaching. When Maya finds herself struggling to find an appropriate assessment tool to use with a creative project she has designed, she turns to her classmates for guidance. Together, they examine Maya's curricular materials, using what they learned in their assessment courses during the fall semester, and design a tool that meets both student and teacher needs. Franklin shares with his colleagues his co-operating teacher's classroom rules, which he feels may not adequately fit his style of teaching. He seeks input into how he might modify them to ensure the academic, emotional, and physical safety of all of his students based on his particular pedagogical approach. Clearly, seminar is a place where all students work together as a community of learners to solve problems.

THE MASTER'S YEAR (TEACHER AS LEADER)

Advisement. During the final year of the program, advisors continue to mentor and guide, helping Maya and Franklin select courses that best fit their specific interests and needs, and to collaborate with them to complete the master's degree plan of study. The portfolio that Maya and Franklin began in the fall of their junior year takes on an additional role during this year. While it continues to be a development tool for assessing and reflecting upon their growth over time, it is revised later in the year into a "showcase" portfolio that, ultimately, helps students gain employment. At the end of the master's year, Maya and Franklin meet with their advisors to present and review the final manifestation of their portfolios. They discuss with them their growth as professional educators and decide how best to display the work that demonstrates their lives as teacher leaders.

Coursework. In choosing their coursework this year, Maya and Franklin have a bit more flexibility. To fulfill program requirements, they must take classes in the areas of multiculturalism, leadership, and research (the graduate seminar discussed below). Their remaining courses are electives that serve their personal needs and interests.

Several classes meet the multicultural requirement:

> *Foundations of Bilingual Education* includes the study of the political, social, and legal aspects of bilingual education.
>
> *Bilingualism and Second Language Acquisition* addresses the developmental sequences and theories of first and second language acquisition.
>
> *Bilingual Education and Biliteracy* describes current methods, strategies, and techniques of reading in the mother tongue (L1), transfer of reading skills into English (L2), and the evaluation and adaptation of L1 and L2 materials.

Multicultural Education explores the interrelationships between education and various sociocultural aspects of cultural diversity and cultural pluralism.

Latinos and U.S. Education examines the conditions of schooling for Latinos in the educational system in the United States through a historical and economic context. Discussions focus on policy issues and theoretical discussions of underachievement and the relationship between dominant and subordinate cultures and the effect of these relationships on classroom discourse.

Seminar in International Education provides a concentrated study of culture and education in a major geographical region (such as Africa, Asia, or Latin America) or cross-cultural studies of educational issues.

Assessment of Bilingualism exposes students to the principles of assessment for bilingual learners, including language proficiency and dominance, (bi)literacy development, and academic content knowledge. The course emphasizes current assessment approaches for bilingual learners in different contexts (e.g., bilingual, ESL classes) and for various purposes (e.g., screening, placement, evaluation).

In the selection of their leadership course, Maya and Franklin may choose to enroll in one of several classes:

Teacher Leadership and Organizations explores the teacher's role in providing leadership that extends beyond the walls of the individual classroom and includes collaboration with other adults.

Women, Education, and Social Change examines the lives of girls and women as students, teachers, and academics, noting, in particular, the existence of teaching as a hierarchically sex-segregated profession; the effect of gender on the status and organization of the profession; and the changing roles and social ideologies related to women's educational aspirations, career achievement, and leadership.

Contemporary Educational Policy Issues involves the study of current educational policy issues, including, for example, school choice, voucher systems, and the effects of federal testing mandates.

Human Resources Administration explores personnel management in education. Topics include current laws, policies, practices, and prob-

lems such as recruitment, tenure, promotion, and retirement; performance evaluation; motivation; salary, benefits, welfare; staff development; data collection; layoff procedures; grievances; and contract
administration.

During this year, Maya and Franklin also enroll in a minimum of four content area or curriculum elective courses that are of interest to them and help
fill any perceived gaps in their preparation thus far. During her student teaching experience, Maya recognized that her knowledge of British literature
could be more thorough. As a result, she chooses to enroll in a graduate-level
course offered by the English department that focuses on Victorian British authors. She also enrolls in courses focusing on the advanced study of young
adult literature, media literacy, and creativity. Franklin, after careful reflection
following his student teaching semester, decides he wants to develop further
expertise in science teaching in the early grades. He also wants to acquire
more experiences in teaching and learning about the environment outside his
classroom walls. He enrolls in *Environmental Education*, a class that offers
new perspectives on learning science through local field trips and authentic
science experiences. In this class, he visits local forests and rivers and actually
does science as the instructor models how to teach science to young children.
To complement this course, he also enrolls in an advanced environmental science course during the next semester.

Clinic Placement. During the master's year, Maya and Franklin's clinic experience involves a twenty-hour-per-week internship in which students assume a leadership role in the school. Here, Maya and Franklin witness the
inner workings of their sites from various perspectives in and out of the classroom, work to implement positive change within the educational setting, and
formally reflect on their work. Internships are designed by teachers and administrators within our partner schools and reflect each school's particular
needs. Maya selects an internship based upon her interest in creating and
maintaining a writing center at an urban high school. In her role, she as-
sumes control of the day-to-day operations of the center, advertises its services, provides guidance to students in need of writing support, and creates
in-service presentations to educate English department teachers about new
theories and approaches to teaching writing in the classroom. Franklin works
on a greenhouse project in a local elementary school. He is responsible for

curriculum development, the day-to-day operation of the greenhouse, and professional development opportunities for teachers. He finds his role challenging as he learns many of the hidden responsibilities of professional teachers.

Seminar. The graduate research seminar in which Maya and Franklin enroll focuses on the nature of the teaching profession and encourages reform-minded thinking. The students read and reference the works of key theorists in education—Dewey, Noddings, Freire, and others. They and their classmates explore answers to such questions as "What does it mean to be a professional educator?" "How can teachers reclaim the power they have lost, as evidenced by popular perceptions of teachers and reduced autonomy?" and "What is the role of research in the educational community?" They explore how the action research process might help teachers reflect upon and improve their practice, as well as empower them as decision makers capable of bringing their own agendas, grounded in their good research, to the table.

To this end, Maya and Franklin each spend the year researching an issue of personal relevance that has arisen out of their individual internship experiences. This inquiry project helps them develop teacher research practices that promote continued questioning and problem solving once they leave the university and begin their careers. We want our students to serve as teacher leaders—as educators willing and able to elicit real change in their schools and communities. We want them to be empowered, to recognize and feel comfortable knowing that they have both the tools and obligation to advocate for reform. To achieve this, they must be able to identify problems and issues in their classrooms and schools, generate questions that are important and answerable, utilize effective and appropriate research methods to collect and analyze data, and articulately disseminate their discoveries. Maya demonstrates her competence as a teacher leader when she successfully completes an inquiry project that examines the reasons why many writing teachers ignore current literature about effective practice and also offers suggestions, supported by her research, for persuading teachers to evolve their methods. Franklin explores the impact of the greenhouse program on fostering third graders' understandings of the nature of science. He finds that, although having students *do* science is an important precursor to understanding the nature of science, he must also explicitly attend to helping students *reflect* upon their hands-on experiences if they are to develop true conceptual understandings. His results will impact the school's curriculum development work next year.

CONCLUDING THOUGHTS

Our program may be likened to that of the medical school model. We maintain a selective admissions process that draws the most talented and committed students from a large pool of applicants. Our students experience various rotations in their clinic placements, specialize in a given subject, receive both content area and pedagogical training in that subject, and complete an internship or residency under the auspices of professionals in the field. Perhaps most importantly, we treat our students not simply as technicians who can perform skills with competence and confidence. Just as a well-prepared physician can remove sutures with ease, our students can ensure appropriate alignment between objectives, activities, and assessment when planning lessons or units. But, they can do much more. The have the ability to *create* good pedagogy based on the real and ever-changing needs of their students and educational communities. They also demonstrate the necessary empathy and compassion—a bedside manner, if you will—essential for making a genuine difference in the lives of kids.

As creators of an innovative program, we have chosen to embrace the tension that exists between specialized knowledge and the affective element inherent in teaching (as noted in Chapter 1 by Rousmaniere). We work to empower teacher education candidates as practitioners and as people. Our graduates possess not only the tools necessary to elicit positive change in their schools, but the desire and passion to do so as well. They recognize the influence of outside forces—local, state, and federal mandates—on their classrooms and students, and they are able and willing to gather data to support the choices they make in response. They are committed to their students, their professions, and themselves. As our graduates work to professionalize the field, they refuse to remain silenced. They demand, instead, that their voices be heard.

BIBLIOGRAPHY

Case, C. W., Lanier, J. E., & Miskel, C. G. (1986). The Holmes Group report: Impetus for gaining professional status for teachers. *Journal of Teacher Education, 37*(4), 36–43.
Goodlad, J. I. (1990a). Better teachers for our nation's schools. *Phi Delta Kappan, 72*(3), 184–194.

Goodlad, J. I. (1990b). *Teachers for our nation's schools*. San Francisco: Jossey-Bass.

Goodlad, J. I. (1994). *Educational renewal: Better teachers, better schools*. San Francisco: Jossey-Bass.

Holmes Group. (1986). *Tomorrow's teachers*. East Lansing, MI: Holmes Group.

Holmes Group. (1990). *Tomorrow's schools*. East Lansing, MI: Holmes Group.

Holmes Group. (1996). *Tomorrow's schools of education*. East Lansing, MI: Holmes Group.

National Commission on Teaching and America's Future. (2003). *No dream denied: A pledge to America's children*. Washington, DC: National Commission on Teaching and America's Future.

Strike, K. A. (1990). Is teaching a profession: How would we know? *Journal of Personnel Evaluation in Education, 4,* 91–117.

Walk a Mile in Their Shoes: A Day in the Life of Professional Educators

David M. Moss with Shirley Reilly, Christopher Burdman, and Sayward Parsons

I vividly recall the first time I saw my teacher, Mrs. Tomford, in the world outside of the school. I was in first grade, and it had never occurred to me that she might exist beyond the environment of Hiawatha Elementary School. She seemed to me as much a part of the school building as the speckled terrazzo flooring and red bricks. Yet, one day, there she was pushing a carriage in a grocery store. Why she would not eat all her meals in the cafeteria puzzled me, regardless of the fact that she might not like pizza rolls, tater tots, and fish sticks. The tale is a common one, and I have heard similar stories told by many individuals over the years. The first sighting of a teacher outside of school typically occurs in the primary grades and is accompanied by an uneasy sense that our teachers are not as we believed them to be.

The naiveté that many of us held at a young age about teachers and teaching is slowly replaced over the years by a comfortable familiarity acquired via what is often described as an apprenticeship through experience. That is, after a number of years of sitting in classrooms as students, and all the while watching our teachers, we develop what seems to be a clear conception of what it is to do that job. I recall thinking throughout much of my high school years that teachers had it made. To proctor a test instead of taking it, to assign homework instead of doing it (nothing seemed more horrible to me than having to do schoolwork outside of school), and to hand out report cards instead of having to bring one home—teaching sure seemed like a good gig to me. My perspective on the life of a teacher could not have been farther from the truth.

I suppose holding misconceptions regarding what people do for a living is not unique to teaching. I imagine that police officers often scoff at the television when they watch cop shows in which perpetrators easily confess in the waning minutes of the one-hour drama. The same is probably true for lawyers; I am told by trial litigators that the banter between judges and virtually everyone else in the courtroom makes for good television but in no way reflects the actual workings of the legal system. In teacher education, we strive to move beyond this so-called apprenticeship as we face the fallacies of teaching head-on, helping students see beyond the sum of their own experiences so that they might adequately serve all populations of students. However, "What's the real harm?" might be a fair question regarding this perception versus reality gap for those not entering the ranks of educators. The potential harm is significant, and the implications of letting these misleading notions go unchecked may impact each and every child enrolled in our schools.

The overarching argument for understanding the actual roles and responsibilities of teachers is embedded throughout the first several sections of this book. The question of whether teaching is a calling, technical vocation, or perhaps some blending of these concepts resulting in the problematic designation of "semiprofession" highlights the lack of understanding about what it is teachers actually do from day to day. The answer to this question has very real implications for those who are considering entering the ranks of public school teaching and what those individuals are able to do once they get there. Legislation is enacted, school board policies are implemented, budgets are voted upon, and countless parents send their children off to school each day with perhaps very little understanding of the complexities and normative dimensions of teaching. Teaching is a profession. As professionals, teachers make difficult and certainly value-laden decisions over the course of each and every day, bringing to bear their judgment and expertise so that all students may reach their academic, emotional, and social potential.

As I alluded to earlier, as a student I mostly saw teachers engaged in the technical aspects of teaching. They seemed to be doing their jobs—they were teaching students. This included administering tests and assigning homework. Yet, even if one were to acknowledge the mostly invisible work of teachers, such as lesson planning and grading, that still only accounts for a fraction of the work. In fact, I do recall a few teachers moving beyond the act of teaching poised in front of the classroom. In my senior year of high school, I remember the advice that teachers like Mr. Coster offered on a frequent basis. He genuinely cared about the welfare of his students and his words of wisdom sometimes came in the form of rather stern lectures. In eighth grade, I recall the creative teachers like Mr. Stewart who sent me out on a "quest" to explore the local geography and history of my hometown. I remember that his invitation to embark on this extracurricular adventure came as an elaborately hand-decorated envelope with the assignment itself beautifully penned on thick parchment paper. We all have our special teachers, but rarely do we see the effort placed into such student-centered, caring acts along with the underpinning knowledge base and skills required to facilitate those meaningful experiences—not to mention the out-of-pocket expenses often incurred. Perhaps most importantly, as I reflect upon what I saw as a student, and perhaps what I didn't see, I realize now that what I witnessed was through the eyes of a teenager; I see the world very differently now than I did nearly twenty-five years ago. Merely relying on one's perspective of the teaching profession acquired through the lens of adolescence is certainly problematic in its own right. The need for a fresh perspective is long overdue.

As the title of this chapter suggests, in this section of the book, you are offered a glimpse into the day-to-day realities of teaching. I invite you to reflect upon these narratives and perhaps contrast them with your own perspectives acquired through years of schooling. The following three vignettes, written by actual school teachers, afford you the opportunity to "walk a mile in their shoes," although, as you will see, that first mile may not get you past midmorning of a typical day! Each of the teachers I approached about documenting a typical school day responded to me in the same way—there is no such thing as a typical day. I fully acknowledge as much on behalf of these professionals and disclose that we make no claims to represent all aspects of what it is to teach in this single chapter.

The following section contains the reflections of these teachers. The first is written by Shirley Reilly, an elementary school teacher currently working in a third-grade self-contained classroom. She has been teaching for over twenty years and is a Master Teacher in every respect. She makes the job appear effortless, although, as you will see, she strives to balance the many and varied responsibilities of her position. The second contribution is by Chris Burdman. Chris is a middle school science and math teacher in Boston who has been teaching for only a few years. He freely discusses the many difficult decisions he makes on a daily basis as he labors to meet the needs of each and every student in his classes. The final piece is authored by Sayward Parsons. Sayward teaches high school English and has also been teaching for several years. She offers an honest and insightful portrait of high school teaching as she strives to help students make meaning from literature and find relevance in their everyday work. Following the three vignettes, I will make a few brief remarks regarding the common themes embedded in these portraits of the teaching profession.

MS. SHIRLEY REILLY
Elementary School Teacher

Friday, 3:45 P.M.

I just finished a week with four days of indoor recess. Anyone who knows (or remembers) anything about eight- and nine-year-olds can appreciate the significance of not letting the twelve boys and six girls in my room run around outside for thirty minutes each day. I should have known on Monday when I walked into my classroom at 7:30 A.M. to find my voice mail light blinking that this was going to be a challenging week. The pulse from that small bulb meant parents left messages over the weekend, and I would most likely have to schedule some parent conferences or find time for extended phone conferences. I delayed listening to the messages and headed straight to the computer to check for e-mails. The news was not good. I found I had five meetings to attend either before, during, or after school that week. The after-school meeting was a triannual review of a special needs student and would likely run two hours or more. I am often asked by people who are not in education what I do with all my free time. Inside, I'm saying to myself, "What free time!" However, I try to politely respond by describing a typical day for me. I'll share with you my Monday.

Monday, 6:30 A.M.

I didn't get in to school to work this weekend. I usually spend an additional six to eight hours each weekend to plan for the following week—preparing materials, organizing my schedule to fit in meetings, writing notes to parents, and taking care of what seems like a million other details such as curriculum committee work, student teacher evaluations, etc. My goal was to get to work by 7:30 A.M. to take care of some of these issues before the students arrived at 8:40 A.M. This is a good time to address the commonly-held misconception regarding the number of hours a teacher works. Although some think this is a nine to five job, I am in the building at least fifty hours each week (not counting weekends or the two hours each night I spend correcting, grading, and record keeping). My daughter is a lawyer with a large firm in Washington, D.C. She is constantly complaining about her twelve "billable" hours each day. I just laugh and remind her I've been doing that for more than twenty years and will never make as much money in my lifetime as she will in just a few years. She will never get stopped in the hallway by a client who shows up unannounced and expects her services. This happens to teachers all the time. And, none of it is "billable."

Another misconception sometimes held by noneducators is that anyone can do my job. We in the profession have always heard the motto: Those who can, do; those who cannot, teach. I challenge anyone out there to take my place for just one day. I guarantee the brave soul will be enlightened to the roles and responsibilities of today's teacher. I prefer the motto: Those who can, do; those who do more, TEACH. To be an effective teacher in today's society means that you must act as mentor, social worker, counselor, facilitator, cooperating teacher, colleague, cheerleader, as well as educator. My daughter once commented that she could never teach young children because you have to be "on" all the time. She thought it would be mentally and emotionally exhausting. She's right.

7:30 A.M.

Two notes are taped to my door (evidence of teachers who did make it in over the weekend). These are from support staff members who need to pull one student for testing and reschedule another student's time due to a PPT, or conference. This means I have to rearrange my schedule to accommodate these changes. I've already mentioned the "blinking light." I check those messages around 8:00. One parent wants to know why her son isn't in the high math group for multiplication. Another wants to know when he can bring in his son's pet rabbit to show the class. A third message asks me to get a week's worth of work ready by Friday because of a planned family vacation to Florida. I take notes and plan on returning these calls during my thirty-minute lunch break. I've learned over the years that parents expect teachers to get back to them expediently. My last message is from a math coordinator in a neighboring district. She had heard about our successful methods to differentiate math instruction (followed by higher scores on the state mastery tests) and wants me to speak to her third-grade team.

8:30 A.M.

A student teacher stops by and says she heard I had some good ideas for science lessons on animal adaptation. Could I show her? Another has a request for a book I have for a math lesson that she wants to use with first graders. A colleague stops by to ask my opinion about a scoring rubric we are using for reading tests. My principal stops by and wants my thoughts on next year's professional development plan and to ask if I could be a speaker at her seminar class this Wednesday. The topic is "How to balance your life." I've only been in the building an hour, and, already, I feel like I've put in an eight-hour day.

8:40 A.M.

The first students arrive. I always go out in the hall to greet them and ask about their weekend. Several hand me notes from home. Some are about a change in transportation or information about whether the mom or the dad will be picking up the student. One note from a parent says her child isn't feeling well and could I please keep an eye on him. (Add nurse to my list of responsibilities.) One dad brings his daughter to school and wants a miniconference on the spot while the children are at their lockers; he asks me to watch what his child eats for lunch because he suspects an eating disorder. Another mom asks me about coming into the classroom to volunteer because she feels "disconnected." Finally I make it back into the room to start my "real" job.

9:00 A.M.–3:45 P.M.

My class has gym first period on Monday mornings. Except for my lunch, this is the only time I will be away from my students all day. Once students return, they read the schedule of activities that I post each day and are as eager as I am to get started. We recently finished a book called The Talking Cloth, *and today the students are making a "talking vest" out of large white paper bags to tell about their own family histories and participate in a fashion show complete with runway, announcer, and music. The "Metric Olympics" will take place in math beginning with the parade of "mathathletes" and followed by competitions in metric measurement. An Olympic-style medal ceremony will conclude the activity. Students are also anxious to share the stories they wrote for Young Author's Day coming this week. Some parent volunteers are coming in this afternoon to help with the final editing phase of this project. Monday is also the day we have science at the end of the day. Students in this class are in the final stages of creating their "amazing adapters" as part of our unit on Animal Adaptation. Some of the parents stay on to help man the glue guns. We end the day with the latest chapter in our current read aloud just as the dismissal bell rings.*

3:45 P.M.

The halls are quiet. Some of us gather to share the day's experiences—the good, the bad, and the ugly. No teacher ever feels completely satisfied at the end of the day. We all seek the unattainable goal of meeting the needs of each and every student in the class. Slowly, everyone fades back into his or her classroom. The first thing I do is "dig out" from the day's activities. I have made mental notes all day to change seating arrangements for some students and to find more challenging reading books for others. I also need to seek out the enrichment teacher for some advice on a student in math. I reflect on the lessons I taught today and make adjustments for tomorrow. I start to grade math and spelling papers and write anecdotal comments on stories written during the afternoon. When I glance at the clock, it is 5:00. I look around and still see at least two more hours of work left to do. But, that will have to wait. I stuff my canvas bag with work to complete at home and hurry to the parking lot.

5:00 P.M.

I have been invited to attend an awards ceremony at a local restaurant called the Aqua Turf with several other staff members. The purpose of the ceremony is to honor exemplary programs in elementary schools throughout the state, and our physical education teacher is being recognized. Nine of us meet in the parking lot to carpool the one hour and twenty minute trip across the state. We have all agreed to talk about ideas for a skit to be performed at the end of the year in honor of our retiring nurse and compare notes at the restaurant. With the end of the year fast approaching, it is the only time we have available to give it some attention.

Talk also turns to summer plans. Most of us are doing district curriculum work or receiving training in new programs and initiatives. I will spend several days developing math assessments and finding ways to integrate more technology into the curriculum. My third-grade colleagues and I are also attending a two-week workshop called "Mentoring Mathematical Minds" held at the University of Connecticut. It is the beginning of a three-year initiative to identify students with mathematical potential in the early grades and teach a new curriculum that is being developed. If a National Science Foundation grant comes through, I will also be spending another week at the University of Connecticut working on integrating science and literature. All of the above will take place during July with hopes of getting away for a week's vacation sometime in between all the summer work. During my vacation, I will spend time on a required reading assignment for a leadership conference I will be attending in September. So much for the teachers have the whole summer off myth! On or about the first week in August, I usually start receiving phone calls from other staff members all as anxious as I am to get back into the building and start preparing for another school year. The first day of school does not magically just happen. An exciting classroom atmosphere takes at least two weeks to create.

10:30 P.M.

Finally home from work, but with a bag full of papers to correct. I make a deal with myself. I'll work for one more hour and do the rest in the morning. That will mean getting up at 6:00 instead of 6:30.

Friday, 3:45 P.M. revisited

The official workweek is finally over. I will spend Saturday and Sunday in my classroom doing next year's budget, which is due on Tuesday, and getting a head start on progress reports, which are due the following week. There will be other teachers sacrificing their weekend as well. Teachers live for the four-day week—not to have one less day to teach, but to have one more day to accomplish all the essential tasks that must be done.

As I reflect on this narrative, I think of myriad details I have left out. As a veteran teacher, the scope of this job becomes almost second nature to me. I am reminded of the depth of this scope when I look into the eyes of a new student teacher that comes thinking he/she is well prepared for the experience. Those eyes start to glaze over with wonder within just a few days. How can you do all this? How can anyone remember all this? How can you know what each and every student needs each and every day? How can you have a life? These are the questions those fresh eyes are asking. And so, a new kind of education begins for those eager, future teachers. I share with them my successes and failures, my strategies and beliefs. I model for them my pride in my profession and my love of my work. My daughter might have billable hours at the end of each day, but I get hugs and sometimes pictures that say, "You're the best teacher I ever had." And, once in a while, a parent will call to say thank you for understanding the needs of a child. And every now and then, one of us gets honored with a dinner at the Aqua Turf.

MR. CHRIS BURDMAN
Middle School Teacher

5:00 A.M.

My alarm goes off at 5:00 A.M. If you had told me that I would be waking up before the sun rose, I would have thought you were crazy. In my second year of teaching in the Boston public schools, I have become accustomed to these early mornings. Although they are routine at this point, I still find them somewhat unpleasant. Now that we are in the month of June, I can at least get out of bed without freezing.

I go through my normal routine—fix a cup of coffee, watch Sports Center for half an hour, and then get into a shower. Truth be told, I really do enjoy the mornings (once I've had my coffee) because each and every day I look forward to going to school. That is one of the best things about being a teacher. Every day is a new day. Even though I have planned for today's activities, I really have no idea what my day will be like. Working with kids means never knowing what will happen next. In my two years in Boston, I have had both the good and the bad. Fortunately, the bad occurs only from time to time. A few knives confiscated, a few fights broken up, and lots of attitude to deal with. But today will be a good day.

I work in West Roxbury, a fairly affluent neighborhood of Boston. My perception of West Roxbury is that it is a predominantly white community with moderately sized houses situated on nice quiet streets with two-parent families. Yet, only a handful of students at my school reside in the community. This is a reality I still find disturbing. In West Roxbury, there are two public middle schools—my school and the other school. The other school, whose campus currently consists of mobile classrooms, seems to be the school of choice for the residents of West Roxbury. The demographic of the school, unlike mine, is predominantly white. At my school, most of the students are bussed in from towns like Dorchester, Georgetown, and Roslindale. The school is made up of 465 students, 56 percent African American, 24 percent Hispanic, 14 percent Caucasian, and 6 percent other in composition.

I am not sure why, but the residents of West Roxbury have a hard time accepting this school as their own. In fact, my school will be closed at the end of the year, and staff will be reassigned to other schools. Boston has decided to close schools whose buildings are dilapidated and/or are failing academically. The students of these schools will be reassigned to one of three brand new, 700-seat schools. This is infuriating and frustrating because my school is a successful, small middle school. Yes, the building is old, but the fact that it is being closed leaves one to think that political pressure from the residents has forced the "bussed" students back to their neighborhoods. Currently, our staff and families are campaigning to keep the school open.

6:15 A.M.

I leave my apartment in Brighton around 6:15. It only is a fifteen-minute drive to school and, at this hour, there is no traffic. Teachers are required to be in at 7:10, but I like to get there early and do any photocopying or correcting that I need to. This is truly my most productive time of the day. I don't need to pick up the students from the courtyard until 7:20, so I have almost forty-five minutes to myself. I accomplish more in this time than I would if I stayed for two hours after school.

This morning, I have papers to correct. I teach both math and science for two classes of about twenty students. I spend the majority of my time on math because of the Massachusetts Comprehensive Assessment System (MCAS). Yesterday I gave a twenty-question math quiz on adding and subtracting fractions. We have been working on this concept for only three days, so I don't expect that the students have mastered it yet. I have the kids show all of their steps so that I can see where they are "messing up." This quiz is more about seeing what I need to stress in today's lesson rather than giving a grade. This makes correcting them a really time-consuming chore. I check that each step was done correctly and that the right procedure is being followed. Most of the students did well, but there are still a few who are forgetting to change the numerator in order to create an equivalent fraction after changing the denominator. For me, this is frustrating because I must have said, "whatever you do to the bottom, you have to do to the top" about 600 times.

7:20 A.M.

At this point, my day really begins. I go down to the school courtyard to pick up the students. They are in some type of formation that resembles a line, and they look eager to start. I am sure that most are here for the social aspect of school and not the academic, but at least they are here. Most say good morning, and a few make a comment about my new Adidas sneakers. I find that it is easy for me to connect with the students because I know what the latest hip hop trends and hot songs are. In some odd way, it gives me credibility with many of the students. I do not fit into that stereotypical "teacher" mold. I am young, I am male, I have tattoos, and I play basketball. I think the kids find it easy to talk to me and confide in me. I am able to joke around with them yet still earn their respect. I tell the kids from day one, "There is a time for kidding around, and there is a time for business. I can be your pal, but I am also your teacher and an adult. Don't confuse me with one of your buddies. If you break the rules, I'm gonna bust you, no matter how much I like you."

After I walk the students upstairs, they go to their lockers and then into homeroom. There, they spend about ten minutes reading a book silently while I take attendance and give any announcements. It is then off to their first period specialty. I use this time to finish correcting the quizzes and to prepare materials for today's lesson. Today, like most days, we will be doing math. With the MCAS just a few days away, most of my time continues to be spent on math. Student performance on the MCAS is seen as somehow reflective of my teaching. Personally, I do not think this is fair. When I get the students, most are below grade level, some as far as two or three years behind where they should be. It is an impossible task to try and catch them up to grade level in only one year. I would be naive to think that I can take a student through an entire year or two of missed concepts while also teaching sixth grade math. Math requires one to build upon previously learned skills. Try teaching adding and subtracting fractions to students who can't multiply. Consider also that the sixth grade MCAS test is questionable in terms of measuring curricular content because it tests material that is not covered by the Boston curriculum until seventh and eighth grade.

8:20 A.M.

At 8:20, the kids come back to my class from gym. They are sweaty and wound up but into a routine by this time of the year. I have the students come in, get out their homework and notebook, and begin working on today's starter problem. While they work, I walk around to see that they did their homework. Today's starter reads, "When we find equivalent fractions, I have told you that 'whatever you do to the bottom, you must do to the top.' In a few sentences, explain why we follow this procedure." I usually let the students work on the starter for about ten minutes. Today, however, I plan on spending at least half an hour talking about this question. Based on their quizzes, I don't think that they truly understand why we do this. I think many of them do it because I tell them to do it.

I begin by asking, "So, who can tell me what I am really asking in this question?" I want to make sure that everyone understands the question before we discuss the answer. After a few of the students respond, most just restating the question before putting it into their own words, I go on to ask, "Does anyone know why I am asking this question?" This question is met by silence. I wait a few seconds and then start to pick the kids' brains.

"What color is the sky?"

"Blue."

"Why?"

Silence . . .

"What is 3×4?"

"12."

"Why?"

Silence . . .

A student finally says 3×4 is 12 because 3 groups of 4 is 12.

"Excellent," I tell her. "Sometimes knowing why we do things is just as important as knowing the answers. On your quizzes, many of you knew how to find equivalent fractions in order to add them, but I am not sure that you understand why we do what we do."

For the next fifteen minutes, I go on to show the kids how any number multiplied by one is that number. A fraction multiplied by one is still equal to that same fraction. So by multiplying the numerator and denominator by the same number, we are really multiplying by one. Therefore, the new fraction is equivalent to the old fraction.

After we have finished reviewing the quiz, we then go on to the next problem in our book. Boston uses a program called Connected Mathematics. All the concepts are taught through word problems. One problem takes about forty-five minutes to an hour to complete. I have the students work in small groups on the problem while I circulate around asking and answering questions. In theory, Connected Math is a good program. Problem-solving skills are essential to a good education and a future career. The problem I am finding is that students whose reading skills are deficient now have two problems to overcome—reading the problem while trying to understand what is being asked and then mathematically solving it. Some groups have finished early and move on to begin their homework while others take the entire class period. With about five minutes to go, I stop the class, clarify the homework assignment, and then send students on their way to their second specialty and then lunch.

Everyday, except for Fridays, the sixth-grade team meets at 10:30. There are seven sixth-grade teachers including myself. We work in two-teacher teams except for one special education class whose members stay with one teacher for all subjects. There are three math/science teachers and three English Language Arts/social studies teachers. A normal meeting consists mostly of housekeeping type items. We discuss upcoming events, talk about problems people are having in their classroom, or any other topic that comes up.

Today's meeting is a bit different and much more important. Today, we begin trying to decide which students need to go to summer school and which should be retained. In theory, this should be a simple task, but it never is. Many of the teachers have different points of view on this topic. Some feel that all students should pass regardless of their grades. The rational behind this view is that keeping a child back is detrimental to that student's social and mental well-being. Other teachers feel that a child who did not perform up to a sixth-grade ability level should be retained. We all do not need to agree, but each team needs to come to a consensus. Regardless of our own beliefs, Boston's promotional policy is somewhat unclear. In order to graduate from middle school, a student must pass only two years of language arts and two years of math. So it is feasible that if a student fails a year, that student will be promoted. This is hard for me to accept. I believe that if I pass a student that is not academically ready to the next grade, I do that student a disservice. I also feel that I am passing my problem on to the next teacher. On the other hand, as our guidance counselor points out, research shows that keeping a child back rarely helps academic performance and can be detrimental to that child's social progress. To complicate matters even more, in my school there are a few unwritten rules. First, if a child has already been retained in the sixth grade, he or she will be promoted unless there is an extremely strong case against it. Second, if a child will be turning fourteen years old during the following school year, he/she will be promoted. After all, a ten/eleven-year-old and a thirteen/fourteen-year-old are at different stages of development. Their physical and social needs are very different, even if their academic needs are the same. There is a surprising number of students who fall into these two categories. Regardless, I need to be able to justify any recommendation for retention that I make. If a child will not fail the course for the year, then he/she can not be kept back. This makes sense from an administrative point of view. I learned this lesson last year.

Last year, in my first year of teaching, I passed a few students who I felt showed effort yet still fell short of making the grade. I wanted to boost confidence in hopes of boosting academic performance. I felt that failure would only cause the students to give up, try less, and, as a result, fall farther behind. But when it came time to possibly retain students, I did not have the choice because I had passed him/her.

This year, I gave the students the grade they earned. I still don't know which is the right thing to do.

In today's meeting, I am joined by the other six sixth-grade teachers, the guidance counselor, and the school's director of instruction. As we begin going through the list of students, we are reminded that this is only an initial list and that it will be modified several times in the upcoming weeks. We are asked to record the name of any student who currently has a D or F for the year. The math teachers need to list all of the students who have not passed five out of eight math tasks. (A math task is an assessment given by Boston after each book we complete. All math teachers teach the same books in the same order and give the same test at the end. Boston tracks the results.) The meeting goes by fairly quickly as there are not too many discussions or disagreements. This is just the first of many meetings on the topic. The closer we get to the end of the year, the more intense these retention and summer school meetings get. Everyone wants what he/she feels is best for the student.

11:05 A.M.

After the meeting, I now have to go to the cafeteria and serve lunch duty. I use this time to eat my lunch and joke around with the kids. For the most part, this time is easy and relaxing. The students are in a pretty good routine of getting their lunch, sitting, and eating. The only real issue is noise level. Like I said, relaxing.

11:30 A.M.

I walk to my class up from the cafeteria and teach the same lesson as I did during my morning class. The afternoon always feels to drag. The kids are a little more wound up than in the morning, and I am a little less tolerant of foolishness. One positive aspect of the afternoon class is that I have already done the lesson once. I am able to clean it up a bit, make it crisper, and make any modifications that I need. I try my best to tailor the lesson to the class. Although students in both classes are at about the same ability level, their personalities are much different. My morning class is chatty but task oriented. I can give them the assignment, and they will get right to work. With them, I just need to keep circulating around the room to help keep the groups on task. My afternoon class hardly talks at all, but they will also sit and do nothing if given the opportunity. So now, I have to go step by step with the activity. I give one direction at a time, let them do it, and then give the next direction.

This afternoon, my lesson stalls. Apparently, there was some type of name-calling altercation in gym class before lunch. I can tell right away that the class is caught up in the morning's drama rather than focused on the lesson. I try very hard not to bring "drama" into my class. From day one, I tell the kids that when you are in these four walls of my class, you are here to do work. I wish they believed me. As for this afternoon, I give the starter and then ask the two girls who are having differences to step into the hallway.

It seems as though Kyma has told "lies" about Regina to a boy that Regina likes. And according to Regina, she's "gonna smack Kyma for talkin shit about her." I think back to peer mediation classes I took while enrolled at the University of Connecticut and try my best to help diffuse this situation. I ask Regina what Kyma said about her. She gives her account, and Kyma denies saying those things. I ask Regina if she heard Kyma telling the lies or if she heard them from someone else. It turns out that another girl told Regina's friend that she heard that Kyma was spreading rumors. Kyma denies saying any of it. I try using the analogy of playing telephone. The more distant the firsthand account is, the more distorted the truth becomes. I don't think they quite get it, but they are both willing to try and let it go.

The rest of class goes as planned. I go through the same question-and-answer routine as done during the first class. I show the kids why we do what we do when we add fractions, and then there is a little time left for today's problem. Instead of doing the problem in groups, we do it together as a class. With this group, a more teacher-centered approach works better. By doing a problem together, I am able to call on certain individuals who I know need a little extra help. Toward the end of class, we don't quite finish, but we can pick it up tomorrow. I give the homework and then it is Drop Everything And Read (DEAR) time. The kids pull out their books and read for about ten minutes. At 1:30, I walk the kids out of the building, and their day is done.

1:30 P.M.

After the kids get on their buses, I spend the next half hour unwinding. I go to the office and check my mailbox, chat with other teachers, and straighten up my classroom. Normally, I would stay at school until about 3:00 planning for the next day. Today, however, I have my last meeting for the National Science Foundation's Urban Systemic Leadership Grant. This is a three-year grant that Boston received from the National Science Foundation (NSF) to improve the science curriculum in Boston. There are about twenty middle school teachers with whom I work on piloting new materials and getting trained as a teacher leader. In the upcoming years, I will be able to train other Boston teachers and provide professional development opportunities in my school.

Despite the fact that I have spent the majority of this year teaching math, this is an important project for me. It has given me the opportunity to be a part of a curriculum assessment team. I have learned valuable lessons on what it takes to implement a districtwide curriculum change. I also feel honored that my opinion, based on two years of piloting materials, is taken into account when decisions are made. Next year, it is my hope to go back to teaching primarily science. I will be *able to offer quality instruction, using an activities-centered curriculum that is based on both the state and national science standards.*

1:45 P.M.

I leave my school at 1:45 in order to get downtown to the Science Center by 2:15. The drive is less than ten miles but will take about a half an hour. I put the radio on, roll the windows down, and let my mind drift away from the school day to what I will be making for dinner. I use this car time to call my fiancée at work. She is not at her desk, so I leave her a message letting her know I won't be home until after 5:00.

2:15 P.M.

The meeting is scheduled to start at 2:15, but, in two years, I don't think any meeting has started on time. I use this waiting time to talk with the other science teachers. We have all heard rumors of significant layoffs that will be coming at the end of the school year due to a budget crisis. Some of the women at the meeting are also on the Teachers Union board. I try and get some info out of them, but it is nothing I have not heard before.

The focus of today's meeting is to come up with a scope and sequence for the Human Body Systems curriculum. We have spent the last two years piloting this curriculum, and it is going to be adopted for the next school year. The problem is that the curriculum takes longer to teach than the allotted time. Although I could have spent the entire year on the kit, we need to cut it down to a ten-week unit. Only eight teachers are able to make today's meeting, so it is easy to listen to everyone's opinion. For the most part, we are all on the same page in terms of what to keep and what to eliminate. We decide to limit the curriculum to the digestive system unit; this includes seventeen activities. The great thing about this unit is that each activity is hands-on. The students get the opportunity to use chemicals and models to learn about how the digestive system helps us process food.

I've talked with teachers who have been teaching in Boston for twenty plus years, and I am amazed at how little support science education has received. Teachers are given outdated textbooks and a minimal amount of materials to work with. Any lab activity usually means that the teacher has to spend his/her own money on materials. With this new curriculum, all materials, textbooks, resource guides, and interactive CD-ROMs are included.

4:30 P.M.

It only takes the group an hour and a half to create the scope and sequence for the upcoming year. After a few brief announcements about the next year's schedule, we all say our good-byes and depart. It is 4:30, and my day is almost done. The drive takes me forty-five minutes to get home this time of day. I stop at the super-

market to pick up some fresh fish and sweet potatoes for tonight's dinner. It is 5:15 before I walk in my front door. An important piece of advice that I received in my preservice program that I will gladly pass on to all teachers is the following: You must separate your personal life from your professional life to avoid getting burnt out and resentful of your job. Tomorrow, I will be in at 6:30 and do my planning. As for tonight, I am done with work.

MS. SAYWARD PARSONS
High School Teacher

My alarm blasts music as I catch a glimpse of the time through sleep-blurred eyes. As an individual who has always abhorred rising from the cozy comfort of bed before 11 A.M., I am smugly proud of my newfound ability to be satisfied with only two hits of the snooze button.

I climb out from under the covers and head towards the shower at 5:20.

It took a full year of trial and error to adjust, but making it to school forty-five minutes early is one of the many routines I've adopted to acclimate to the life of a teacher. As much grading as I commit to completing each night, sleepiness inevitably thwarts my plan, and I have to make up for this each morning before classes begin. That, and procuring my place in line at the copying machine, require that I walk through the school doors with the kind of energy that seems to hit naturally at 10 A.M.; therefore, I have started eating breakfast each morning as well. Sometimes fifteen extra minutes of sleep sounds irresistible, but I have finally learned that a bowl of Shredded Wheat before I run out the door will aid my morning class instruction as much as those hour-long college lectures on pedagogy. Today, it will be microwaved oatmeal once I get to school.

Unfortunately, I lack the discipline required to keep a daily written reflection of my classes and teaching practices, though my teacher preparation program instilled the importance of this into my brain. It's not that I don't agree with the value of doing so; it's simply a matter of personal history. Varieties of diaries lay scattered underneath my bed and clutter my bookshelves. From the pink vinyl padlocked diary of my second-grade year to the leather bound personal journal that chronicled my semester abroad, each journal was purchased with the sober intention of devoting time to recount each day's events. The best of intentions don't always pan out, however, so I relish my twenty-five minute commute to and from school each day. It has allowed for commitment to a sort of mental journal where I plan my days on the way to school and catalogue each day's events on the way home.

This morning, I strategize ways to reign in the energy of my G period freshmen. I've been impressed by their writing skills and the insightful comments brought up during discussions; their energy, most of the time, invigorates me. I've had slightly less admiration for their highly developed skill of veering our class away from the intended focus. The other day, a student smeared lip-gloss under his eyes and said, "Ms. Parsons, it's war paint." As the smell of passion fruit pervaded the air, he tried to bargain his way to the bathroom, "I'll be quiet for the rest of class if you let me wash this off." I turned to him and snapped, "You'll be quiet now, and you can wash your face after class." Next thing you know I'll be saying, "Because I'm the teacher," or, "Because I said so." I shudder at the thought of those tyrannical responses becoming second-nature and vow to continue trying new approaches to handling discipline concerns. Being commanded to behave makes me want to do the exact opposite, so why should it be any different for my students? My methods classes taught me to place myself next to unruly students; my mere presence, I believed, would calm them down and keep them focused. I wonder what to do when this technique fails miserably.

While preparing for today's classes, I catch snippets of stories from my car radio. NPR morning news replaces my former early morning staples: pop songs and reports on the latest celebrity scandals. I've begun to realize that only through broadening my own knowledge of global issues can I expect to convey to my students the importance of caring about the world beyond New Canaan, Connecticut. I take note of a brief segment about South Africa's AIDS crisis; this may interest my Model United Nations (MUN) club members who will be representing South Africa and Kuwait at the Yale MUN conference at the end of January. Today, I am also lucky enough to hear of a Tennessee Williams festival held every year in New Orleans. A recording of a southern-drawled husky voice shouting, "Stella!" at the top of his lungs crackles from the speakers as the reporter describes the variety of people who gather together to rip off their shirts, bellowing the infamous name. I will share this with my juniors when we read A Streetcar Named Desire. I question whether it is fate that constantly brings me these juicy connections I can incorporate into my classes. This philosophical question nudges my brain into thinking about planning a Romeo and Juliet unit for the state-required second-year teaching portfolio.

I pull into the school parking a lot at 6:50.

The second-year-teacher label instills in me a confidence that helps me handle my daily tasks with ease; however, I think that twenty-five years at New Canaan would not be long enough to conquer the schedule. We have eight rotating periods with one class dropping every day, and I have developed the habit of obsessively checking the cheat-sheet posted in my classroom. One final glance at the schedule assures me that A period is first today.

I am lucky enough to have only two class preps, but inevitably at least one of my three freshman classes is in a different spot because of the rotation. We are reading To Kill a Mockingbird, and I am excited to teach a lesson that I've modeled after a workshop I took recently through Bard College's Institute of Writing *and Thinking. Bard's writing program, founded by Peter Elbow, teaches teachers how to realistically blend theory and practice. Through my participation in two workshops, I've learned countless new ways to teach reader response, a theory embraced by my school's English department.*

Today I have chosen two passages from To Kill a Mockingbird *that I read aloud. My sleepy A period always occurs in the morning and that, combined with the quiet personalities of most of these students, makes for a low-energy class. I love reading aloud and have fun with Burris Ewell's speech, "Ain't no slut of a snot-nosed school teacher gonna make me do nothin'." A few students glance at each other, and I hear a chuckle or two. I ask the students to take twelve minutes to respond in their writers' notebooks to the two passages I've read, exploring what each revealed about the Finches and the Ewells. I write with the students, in my own writer's notebook, and, when time is up, I ask everyone to choose about ten lines they will read aloud. This is a way to ensure that I hear from everyone in a class where only a few students regularly volunteer to share their ideas. I read a segment from my notebook, as well, and take notes as the students read theirs. In the end, I have a number of points to return to, and I make sure to give credit to the students who brought up those ideas. This was a great success, and I notice as we begin discussion for the last fifteen minutes of class, students seem more involved. I suspect this is because we are discussing what they've noticed and not necessarily what is on the teacher's agenda, or so they think.*

When I ask why I had everyone write and read, Brendan raises his hand and says, "It's so everybody can have something to talk about." Mission accomplished; they know what they did and why they did it. Before the bell rings, I share with them my experience at the Bard workshop. I told them how my department chair had been with me and that I felt intimidated because she was so much more experienced; furthermore, we were discussing a book by an author named James Joyce, which had been difficult for me to understand. I explained that we did this same activity, and, as it approached my turn to read, I felt nervous and couldn't really pay attention to what other people were reading. I saw some students nod in agreement, and we talked about the benefits of practicing something that makes us nervous. Overall, I couldn't have asked for a better class. Things do not always work out this perfectly.

Last year, I requested that one of my teaching assignments this year be in the Academic Center (AC). All bright-eyed and innocent, I entered the AC excited to offer individualized instruction in social studies and English. I would have a total of six students assigned to me and would meet with them in groups of two or three, every four days. The AC is a relatively new endeavor, and this is the first year students are placed there if they did not receive a satisfactory grade on their freshman year English writing portfolio. Previously, the AC had been open to any student seeking extra help or for teachers who wanted to send down individual students or small groups during class. We still accept walk-ins, but to me, the focus now seems to be on students assigned there. I thought that this intimate setting would give me an opportunity to help these students improve significantly, but it is not that easy.

Today I will see Adam, Jake, and Tyler. Few students see the AC as an asset; to them, it is more like a chaperoned study hall, not welcomed by students who are used to an open campus and free-roaming privileges. Adam, who is good-natured and fairly positive, comes in and asks me what I think about the CAPT (Connecticut Academic Performance Test) because he is writing a persuasive essay for his English teacher about it. I spout an edited version of my CAPT sermon, and then he logs on to the computer and looks for some articles for his research. Jake sits on a couch in the corner and takes out a book, but it is Tyler with whom I struggle endlessly. His routine is to spend the first part of the period talking about how unfair it is that he is in here. He looks for ways to avoid doing anything productive and often manages to pull Adam and Jake away from their tasks as well. Tyler has helped me master the art of patience, the greatest asset a teacher possesses. "You were pissing and whining at me last week because you were in a bad mood," he claims this morning. I choose to let this comment dissipate without a response. I indulge myself by pretending Tyler really wants help; I just have to build his trust first.

One challenge I face is to keep up communication with my AC students' regular classroom teachers. It is best if I can stay one step ahead of them, seeking out their assignments on my own, but there is simply not enough time to do this. As a regular classroom teacher, I also understand the present demand to communicate with parents, special education teachers, learning strategy teachers, and academic workshop teachers of struggling students. Another obstacle is seeing these students every four days because assignments are often given and collected before I have a chance to help them. The bell rings, and the boys are still lounging on the couches. "You hate it here," I tease, "So why are you still sitting around?" "It's not that we hate it here," retorts Tyler with a smirk spreading across his face, "We just hate you." "Oh, I see," I answer and walk out the door, waiting for them to follow so I can lock up the room. On his way out, Tyler makes a point of saying, "I was just kidding; I don't hate you." He heads down the hall. This seems inconsequential, but the fact that he bothered to say anything at all gives me hope. I can be optimistic, can't I?

I dart upstairs and get to my C period juniors right before the bell rings at 9:16. When I received a copy of the roster for this American literature and creative writing class a week before school started, I feared the worst, as the names of twenty boys and four girls stared back at me. This, along with the fact that my deficiency in American literature had become glaringly obvious last year, filled me with apprehension. (While I should have been reading Hawthorne and Twain to prepare myself for teaching, I was filling my elective slots with African and Caribbean lit-

erature of the 1990s, not yet a focus of most high school curricula.) At the end of last year, I asked students to write evaluations of their class and my teaching practice, something that was helpful, but that I will not do again until my skin has thickened a bit more. Students noticed my unfamiliarity with the text, mostly because I had made the mistake of being completely honest with them. I felt my inability to push them and their thinking was more apparent. I couldn't challenge them to look beyond the words on the page and seek new meanings beyond their initial understanding. When a student in this year's junior class wrote in a portfolio self-reflection that we were spending "too much time analyzing books," I realized that I had succeeded in making literary analysis and interpretation one of my main focuses for the semester. I recognized this as a good thing, even if my students could not. I then obsessed for the next week about not having done enough creative writing and tried to spend the last part of the semester integrating that as much as I could. It is important for me to understand the fact that, as soon as I strengthen one area of my teaching practice, a million more weaknesses are exposed. I just have to accept that that's the way it is and see it, not as an obstacle that must be conquered, but the driving force behind why I work at teaching.

A free period comes and goes, and then I have computer lab duty. The lunch bell finally rings. I remember visiting New Canaan High School a month after I was hired. One lunch with members of the English department affirmed that I had made the right decision. Lunch here oozes with warmth and collegial chatter. The English office has been turned into a mini-lunchroom where at least eight teachers crowd around the table on any given day. The discussion dashes from a passionate debate regarding the Democratic Party nominees to a short story a few of us have recently read. A new teacher talks about her plans to adopt a dog and enroll him in dog daycare as my department chair's laughter surges down the hall. Others discuss their plans for the weekend: the opera in New York City, a visit with college friends, a quiet day at home with a five-month-old daughter. When the conversation turns towards work, lessons, and classes, I rarely hear the grumbling I had been told to expect from a high school lunchroom. I don't mean to give the impression that no one in my department gets frustrated or complains. We are human, after all, but complaints are rare and frustrations are nearly always resolved.

Lunch ends at 12:20, I teach two more freshman classes, and the final bell rings.

I grab a notebook and head back downstairs to the AC where the two social studies and five English teachers who staff the AC meet each Monday. One of the few interdisciplinary classes New Canaan High School offers is an American studies course available to juniors. The AC's goal is to provide a stronger link between the social studies and English departments, ideally as a precursor to more integrated instruction. Our current goal is to help students improve on the Reading for Information section of the CAPT, so we discuss which AC teachers will pair up with which sophomore social studies teachers to administer our second practice test this year. At times, I question why the AC seems to be focusing so much of our attention on raising standardized test scores, but my concerns are assuaged by the relative authenticity of CAPT tasks, and the fact that the better our kids score on their own, the less pressure we will feel to devote all of our time to test preparation. I have paired up with my Model United Nations coadvisor and will visit her class next week. I'll be teaching her students how to understand the CAPT task: taking a position on a pressing global concern (this time it's whether ATV (all-terrain vehicle) use should be limited on public lands; I suspect students in New Canaan represent the small part of our country's population that will be familiar with this activity).

After the meeting, I pack my bag with a stack of papers to organize and three stacks I need to grade. I've been waiting to get a bag like this since I decided to be a teacher: the big beige bag with green handles and green embroidered initials across one side. My mistake was buying the biggest size. So each day, I lug home more work than I could possibly finish, simply because it all fits in my bag. I stop at Dunkin' Donuts as I near my apartment for my much-needed afternoon caffeine boost.

It is nearly 4:00 P.M.

I settle at my kitchen table to read junior literary essay rough drafts on Herman Melville's short story, "Bartleby." In my zeal to expose my juniors to challenging and classic texts, I didn't have the foresight to see that reading twenty-four essays on Melville's purpose for creating a romantic hero would be, at the least, exhausting. I struggle through three and vow to reevaluate my reasons for assigning this. I think the students would have done better with an essay addressing issues in a more easily accessible book like O'Brien's Vietnam novel, The Things They Carried. *The rest of my night should be consumed by grading. I remember bringing a batch of oatmeal chocolate chip cookies to our department office and having a veteran teacher exclaim, "How do you have time to bake?" I suddenly felt guilty and wondered if I were not as committed to this job as I should be. But then I took a bite of a cookie and realized that I can be committed to this profession and still take time for myself.*

Around 11:30, I decide it's time to go to bed. There are eleven more essays to read and freshman homework assignments to enter into my grade book. I should really type up that creative writing assignment for my juniors and read ahead in To Kill a Mockingbird. *With complete awareness of all that's left to be done, I climb into bed and pick up a collection of short stories by Jhumpa Lahiri. I've taken the book from the school's book room, but not because I will be teaching it; it's a senior text. I've been curious about the book since it was discussed in the lunchroom a few weeks ago, and I recently heard an interview with Lahiri on NPR last week. I snuggle under my covers and open up to the title story, "Inter-*

preter of Maladies." I feel a pang of guilt as I evade my remaining schoolwork, but it is quickly veiled by the delicious satisfaction of reading a book just for me. I read only two and a half pages before I decide to turn off the light, but it is five minutes of tranquility, just enough to end the day.

CONCLUDING REMARKS

Although there is no typical day that is representative of the full range of what it is to teach, each vignette shares certain common elements. Collectively, these notions offer insight into the dedication, emotional toll, and knowledge base required of today's teachers.

Perhaps most significant is the effort expended by each of these educators with respect to the desire to meet the needs of each student in class. Whether it is scheduling meetings to coordinate student support, revising lessons over the course of a single school day in response to the learning styles of students, or developing curriculum materials to capture student interest and sustain motivation, there is an underlying element of respect and personal attention for students expressed by each teacher. Differentiating instruction, attending to students' needs and interests, and providing support beyond the confines of traditional classroom time are all measures designed to meet the needs of *each and every learner.* This attention given to each individual person who, together with classmates, forms a collective, as opposed to considering each class as an amorphous whole, is often overlooked by those not immersed in the profession. This consideration for all students is the hallmark of excellent instruction. Knowing your students as learners and individuals is a fundamental precursor to effective teaching.

This need to know one's students invokes another common theme seen throughout these descriptive essays—effective instruction demands contact time with students. As seen, this can take on many forms, from using student-centered pedagogical strategies in class to sitting lunch duty. The "chalk and talk" style of teaching that sees the teacher lecturing at the front of the room can meet some of the needs of a few learners in each class, but, by and large, there exists a disconnect between teacher and pupil in this approach. Educators do not consider project work, discussion groups, etc., as more effective means of facilitating learning because these tasks fall into an arbitrary category of "student-centered" methods, but because they actually take into account the student as learner and person. These methods shift the emphasis of instruction away from teaching and toward one of learning. Clearly, the teachers whose words are shared here go to great lengths to move beyond the attempt to infuse information into their students' short-term memories. They are committed to meeting their students on their own terms and facilitating actual understanding.

Ongoing professional development serves as an additional theme. Two of the teachers are involved in large-scale professional development and curriculum work sponsored by the National Science Foundation, while a writing institute provides a setting for professional growth for the third teacher. Although schools offer mandatory professional development days for their professional staff, the several days are often not adequate for teachers to keep abreast of current thinking in curriculum, assessment, and organization and management issues, just to name a few. In fact, the current professional development paradigm of one-shot workshops is a borderline complete waste of resources given the complexities of today's classrooms. There are few easy fixes. Professional development must serve the professional. It must provide a sustained opportunity for engaged professionals to pose timely and relevant questions regarding aspects of their own practice. Teachers should be empowered to seek professional development, in part, on their own terms and be afforded the resources and time to pursue those much-needed experiences. The one-size-fits-all model currently employed by many districts serves neither the teacher nor students well. In the case of our teachers, each sought experiences that each believe will ultimately have a real impact on practice.

Although additional themes, including the role of a professional teacher as mentor, counselor, and advisor, along with the extensive "hidden" responsibilities of the job, such as grading and meeting with parents were prevalent, I will mention the issue of time as I conclude this chapter.

This is a tricky concept to address because the argument that there is not enough time does not seem especially compelling to me given that we all have the same amount of time each day to manage. The real issue for teachers is less about time management per se than it is about the underlying implications of power and autonomy given the structure of most public school days. It seems that, as a society, we only value the direct contact time that teachers have with students. If teachers are not engaged in the traditional practice of standing in front of a class and actually telling their students things, then whatever it is teachers are doing, it doesn't seem to count as teaching.

This brings us full circle. If teaching were merely a technical enterprise, one in which students are widgets and learning is automatic, then the issue of time could be minimized. We must abandon, however, any simplistic notions that we hold about teaching and teachers developed through our apprenticeship of experience, including our perceptions of how teachers spend their time. As these three professionals have demonstrated in this chapter, to teach is to establish and maintain relationships with students, colleagues, and parents. It is to advance one's own skills and knowledge. It is to be a role model, counselor, mentor, and advocate. Teaching involves early mornings, late nights, weekends, and, yes, even summers. Assessment, curriculum, pedagogy, management, organization, discipline, and sometimes lunch duty are but a few of the daily responsibilities. Split-second decision making is routine. The stakes are real. Respect is elusive. The pay is poor. The rewards are tremendous. The dedication is real. To come to really know the profession—walk a mile in their shoes.

Key Challenges for Teachers: Windows into the Complexity of American Classrooms

John Settlage and Karl F. Wheatley

INTRODUCTION

What does it mean to be a teacher? Some would reduce teaching to possessing just two elements: subject matter knowledge and verbal communication ability. Yet, we all know from experience that a smart person who is eager to talk to others is not necessarily a good teacher. Such intangible traits as the zeal for learning, enthusiasm for education, and a genuine interest in students are also key features. Identifying someone who is an effective teacher is a task most of us could do. Defining the traits that define a good teacher— this is not such a simple task. For example, even though a sense of humor would seem to be a powerful trait in a classroom, having a funny streak is not sufficient. We recognize that our knowledge about teaching is flawed and incomplete. Perhaps the most simple and accurate statement we can make about teaching is this: Teaching is incredibly complex.

The authors of this chapter have worked with a large number of teachers and spent time in countless classrooms. And we have been teachers ourselves. Currently, we serve as teacher educators at two different universities, and we continue to maintain close ties with schools. These connections take the form of research in classrooms, preparing college students to become teachers, conducting ongoing support to practicing teachers, and sharing our growing knowledge with colleagues and community through conversation and writings such as these.

When we were new to the teaching profession, our views of teaching were influenced by portrayals in the popular media along with romanticized recollections from our own educational experiences. Having spent many hours educating others, we now have a much more accurate view about the perspectives that influence the year-to-year, day-to-day, and moment-to-moment lives of classroom teachers. We have organized these perspectives into three groups: the practical, the political, and the personal. The three perspectives will serve as windows through which we can look into the world of teaching. The first window gives us a glimpse into the practical, the realities that are automatically present within every teaching act. These issues may seem mundane, but they are legitimate and cannot be explained away or waved off. Examples of practical issues are constraints of time and space and the inevitable variety of demands that comes with working with people. The practical issues are often invisible to those who never cross the classroom threshold in the role of teacher but are relevant to teaching. The second window into teaching is the political. In this category, we include issues both local (such as the give and take between people and groups within any workplace) and national (such as changes in federal requirements for special education). Political issues are more than the battles that occur during an election year; they include the struggles for power and voice that are inherent within every social organization. The third window into teaching is the personal, the individual and emotional elements of teaching: the desire to help students less fortunate than oneself, the belief that schooling is more than just teaching about subject matter, and the convictions that are drawn upon when decisions need to be made. While personal issues are subtler than practical issues, they are similar in their influence. Denying the significance of personal issues is foolhardy because often these issues are the factors that attract individuals to a teaching career; one cannot dismiss these challenges because they are an essential part of America's education system.

Consider these three perspectives—the practical, political, and personal—as windows into the classroom, each providing a slightly different way of looking at and thinking about teaching. These windows shed light onto teaching even as they give us a way to peer into this world. By looking at the challenges through multiple windows, we can better appreciate what it is like to be a teacher in the midst of the swirl of energy, expectations, and excitement that characterizes America's classrooms.

THE SIX CHALLENGES OF TEACHING

We have identified the following as challenges that we believe capture the complexities of teaching:

1. The challenge of teaching anyone anything

2. The challenge of deciding what to teach

3. The challenge of teaching what you decide to teach

4. The challenge of teaching each and every student

5. The challenge of doing unnatural things

6. The challenge of teaching day after day

These six challenges provide insight into the reality of the profession. To be a teacher means responding to a variety of demands and requires a careful and constant attempt to find a middle ground between often contradictory expectations. We will present each of the six challenges and then consider them from the perspectives of the practical, the political, and the personal.

The Challenge of Teaching Anyone Anything

An antiquated notion of teaching is that it involves dispensing knowledge from source to recipient. Another way to think about this is to consider the difference between information and understanding. A vast amount of information does not necessarily dictate what is known. A computer disk full of data is not knowledge until some person makes sense of the information. Buying books to create a personal library does not make one an intellectual. The books have to be opened, read, and understood before we would suggest that someone is educated. Teachers must guide students to incorporate new information into their existing ideas. The mind does not simply store information—it organizes, arranges, and catalogs the information so the knowledge can be used to sort through new experiences. Instead of absorbing or accepting the information presented to them by their teachers, students are expected to be able to *do* something with the knowledge they gain. Knowledge cannot be treated as something inert. Knowledge, if it is worthwhile, should be applicable in settings beyond the confines of the classroom.

Practical Issues

Taking the knowledge learned in one instance and applying it to another situation is the essence of understanding. When we truly understand, we can use this idea or apply that skill in a wide variety of circumstances. In physics, this means knowing how to solve a problem that is not exactly like any ever experienced before. In athletics, understanding means knowing how to apply a strategy when facing a brand new opponent. If a student can take what he or she learned during a lesson and then correctly apply it to a novel situation, then we say that he or she can transfer his or her knowledge. When a student can successfully transfer knowledge, then he or she clearly understands what was taught.

With a little contemplation, you can name a physical skill that you had to repeatedly practice in order to finally do well—backing a trailer into a driveway, using a pastry bag to decorate a cake, performing an overhand tennis serve, hitting a golf ball so it did not veer to one side, or one of a thousand other actions. Imagine that it was your job to train twenty-seven people to become masterful at this skill. Seeing how an expert does it is not sufficient; each trainee would approach the task in a slightly different way. Some would be easily frustrated, while others would be tirelessly determined. What would be required to eventually have everyone master the task? A good trainer could identify each individual's strengths and weaknesses in order to provide the type of instruction each requires. Learning a skill for your own benefit is one thing—helping an entire classroom of twenty-seven or more individuals is substantially more demanding.

Within the challenge of teaching anyone about anything is the issue of the potential match between the information and the student's way of thinking. Students do not arrive at school with empty minds; they have experienced the world for several years before beginning kindergarten. While the lived experiences of a five-year-old may not seem especially scholarly, even such a young child has ideas about what causes rain, the destination of those who die, and the reasons the moon changes shape. Although these ideas may not be accurate from an adult perspective, they are ideas upon which new ideas will be built.

Teaching one child a new idea means that we need to help connect established knowledge with something fresh for him or her. The complexion of this task changes when the teacher first accepts transfer as the goal and then is faced with 27 elementary school children or 150 high school students (typical numbers for teachers), all of whom bring different background knowledge. Good teachers recognize that teaching the material once is insufficient. Instead, they give the students opportunities to learn in several different ways, through reading, through conversation, through hands-on activities, and maybe through technological means such as computers. Even though students arrive with different background knowledge, coming into contact with the subject matter in multiple ways allows the students to understand the material well enough to transfer it. How to create these multiple methods of teaching the subject, and to do it so all students will be able to transfer their knowledge, is a practical and persistent challenge.

PERSONAL ISSUES

We all learn in different ways. Some prefer to be told first exactly how to go about doing something, from start to finish, and then give it a try. Others would rather be given a general idea and then try it on their own. The variability in how people prefer to learn suggests that there isn't one "right" way to teach. Each of us learns in ways that work best for us, from subtracting with borrowing to tying our shoes. When we look at how someone else does these tasks, it seems odd, foreign, but still somehow correct. If we are skillful at performing a certain task because we learned it in one way, what would make us think that this is the way that would work equally well for everybody else? This challenge of teaching requires knowing many ways of helping students develop an understanding of the material.

By virtue of the paths they took to enter the profession, teachers have proven to be good at learning. Along the way, they found techniques that helped them to learn, but this does not mean that these same modes of learning will work for all 27 or 150 students. Teachers are challenged to invent a variety of strategies to teach the material, even when they may only have their own learning experiences to draw upon. While we might expect that teachers would obtain these strategies from courses during their college training, the reality is that it is impossible to learn all that is needed. If future teachers are responsible for multiple subject areas, if they need to develop skill in multiple teaching techniques, and have to do these tasks for all of their students, it is unrealistic to expect them to learn all they need as an undergraduate. Instead teachers are challenged to continuously develop their skill at applying a range of techniques to the wide variety of topics they are to teach.

In teaching her fourth graders about geology, Mrs. D. begins by providing her students with pails of rocks. Within their groups, students are challenged to classify their rocks in as many ways as they can invent. Ultimately,

Mrs. D. suggests some features of the rocks that they might use, such as the presence of layers. After exploring and examining the rocks, Mrs. D. supplies the children with a collection of books and other printed resources about rocks. Subsequently, she orchestrates a class discussion in which children share their discoveries with each other. As a class, students design a poster showing their understanding of rocks and their formation and transformations. After about a week of this sort of learning, the class eventually creates a chart of the rock cycle. Quite amazingly, Mrs. D. never directly supplied the facts or answers to the students. Because of her wise and responsive selection of activities, she was able to guide the students to learn the targeted ideas.

Political Issues

To teach for transfer is an ambitious goal since it places considerable responsibility upon the students as well as the teacher. Understanding a subject requires that students demonstrate how well they can extend their knowledge. This is a considerable departure from memorizing multiplication facts wherein the mastery of the information is revealed by recalling correct answers. By showing that they can apply knowledge in a novel situation, we are able to discern whether the students genuinely understand what was taught. We might want to consider where we expect students to transfer their knowledge. The expected response might be that we want them to demonstrate transfer to a host of different scenarios, but, increasingly, the answer for teachers is that the students can transfer their knowledge to a multiple choice test. However, the idea of transfer is that students can use their knowledge in a host of situations, not for something as restrictive and unnatural as filling in bubble sheets.

One of the many balancing acts teachers must perform involves the desire to teach students for understanding and transfer versus teaching students to be successful on standardized tests. While tests are important mechanisms for sorting students (into subsequent courses, into reading groups, into colleges), tests are really not part of the daily life of most people's careers. On the surface, it might appear that teaching students to write persuasive essays and then evaluate a writing sample provided by the teacher are parallel skills. However, the thought processes are not identical. Moving from one skill (such as creating) to another (such as critiquing) is an example of transfer, and transfer does not occur automatically. The political pressure that teachers feel to raise test scores can conflict with their desire to teach students to transfer their knowledge in ways more meaningful than to answer multiple choice questions.

The Challenge of Deciding What to Teach

What students learn in school profoundly influences society, as indicated by an engraving outside many schools, "The Foundation of Every Society Is the Education of Its Youth." Given this crucial role of education in society, what should teachers teach? For many people outside education, the answer is seemingly obvious: teach my kid so she knows as much, if not more, than what I had to learn when I was her age. Yet, conflicts over differing opinions about the purposes of school are regularly played out in school board meetings, in the media, and in public policy. Because the subject matter students are expected to learn, also known as the curriculum, is the most political aspect of teaching, we will begin with the political dimensions of the challenge of deciding what to teach.

POLITICAL ISSUES

If educating youth provides the foundation of society, what exactly is the purpose of the foundation? Employment? College? Testing? Citizenship? The question, "What should teachers help children to learn?" is deceptively simple because a complete answer is very close to "everything." Because teachers are those who ultimately translate the rhetoric about education into classroom practice, they must respond to the multiple purposes of education. In what follows, we identify the conflicting pressures placed upon teachers as a result of the politicized aspects of education.

Preparing New Workers. One way to create a strong society is to prepare all citizens for their future jobs. Businesspeople and others who would push for cost-effective education suggest that teachers should train students for the jobs that fit their aptitudes. This sounds practical and efficient, but who is suited to make career decisions for every student? Educators and aptitude tests have a long history of grossly misjudging students' personal potential and future careers, a situation detailed by Peter Sacks in his book *Standardized Minds* (2001). Furthermore, since many adults hold several different jobs over their lifetimes, for which job should teachers prepare students? And to make this point even more personal, who would *you* have allowed to decide your profession for you? Finally, isn't this whole approach undemocratic, since it would reduce the individual's chance to pursue the American Dream? On the other hand, if, in educating children from kindergarten through high school graduation, schools and teachers ignore occupational training, how will the next generation of workers know how to function in the workplace? Is there some content that is generally useful to teach to the future scientist, janitor, poet, travel agent, and businessperson?

Teaching the Basics. Many conservatives and subject matter experts believe that every teacher in America ought to teach the traditional, basic content for their grade level. The "back to basics" movement is supposed to provide a firm foundation for postsecondary vocational or professional education. Some even argue that having this shared educational experience is key to preserving a democracy. One problem with this traditional approach is defining what "the basics" are. Yes, children should learn to read, write, and compute, but beyond that, agreement is difficult to achieve. For example, what books should every child read? *Charlotte's Web? Aesop's Fables? A Lesson before Dying? Hamlet? Harry Potter?* Similarly, school textbooks from different publishers often focus on different content, and in a different sequence, for the same grade. Whose idea of the basics should teachers follow? Who would we be willing to give the authority to make the ultimate decision about the basics for every child?

Meeting the Standards. Another approach to determining what should be taught is to align the curriculum with the standards, the key outcomes in each subject area developed by subject matter experts, teachers, and teacher educators. Because content standards represent expert opinion about critical content, teachers might teach to the national standards for the subjects for which they are responsible. However, national content standards often offer only general guidance about what is to be learned and typically do not identify the specific content to be learned in a specific grade. For example, in the National History Standards, we find this goal for students in grades seven to twelve: "Distinguish between the old and new immigration in terms of its volume and the immigrants' ethnicity, religion, language, place of origin, and motives for emigrating from their homelands." On the surface, that seems reasonable. After all, our nation originated as a result of immigration and is continuing to be shaped by these processes. But if pressed to teach to this standard, we would be scrambling to know how to meet that standard. Where would you begin and what limits would you necessarily place upon the depth of study?

Boosting Test Scores. High-stakes testing has infiltrated the curriculum debates and, like an 800-pound gorilla entering a crowded room, has easily elbowed aside other contenders in the battle. In essentially every state, high-stakes tests have become the standard for assessing student outcomes and, thus, measuring teacher and school success. With the pressure on schools to perform in light of the No Child Left Behind Act, and in response increased local political pressure, teachers are pushed to focus almost exclusively upon these tests. This is understandable, because the fate of teachers, administrators, and entire schools often rests on these test scores.

Is this a bad thing? For many noneducators, test scores are simple and clear indicators of school success. However, these tests only assess those student outcomes that can be measured on standardized tests, and many of the most important educational outcomes (e.g., creativity, ability to solve complex problems, conceptual understanding of subject matter) cannot be adequately assessed on these paper-and-pencil tests. Someone once said that test scores are the best way of measuring how well people can do on tests. In other words, because most standardized tests are based upon choosing a correct answer from a list of three or four options, they are unavoidably limited in what they can measure and reveal about individual intellect. Many skills we would like students to master, such as the immigration standard presented earlier, are difficult to distill to a multiple choice test item. Imagine if we tested for drivers' licenses without ever giving actual driving tests! Do you want your life in the hands of a lifeguard (or heart surgeon) who has only passed a written test on the matter? This is just the type of dilemma that teachers face and must attempt to negotiate.

Developing Good Citizens. Another direction in which teachers are being tugged is in response to the desire for schools to prepare students to become active members of a democratic society. Many teacher educators and other academics embrace this mission for schools. From this view, students should learn to be good problem solvers, critical thinkers, and effective advocates for improving society. While the back-to-basics and standardized-test movements demand that students master content others deem important, those favoring a democratic education want students to assume a role in deciding what they should learn and how they should learn it. Teachers who opt for this path may be gratified that students learn to take on complex problems with creativity and maturity and become self-directed learners. However, this is a risky path in schools where the principal demands that every lesson plan relate directly to one of the "standards" to be measured on the state tests.

While responsible for educating other people's children, teachers are in the middle of a dozen tugs-of-war about the proper goals of education. Whatever path teachers choose, it will be perceived as misguided by someone. As has been true for decades, even in the so-called "good old days" of the 1950s, these disgruntled individuals fill editorial pages with their laments about curriculum content. Unaware or uninterested in the dilemmas and constraints schools face, there is always a segment of the public that is all too eager to complain about the current condition of schooling, always suggesting that their own educational experiences were far superior than what students are currently receiving. By considering their personal educational experiences as "normal" and in wanting to preserve their interpretations of the status quo, these isolated individuals fail to recognize that communities, cultures, and societies are in a continual process of change.

PRACTICAL ISSUES

There are many practical issues that influence curriculum decisions by teachers. Because teaching is so phenomenally complex and time-consuming, teachers often must do what is practical or expedient. This practical consideration pulls teachers towards teaching that which they have the tools to teach. At first glance, simply following the grade-level text for any subject, for example, may seem to be the most practical thing to do. However, these texts contain too much content to be learned well in a year. This leads to a content-heavy curriculum that undercuts students' natural curiosity and motivation to learn. Unmotivated students misbehave more, diverting teachers' energy away from teaching. Furthermore, the adopted texts don't always align with district or state standards, making it difficult for teachers to be sure the curriculum is addressing the outcomes for which they are being held accountable. Moreover, the organization of texts is sometimes very different from the way in which teachers are accustomed to teaching and may present content that is unfamiliar to teachers. All of this makes using even well-structured textbooks an enormously challenging and time-consuming task.

Following students' interests, pursuing meaningful problems, or promoting students' abilities to engage in democratic processes create practical problems. Teaching in these ways is very messy and unpredictable and may not permit teachers to cover all of the specified standards. They may feel such teaching methods are more effective in that students explore matters in depth rather than just skimming the surface. However, at the end of the year, teachers will probably have not covered some of the curriculum content, which is often seen as irresponsible.

PERSONAL ISSUES

Further constraining teachers' abilities to choose appropriate curriculum goals is the fact that teachers sometimes don't know well the content they are expected to teach, even in the primary grades. In a very fundamental sense, teachers are being asked to teach a great deal of content they never learned. The authors of this chapter address their respective states' content standards in their teacher preparation courses. Despite holding two advanced degrees, they are sheepishly ignorant of much that students are supposed to know by the end of sixth grade. History, science, economics, geometry, literature, and geography are all the purview of the elementary school teacher, but it's a rare individual who has mastered all of these subject areas.

There are also the fear factors—fear of losing control of the class and fear of looking foolish. No one likes losing control of the group one is leading or looking stupid. Anyone who can imagine the nightmarish possibility of a classroom careening toward chaos while trying to implement something new will understand the reluctance to push at the edges of one's comfort level. Content that requires risky teaching approaches or approaches where the class could get loud and out of control may be avoided because of these risks to the teacher.

Finally, there is the stress that teachers face by not being able to please everyone. Teachers spend their days teaching—where many are told that preparing their students for the standardized tests is the responsible thing to do. Then many of them spend at least one night a week taking classes—where university professors charge that teaching to these tests spells the death of effective and meaningful education. Is it any wonder, then, in the midst of these conflicting messages that teachers whisper, "All I want to do is teach my students."

Teachers chose their profession primarily to make a positive impact on children's lives. To have different groups telling you you are doing a lousy job is no picnic and can foster feelings of helplessness, depression, and burnout. Teachers have never before been under pressure as they are today, and the faces of many teachers, even young teachers new to the profession, have taken on the look of individuals forced onto a long march. Even achieving high test scores offers no sure relief, since many teachers know (and university professors remind them), that the tests do not measure much of what matters, and achieving high tests scores may require giving up on more important student outcomes.

The Challenge of Teaching What You Decide to Teach

Deciding how to teach something should be easy once you have decided what to teach, right? Unfortunately, it can be as complex. Within this challenge, we are no longer talking about just the "stuff" that needs to be taught but also the ways in which it is to be taught. There are countless ways to teach any topic, none of which guarantees success. People who believe teaching is easy often confuse teaching with telling, as if telling someone how to do something translates into instant knowledge and skillful performance. If that were true, then young children wouldn't need to hear *Goodnight Moon* read endless times, teenagers would keep their rooms clean without any reminders from parents, and students would learn subject matter easily. Instead, teaching the content you choose to teach is an enormous challenge.

PERSONAL ISSUES

Making the Time to Plan. Wearied from teaching and other life responsibilities, the teacher tries to find enough time to plan how to teach what she decides to teach. Preparing to teach content well generally takes more time than learning the content itself. There is never sufficient time to prepare for teaching, and K-12 teachers are faced with teaching something they have not taught since a full year ago. Even if they had a terrific plan and wonderful materials for teaching the content, time will be spent locating and getting those materials out of storage, making sure there is enough of everything, and reviewing the teaching procedure. Further, teachers are not often entirely satisfied with how they taught something before or are otherwise obliged to modify their methods. Creating a new teaching approach and gathering the necessary materials can take as much as one to five hours for every hour of instruction; the unreality of the situation seems obvious. Thus, some teachers may skim the materials they have available, assemble a very rudimentary plan for teaching, and hope for the best. "Winging it" may not be the best way to improve American education, but many teachers do quite a bit more of it than they might like to admit.

The Expertise Predicament. As noted in the previous challenge, teachers are not always experts in the content they are expected to teach. Even if they are brave or compliant enough to try to teach it, it takes time to learn the new content—in addition to time to plan to use the new content in the classroom. Further, teachers are often being asked to teach students using techniques they did not experience themselves as students. This leads to the double-edged difficulty; teachers are supposed to instruct about content they have never been required to know AND are often directed to teach using methods they have never tried before. The ordinary teacher is faced with the predicament of needing to be concurrently a subject matter expert and skillful with novel teaching strategies.

This would be an ample challenge for teachers wholeheartedly devoted to teaching this particular material. However, in situations where teaching has deteriorated into a purely test preparation activity—which often leads to less stimulating teaching methods—teachers are likely to become discouraged and undermotivated. Motivation allows an individual to persist even when the situation is discouraging. When motivation is weakened, teachers have a harder time facing the dual expertise demands along with the political issues they must face.

Practical Issues

Instructional Sequence Uncertainty. What aspects of a topic should teachers teach first? Those outside education might assume that educators know the best order for teaching basic content. While reasonable sequences for teaching some content have been identified, others have not. Imagine teaching the alphabet. It might seem logical to teach children the letters in order, from A to Z, as some commercial programs do. However, children named David and Monique may be much more interested in learning the letters, D and M, respectively. This is a classic problem in teaching. What appears to be a logical sequence for teaching is often different than the sequence that meets the psychological needs or characteristics of learners. Following a seemingly logical sequence for teaching may mean that the content only reflects the current interests of a small minority of students. Repeat this process all day for a few months, and students quickly learn that what seems meaningful to them is not the same as what the schools want them to be learning. As with so many other aspects of traditional schooling, this makes students less motivated to learn.

Another component of the practical issues is deciding whether to begin by engaging students in some meaningful task or project—writing a story, conducting an experiment—or by first teaching them the basic knowledge or skills they need to do the task. Should children just jump into writing a book and discover as they go what they need to learn to make a good book? Or do you first teach them spelling, grammar, the parts of a book, the main parts of a story, plot, character, and so on before letting them begin to write? Following the first path makes for less predictable and more complex teaching, as students discover at different times what they need to know about various aspects of writing. Following the second path can be deadly dull. Since they aren't doing any real writing, students wonder about the relevance of grammar, punctuation, etc. Follow this path often enough, and, you guessed it, students become less and less motivated to learn.

Matters of Timing. When learning new material and skills, students may lack significant background knowledge. Clearly, a teacher should intervene to guide students along the correct path, but *when* to apply that intervention is not obvious. If the teacher doesn't immediately correct the children when they say or do something wrong, there is the worry that students will think they did it right and will have had the wrong way reinforced in their minds. However, if the teacher corrects every error students make at the instant the mistake is made, students can quickly lose interest in sharing their ideas, or even stop trying at all. Sometimes correcting one student's misconception shuts down a whole discussion.

American textbooks are notoriously thicker than the texts in other countries, so teachers have to race to cover the content. This means the content is often not taught thoroughly, it is quickly forgotten, and the teacher in the next grade often teaches the same content all over again. The standards are similarly overwhelming. One might expect teachers to recognize the flaws with this approach and abandon it, but teachers are under pressure to bring all students up to grade level—by the end of that year. This misguided version of "higher standards" only perpetuates the self-defeating teaching behaviors described above. Teaching that is directed solely at test preparation often pushes teachers to cover too much content at too fast a pace. In short, teaching in contemporary classrooms is inevitably a race against the clock and the calendar.

Unsatisfactory Resources. Whatever they choose to teach, odds are that teachers don't have all the instructional materials they need to teach it. Teachers are forever buying supplies with their own money, spending hundreds of dollars each year, making teaching materials in their spare time, borrowing materials from other teachers, or simply teaching lessons without the materials that would make the lesson more effective. Textbooks frequently suggest activities that require materials teachers do not have.

In addition to material resource problems, teachers often suffer from insufficient or inappropriate teaching practice resources. Learning how to teach is a highly social process with many novice teachers learning from the wisdom of their more experienced colleagues. Unfortunately, advice from old-timers (and this does not just apply to the teaching profession) often focuses on getting by with gimmicks and tricks. Here is an example: a teacher is provided a handy tip sheet promising "One Hundred Ways to Praise a Child" (e.g., Good job, You're so smart at math, and so forth). While children often respond favorably to such praise, it can simultaneously reduce student motivation. Telling children they are good or smart at something can instill the belief that intelligence is something an individual simply has or does not have, rather than as something that can always be improved through effort. Children who develop this kind of view of ability tend to avoid challenges, giving up easily when they feel as if they will not be immediately successful. While the praise sheet might appear to be a marvelous teaching resource, it has the potential for causing motivational problems for students. As if teaching was not difficult enough without the abundance of bad advice!

Political Issues

Keeping on Pace. As noted earlier, it is a substantial challenge to teach everything one sets out to teach. As deadlines approach, whether the end of a grading period, the arrival of a scheduled test, or even the end of the year, teachers realize they cannot cover all that they had hoped to teach. What can be done? They might try to speed up and teach a little bit about all of the remaining topics but not with any depth. This might satisfy a need to have "covered the curriculum," but students typically retain little of what they learn when teachers teach that way. An alternative is to continue to teach at a pace that increases the chance that the students will learn the material, but that ensures not teaching it all. Although this is a reasonable decision, it has consequences. The teacher in the next grade level may be inconvenienced by the fact that you did not teach some content, meaning those students will be behind when they reach her next year. She may feel pressured to begin the year by teaching some of the content you did not get to, and cramming this material into her too-full curriculum puts her at risk of not covering content she would normally get to. Thus, political pressure tends to flow down the grades in schools, with teachers of any grade pressuring teachers in previous grades to teach more, so that children arrive the next year fully "ready" for the content that will be expected to learn.

Preserving the Peace. Another political issue is noise control. Traditional teaching methods have been vilified for all their weaknesses: They are boring, students quickly forget what they learn, students do not understand much of what they do remember, and so on. Nevertheless, traditional teaching is usually quiet. The teacher talks, and students listen and write down what the teacher says. Or the teacher may pose a question, call upon one student at a time to answer, followed by everyone quietly doing seatwork. More progressive teaching methods, including cooperative learning and hands-on teaching, are often more effective than traditional methods, but these newer methods are also noisy. Parents may be exasperated by the noise their own children make as they play, or whine and argue. Imagine enduring the sounds of twenty-seven students while teaching in a way that expects children to be pretty vocal. On a political level, the noise from your class may disrupt others' classes and vice versa. Teachers are often very careful not to criticize other teachers in their building but often will tactfully ask other teachers to keep their class quieter.

Teaching what one might choose to teach means navigating a turbulent sea of ever-changing policies, overcoming a lack of appropriate resources, and avoiding any practices that might incur a political backlash. Up until this point, our attention has been upon teaching subject matter to an entire group of students, an admitted oversimplification of teaching. In the next section, we will consider the implications of teaching not just entire groups of students but teaching each one of the students who inhabits the classroom.

The Challenge of Teaching Each and Every Student

The teaching of 27 or 150 students occurs within particular spaces. There is the physical space, the classroom, where students variously sit, discuss, and think. In order for learning to occur, the physical space must be arranged to allow and encourage learning to happen. When writing, students need solid smooth surfaces for their paper. When discussing, students need to be positioned so they can see the face of each person who is speaking. When doing activities, students need facilities that support their scientific inquiries (lab tables and sinks), instrumental performances (music stands and instruments), and technology uses (personal computers and printers). In short, for learning to occur, the physical must be properly organized.

Likewise, the intellectual space must be organized to support learning. The climate should allow students to venture their ideas and interpretations within the context of the subject at hand. Students should feel as if they are able to contribute to the discussions, even as the teacher maintains some measure of control and decorum. Requirements in terms of behavioral norms, homework expectations, attendance policies, and so on must be sufficiently clear and accepted so that their presence rarely interferes with the learning agenda. Only when the physical and intellectual space unambiguously suggests that a particular classroom is the setting for genuine learning will a teacher be able to address the challenge of teaching each and every person in that classroom.

PRACTICAL ISSUES

By definition, a teacher is someone who has successfully negotiated the educational system. Sufficiently intelligent to obtain reasonable scores on standardized tests, these individuals were smart enough be admitted into a teacher preparatory program, they were able to complete their college courses, and so on. Along the way, and you could imagine these as checkpoints, some peers of our now-practicing teachers fell short of the various requirements that are used to screen teachers. This is a reasonable process since we would like our teachers to be those who have succeeded in the academic world. With these skills, they will serve as good guides and mentors for their students.

The catch to this scenario is that classrooms contain a wide mixture of students. With which students would we expect our teacher to be most effective? Those who are most like who the teacher was at that age. But what about the others, the students who are better at speaking their knowledge rather than writing it, or the students who prefer to learn by reading the material rather than hearing about it? And the list goes on. For students whose styles of communication and learning are in alignment with their teacher's, we would expect greater rapport and harmony. But teaching children with different learning styles, let alone different language backgrounds or cultural heritage, is a practical problem when the teacher intends to teach every student.

Certainly, we would hope that teachers would not focus upon just a segment of their students but would find ways to individualize their instruction. But to meet with individual students for only two minutes apiece would, in itself, require an hour. Furthermore, it is difficult to keep the rest of the class working productively while a teacher provides individual attention. Outside of school, many of us are challenged to find sufficient quality time with our families. Envisioning a classroom as a family, albeit with twenty-seven or more individuals, provides a sense of the desperation teachers feel when they attempt to make substantive contact with every one of their students on a daily basis.

POLITICAL ISSUES

Teaching all the children and each child has complex political dimensions. The simplest thing is for teachers to spread their attention equally among the children, but even that takes considerable thought, effort, and self-monitoring. Other complexities await. Within the classroom, friendships and cliques form. Some kids are popular, whereas some are rejected. Some kids work well together, while others do not. As they become older, boys and girls start noticing each other more and noticing learning less. Teachers have to manage all of these social dynamics in a way that is respectful to each child but also allows the whole group to function. Such are the political dynamics within the classroom, especially when we view politics as the distribution and exercise of power within a community and accept the possibility that a classroom represents a community.

If we could identify a potential strength of the current standards movement, it would be the belief that every child is capable of learning and that schools should take this expectation as a very serious responsibility. Such a push for accountability ought to translate into making efforts to improve every child's learning. The antiquated practice of sorting students, with the tacit understanding that some are naturally more capable than others, runs counter to the philosophy of maintaining high standards for all students. From a purely statistical standpoint, it makes great sense to raise the achievement of every child.

Imagine a school where test scores reveal that students are underperforming, and we are able to offer advice about where to direct the limited supply of resources. If we focus upon advancing those students who are already at the upper end of the testing scale, we have two problems. First, they are already performing so well on the tests that it is hard to raise their scores. Second, pulling up the scores of only the students on the high end will have only a slight effect on the average of all students' scores. Far better to try to raise all students' achievement, even if only by a small amount. The impact upon the average test scores will be much greater since elevation of one subset's scores won't be washed out by the marginal performance of many others.

Unfortunately, those in leadership positions who do not appreciate this rather fundamental statistical factor may lead decision makers in the wrong direction. Aside from the moral issue of only focusing upon those students who we sense will be successful, giving attention exclusively to the high end of the academic curve is a foolhardy strategy. This is not meant to denigrate gifted and talented programs. However, in a climate with limited resources (e.g., enough qualified teachers, finite amount of money to spend upon supplies) to invest solely at the high end, thereby not trying to teach everyone, solves few problems.

As more and more schools admit students with disabilities into "general education" classes, many teachers who have had little or no preparation to teach these children are winding up with them in their classes. This practice, called "inclusion," is probably appropriate in many instances, at least in a theoretical sense, but teachers often feel hopelessly underqualified to provide specialized instruction to some of these students. The exploding percentage of children diagnosed with specific health or psychological problems (asthma, food allergies, attention deficit disorder) gives teachers an additional set of issues to handle. A child with a severe food allergy to peanuts could die from a single bite of a peanut butter cookie if not treated fast enough; running around at recess could bring on an attack for a child with asthma. Thus, teachers wind up vigilantly monitoring a significantly wider range of issues that went undiagnosed a few decades ago.

Personal Issues

Teaching takes an enormous amount of energy, including a great deal of self-control. Be it the anxieties and need for attention expressed by young children, or the indifference or traumas of adolescence exhibited by older students, there is a considerable quantity of human drama for teachers to manage and withstand. Beyond subject matter and teaching strategies, the emotional forces of everyday life, forces compounded by being in close contact with children for several hours each day, deluge teachers. Children may vent frustrations that are rooted in family issues, they may be uncontrollably excited about an upcoming holiday, they may be confused by social interactions that are less than friendly, they may be angry because the subject matter is too difficult (or too easy), and they may simply be dealing with the ordinary rise and fall of emotions that everyone experiences.

The Challenge of Doing Unnatural Things

One often-overlooked challenge of teaching is that to do it well often requires doing things that do not come naturally, or that are very different, even contradictory, from the habits or attitudes teachers learned before they began teaching. Research has identified many common cultural practices that, when applied in a classroom, are actually counterproductive to the goal of advancing children's learning. While a teacher's common sense may suggest she do one thing, careful studies of classroom practice reveal that not doing this would be more beneficial to the students. For lack of a better phrase, we label these counterintuitive strategies as the challenge of doing unnatural things.

PRACTICAL ISSUES

Many individuals, when they take on the role of a teacher or parent, unthinkingly turn into bizarre question-asking machines, churning out question after question for youngsters to answer (What color is this? How much is seven times eight? What's the fourth article of the Constitution?). Quizzing kids is not the same as teaching them. Communication research suggests that more effective discussions typically result if the leader/teacher substantially reduces the quantity of questions. And yet question-posing appears to be a defining characteristic of teaching. If we appreciate that teaching is more than an interrogation, why do we continue to ask so many questions?

A natural human response when asked a question is to answer it; it feels good to know an answer. In addition, there is a sense of personal satisfaction when others discover we are knowledgeable and that we are willing and able to share that knowledge. For teachers, the tendency to give answers when asked is powerful. It feels like you're helping the students. It *feels* like teaching. It feels like the right thing to do. Unfortunately, always giving students the answers can unintentionally encourage them to become more passive, relying solely upon the person in authority for their questions. When this continues, students are not learning how to learn because they are being prevented from practicing the self-discipline of working for learning. Students often understand less well that which is simply given to them than that which they figured out themselves. Typically, students forget much faster the knowledge that was simply dispensed to them compared to knowledge they acquire through their own efforts.

Another natural habit in teaching is to praise others for good work. Depending upon the use of praise (how it is given, to whom it is directed, and how it is interpreted), praise can benefit students, be counterproductive, or have little effect at all. Praise can enhance students' intrinsic motivation, but it can also undermine it; it can foster creativity and performance or squash it. Over time, using praise and other rewards can create a "reward addiction" in students. Eventually, when asked to do something, students may respond by asking, "What are ya gonna give me for it?" Teaching and learning regress into a pay-for-performance labor arrangement in which students consent to learn or behave only when they will be given something in return. Toning down one's use of praise in the context of a reward system is another case of the challenge of doing unnatural things.

Another common teaching practice is to use competition as a way to capture a group's interest or jazz things up. Some teachers can seemingly turn anything into a competition. There are many misunderstandings about competition because of the many and imprecise ways we use words such as compete and competitive. However, restricting our discussion to true win-lose affairs, classroom competition is frequently less effective than noncompetitive alternatives, especially if complex learning is involved. Also, student-versus-student competition consistently results in lower self-esteem and has been associated with dramatic increases in student misbehavior. Even though it might initially seem unnatural, it is to the students' benefit to reduce or abandon use of competition as an instructional strategy and replace it with noncompetitive alternatives.

POLITICAL ISSUES

The effort to change teaching practices in response to the issues raised above would not necessarily create any political fallout. It may not show up on anyone's radar if a teacher deliberately reduces the frequency of questions used during class discussion. However, doing many of these seemingly unnatural things may raise opposition from parents, administrators, or students themselves. The generally conservative nature of schooling opposes change that threatens tradition, and teaching by telling, using rewards (including grades) to motivate students, and encouraging competition are all part of that status quo.

Many people grasp the claim that students should have to work for the answers. Nevertheless, those same people will express the belief that teaching is not occurring unless the teacher is dispensing facts and allocating rewards (and sanctions) to students. There are many instances of school routines that we accept as natural aspects of schooling, but they can perpetuate problems we have not recognized. Competitions are defining moments within many schools: Who is finished first, which classroom has the fewest dress code violations, what school has the best attendance? Then there are all the forms of praise: homework ribbons, pizza parties, and even gold stars. Natural parts of teaching? Probably so, but each may have only immediate benefits and, over the long term, create academic and emotional confusion.

As a society, we believe that competition is part of what made America great. Proving to be the best on the battlefield or the basketball court is a source of pride and has come to be a defining aspect of our culture. Consequently, there is the widespread belief that competition is an important aspect of education, in sports and in academics as well. To suggest that competition, as "natural" as it may seem, could be other than a wonderful technique might be perceived as un-American. These unspoken assumptions about naturally good teaching may translate into expectations that run afoul of the beneficial yet unnatural approaches we identified in the preceding paragraphs. There are political implications for teachers who resist these traditions and attempt to do otherwise.

PERSONAL ISSUES

There are two tough personal issues to deal with regarding the challenge of doing unnatural things. One is unlearning old habits even as one is learning suitable replacements. Teachers are accustomed to giving praise, and it is often infused into their training. It is a genuine struggle to avoid giving global praise (e.g., "nice job" or "good work") and instead replacing generic comments with statements indicating what it was about the student's work that makes it noteworthy. For many teachers, praise just pours out automatically; it requires a concerted effort to regulate its use. Because habits are things that are done without thinking, to overcome a habit requires diligent self-monitoring. In this way, a teacher can catch him- or herself before using habitual behaviors and try out these new alternatives instead. This is a struggle because it necessitates being attentive to actions and utterances that normally go unchecked.

The second issue is facing opposition to these ways of teaching. Students, parents, and others may expect teachers to give more answers, rely upon traditional praise and other forms of token rewarding, or incorporate competitive games as a purported means for generating excitement about learning subject matter. Taking a stand against teaching approaches that are "tried-and-true" requires a great deal of personal resolve. If colleagues claim that practices such as competitions and reward systems are good because "the kids respond to them," then it is hard to argue that some students feel demeaned and discouraged by these. To push oneself to do unnatural things can be a lonely endeavor that can deepen the isolation that is an inherent part of teaching. Better teachers develop the resolve to continually question their assumptions and to revise their practices. The general public might interpret this as an improper form of uncertainty when it actually characterizes a healthy disposition of the practicing professional.

The Challenge of Teaching Day after Day

The next time you visit an older school building, take a moment to notice the wear patterns on the steps. If the school is several decades old, you can see the places where children's shoes have rubbed the steps. Where the edge of a stair tread was once sharp and distinct when it was first installed, today the edges are rounded over. Had you visited this step at the end of the very first schoolday at this building, you wouldn't have been able to detect any wear. By now, we can recognize that each little shoe that brushes this stair rubs away a small bit of the tread. It is not much that is worn away in one day. But as shoes continue passing across that spot, the cumulative effects are obvious.

The scuffing of the stairs is similar to the wear upon a teacher. We may not appreciate the effects of a single day. We have to remember that neither stairs nor teachers are used only once. Our expectation is that the steps in a staircase and the teachers within a faculty will be reliable and solid. A stair tread that is weak is very unsettling. Similarly, we expect teachers to be consistent and steadfast. As time passes, the stairs age, and the teacher matures. The slight effects of friction begin to have a discernible influence over the years. But we still want the stairs we tread and the teachers we employ to be reliable.

Personal Issues

Several years ago, a college professor took a year away from his university responsibilities to teach high school social studies (Palonsky, 1986). The book's
title began with the phrase, "900 Shows A Year," which gives a sense about
the number of performances a teacher must make, in this case five classes per
day, over an entire academic year. Teaching one lesson is not overwhelmingly
difficult. We can imagine how we might engage the students' attention to ini-
tiate the lesson. We can sketch out several examples to illustrate the idea we
are presenting. And, if we are exceptionally wise, we will give the students the
opportunity to practice the ideas they are supposed to learn (this is where
teaching is different from a performance: The "show" is only as good as the
effects it has on student understanding). It seems reasonable to muster the
resources and energy to provide an interesting and informative lesson to our
group of twenty-seven students. If we think about teaching a high school lesson, we might suspect that one day of teaching would require teaching essentially the same lesson to a series of classes that may total 150 students by the
end of the day.

We may not think of teaching as a physically demanding profession, but the
reality is that teaching requires a surprising amount of stamina. One of the
striking features of being a new teacher is the awareness that one is always
"on" and that there is little downtime. Everything seems to occur in a rush.
The time that teachers have for lunch is notoriously short with twenty minutes being a luxuriously long time. Likewise, the opportunities for other crea-
ture comforts are rare. An elementary school teacher really cannot leave his or
her twenty-seven students unattended for a quick bathroom break; the liabil-
ity issues are frightening. Even though high school teachers would seem to
have time between class periods, the expectation is that they are to monitor
hallway traffic to prevent minor incidents from escalating. These may not
seem to be substantial issues if you are at a school for one day as a substitute
or guest speaker. But the challenge begins to enlarge when the days string together into weeks and those turn into months.

From a personal perspective, the challenge of teaching day after day has a
collective effect that can parallel the erosion of a stair tread. The recurring
presence of students one day after the other cuts into activities that are known
to contribute to teacher effectiveness. Spending time reflecting upon one's
practice, using the Internet to seek new ideas, talking with colleagues to coordinate efforts, attending professional development to enhance one's teaching

repertoire—all of these are pushed to one side by the perpetual and daily demands of teaching. This is not to suggest that teaching is onerous or burden-
some. Instead, an imperceptible amount of wear and tear will begin to have
effects over an extended amount of time.

POLITICAL ISSUES

The erosion metaphor applied to teaching day after day extends to the political
issues teachers must face. First are the internal politics that emerge as teachers, principals, and schools are constantly reminded that they need to improve. These demands elicit different types of responses. The teachers we
admire believe that there are ways to help a wider range of students learn even
more. Such teachers aren't fearful of the idea that they, too, may have room to
grow. However, another segment of the teaching population is resistant to
change. Such individuals feel that all requests for reform are politically motivated (which may have some truth to it). The naysayer believes that the inability of schools to effectively educate all students has its roots in problems that
are beyond the control of the teacher.

Unfortunately for the teacher who has the ambition to continually improve
her practice, the pessimist's voice is insidious. If one believes that certain students (often labeled as "those kids") cannot be successful for such reasons as
a lack of parental involvement, insufficient motivation, or some other inherent flaw, then this becomes a self-fulfilling situation. When we expect to find
problems in students, then we are predisposed to consider their actions as evidence that they are defective. And while this may seem to be just a matter of
perception, the constant restating of such dogma can erode our idealistic
teacher's ambition. On one level, the grumbling teachers are correct. They
have constructed a way of thinking that reinforces the fact that THEY are unable to teach the students in their classroom. But the frequent voicing of those
complaints, despite a good teacher's efforts to resist or ignore, has a corrosive
effect. Once again, it is not simply the single event or conversation but the in-
exorable toll it inflicts upon others (see Figure 5.1).

Political pressures related to the challenge of teaching day after day extend
beyond the faculty lunchroom. Because education is such a hot topic, both in
the government and in the media, teachers are constantly hearing messages
about how the schools are failing. The standards and accountability movement has had an especially powerful effect. Only rarely are principals or superintendents satisfied by test scores. From a statistical standpoint, there will

FIGURE 5.1: Vignette describing the impact of teacher expectations on student achievement.

At a California elementary school in 1968, researchers gave an intelligence test to all of the students and informed teachers of those children whose scores indicated a pending burst of intellectual development. By the end of the school year, those 20 percent did indeed show significantly greater test score performance. However, these findings do not validate the test as a good predictor of pending intellectual growth. In reality, the 20 percent of the students were randomly selected without any reference to their test scores. Many in education use this as evidence that teacher expectations have a powerful effect upon student learning. When teachers expect students to be successful learners, the teachers tend to interact with those individuals in ways that are different from how they interact with students that the teachers are less certain about. This study suggests that by holding genuinely higher expectations, students will achieve more than when expectations are not as high. For more detail, take a look at the classic *Pygamalion in the Classroom* by Robert Rosenthal and Lenore Jacobson.

always be scores that are above the average and some that are below the average. But no one is willing to be considered "just" average. A classroom or school or district that has average test scores is immediately thought to be mediocre. Then there are the inevitable comparisons between classrooms and schools and districts, even across states, and the push is to always be the best. What many fail to acknowledge is that it is impossible for everyone to be in first place. This doesn't mean that we should lower expectations. But to constantly draw comparisons to the highest test scores is too much of a burden to place upon students and their teachers. The persistent reminders about how our test scores compare to someone else's can eventually lead to a sense of futility.

Many exemplary urban high schools have created alternative accountability systems focused, for example, on in-depth graduation portfolios. While such alternatives to standardized tests are appealing in many ways, they have generally succeeded in schools in which multiple aspects of traditional schooling have been fundamentally altered. To achieve such profound change in most American schools, teachers across the country would need to advocate strongly for these changes and engage in years of intense school restructuring work. Even those teachers who favor such changes face long odds in convincing students, parents, and colleagues to engage in such revolutionary changes.

Practical Issues

Teaching day after day also presents challenges from a practical perspective. Teaching requires great stamina beyond just physical endurance; there is also a need to maintain emotional stamina. One has to be positive, one has to be motivated, and one has to be ambitious for one's self and for one's students. This is not hard to accomplish over the short term, but, over time, it is difficult to maintain a consistently high level. Adding to this situation, American teachers generally spend more contact time with their students than teachers in other industrialized countries. This means they have less time they can devote to planning for instruction than their counterparts in other countries.

Teachers are often faced with differential abilities in students. While certain concepts seem to quickly take hold in some students' minds, there are other students who have a more difficult time. The teacher wants to push forward, yet some students need more time to master the material while others are ready to go ahead. This variability in learning is subject matter dependent. Just because one student is very successful in language arts does not mean that he or she is going to be equally successful in math. Teachers face the practical challenge of remembering which students struggle and which ones ease through each subject. For elementary school teachers, the challenge is to keep track across subjects, while the high school teacher, even with fewer subjects to be concerned about, has to keep track of the learning of 150 students.

The practical perspective of teaching day after day can be reduced to the simple wear and tear of teaching. It is difficult for a teacher to remain upbeat in the face of the constant need to prepare lessons, gather materials, adjust to the different rates of learning, not to mention all the record-keeping required to document individual student progress. When considered independently, no single demand is substantial. But, just as for the stair step, minor abrasions over a long period of time lead to obvious patterns of wear.

AN EXAMPLE OF THE CHALLENGES IN ACTION

The principal of an elementary school has a vision for her newly opened building. She would like for science to become central to the school's mission. One motivation for this is that the students who will attend this school tend to come from low-income families, many of which have immigrated here over the past few years. While the community at large has not been accepting of the change in the local demographics, the principal and her staff know that the ethnicity and language backgrounds of the students are not necessarily barriers to academic success. By showing that the students can be successful in science, the staff hopes that the community will come to recognize that "those kids" are intelligent and will perhaps soften the defensive stance toward families from other cultures moving into the district.

Becky holds a master's degree in reading from the local university. She is one of three sixth-grade teachers in this school, all of which are teaching for the first time. In addition to the principal's commitment to science, the school district has dictated that every elementary school select an established literacy program as a way to raise reading test scores. Becky's ambition is to find ways to blend the reading and science curriculums so she can avoid pitting one against the other.

As is true in most states, a list of science standards is available for Becky to guide her curriculum decisions. The topics sixth-grade teachers are expected to address include: Astronomy (moon phases, the solar system, and the universe), Microorganisms (beneficial and disease-causing), and Energy (heat, light and sound). One by-product of the district's emphasis upon reading is that money has not been forthcoming to purchase science materials, including textbooks. In her teacher preparation courses, Becky was told that elementary school science could, and perhaps even should, be taught through the use of concrete materials, so not having a textbook was not especially troublesome. Furthermore, the state science office was intent upon posting a locally developed electronic science textbook on its Web site that could be used as a resource for teachers and students.

One challenge that Becky faces is how to teach these science concepts to her twenty-seven sixth graders. The state standards contain lists of objectives, including such expected outcomes as, "Students should be able to describe the movement of heat from warmer objects to cooler objects by conduction and convection." The state science Web site has not posted the electronic textbook, so Becky checks two national science organizations to find out what each has to say about this concept. While these documents clarify for Becky the meanings of conduction and convection, she also discovers that study of these concepts is more suited for students much older than her eleven- and twelve-year-olds. After consulting her former science education professor, Becky's uncertainties about how to teach this material are confirmed. Despite the push to teach science through hands-on materials and use an inquiry approach, the concepts her students are to learn are notoriously fraught with misconceptions and are very difficult to teach through direct experiences.

Even before meeting her students, Becky is faced with several uncertainties. How can these abstract science concepts be made understandable to sixth graders, what materials can she gather so she is not the sole source of information (there is but one Internet accessible computer in her classroom), and what teaching strategies should be used so students' initial and unscientific ideas about germs and planets and heat are not further entrenched? To compound her anxiety, Becky is responsible for teaching not only science, but also math, reading, computers, social studies, writing, and health to her students.

One reason that Becky applied to teach at this particular school was the potential to teach a diverse group of students. The school is situated in the midst of a neighborhood that has gone through a construction boom with a variety of families moving in, many from beyond the United States. Even though she doesn't speak Spanish, Becky is eager to put into action the strategies she has learned for teaching ESL (English as a Second Language) students. Knowing the principal is looking to the sixth grade team to spearhead a spring science fair, Becky is optimistic that she has the skills to lend support to students whose English is not especially strong so that every student will be able to conduct his or her own science experiment.

Even though the school is situated in a suburban community, Becky is nevertheless surprised by the variety of students entering her classroom door the first day of school. One boy has had his hair shaved from the sides of his head; the remaining strands are styled to stick straight up. Another boy is as tall as Becky and built like a football player. Among the girls, there is equivalent variety. One girl with thick glasses, long brown hair, and a conservatively cut skirt comes into the classroom just before Bianca, who is sporting large hoop earrings, chewing bright blue bubble gum, and wearing tight jeans. Generally well-behaved, Becky is able to eventually get the students settled so they begin their introductions.

As they sit in a large circle, Becky realizes that not every student shares the enthusiasm for school she once had. Thomas slumps in his chair with his legs sticking way into the center of the group, and Charlene conveys how disappointed she is that her friends are down the hall in another class. Two students are originally from Croatia, and one is from Sudan. And a student who is escorted to the room by the secretary a half hour late is from Mexico and can not speak any English. And so Becky's first year of teaching begins.

Becky is challenged to rethink her role as a sixth-grade teacher. She develops a greater appreciation for the fact that every student has different experiences, quirks, aspirations, talents, and inclinations filtering every topic that is studied. Some students prefer learning by listening to the teacher, while others want to try it out first without much introduction. Some students enjoy learning by first reading about the topic, whereas others came to understand something by discussing it in a group. Becky realizes very early in her first year that her planning, her teaching, and her self-evaluation have to necessarily account for each and every child, not the class as a single group.

Despite the ominous beginning, the school year ends very well. Every student creates a science fair project, and Becky's students' scores on the spring standardized tests are close to the district averages. There were many times during the year when Becky wondered whether she was suited to be a teacher. Every evening was spent planning for the next day, she was overwhelmed by the irregular attendance that caused some students to fall behind while others were anxious to move forward, and spats sometimes deteriorated into shoving matches which, in accordance with the zero tolerance policy, led to students being suspended (and also falling behind). The Mexican girl returned to her home country in October, reappeared in February, and left again in April, but otherwise the class membership was fairly consistent. Becky's interactions with parents were sometimes strained, as many worked long hours and were unable to attend the scheduled parent conferences. A few parents expressed dismay that their child was forced to be in the same room with children who were not as bright as their own.

All in all, Becky felt she had a successful year and considered herself fortunate to be offered a contract in the same building the next school year. But she was also beginning to appreciate how teachers become burned out if they have to experience the same stresses year after year. One realization she came to is that she must reconsider who she thinks she is teaching. In her mind's eye, she had envisioned herself teaching a classroom of students. There was a teacher, and there was a class. The flaw, she discovered during her first year, was thinking about the class as a collection. What became evident was that, in many ways, she must teach the same ideas twenty-seven different ways. And Becky's measure of a lesson's success is not whether the class as a composite understands what was taught, but whether Jacob *and* Charlene **and** Thomas

AND Bianca **_AND_** every single student learns the material. As Becky prepares for her second year of teaching, she is grateful for the skills she has developed in her first year that have become part of her teaching routine. But, in the back of her mind, she knows that, in many unknown ways, her new class will be very different and that she will be perpetually challenged to find ways to help each student make a connection with science along with all the other subjects he or she is to study and ultimately be tested upon.

CLOSING THOUGHTS

Our ambition for this chapter was to provide a clear sense of the complexities of teaching, especially in regards to issues that may not be obvious to those outside the profession. We employed the metaphor of windows through which you might peer into the world of the modern American classroom. We selected three windows to illustrate the different perspectives you could take as you look into the lives of teachers: the practical issues, the political issues, and the personal issues. Using these three windows, we presented six categories of challenges that teachers face.

Education, in general, and teaching, in particular, is the focus of a great deal of attention. Meanwhile, the demographics of our schools continue to change as we experience perhaps the largest wave of immigration in the history of the planet. The more that the general public is aware of the nuances and complexities of teaching, the more likely we can collectively move education forward. The goal of helping every child rise to his or her greatest potential is not something that we can leave to only a certain segment of society. No group has a monopoly on the wisdom needed to continue to reform and improve our schools. The small part that this chapter and book might play in shedding light upon the educational system is seen as an important component of a larger agenda to make our schools the best that they can be.

BIBLIOGRAPHY

Meier, D. (2002). *In schools we trust*. Boston: Beacon Press.
Paley, V. G. (1998). *The girl with the brown crayon*. Cambridge: Harvard University Press.
Palmer, P. (1997). *The courage to teach*. San Francisco: Jossey-Bass.

Palonsky, S. (1986). *Nine hundred shows a year: A look at teaching from the teacher's side of the desk.* New York: McGraw-Hill.

Rose, M. (1999). *Possible lives.* New York: Penguin.

Rosenthal, R., & Jacobson, L. (2003). *Pygmalion in the classroom: Teacher expectation and pupil's intellectual development.* Norwalk, CT: Crown House.

Sacks, P. (2001). *Standardized minds: The high price of America's testing culture and what we can do to change it.* Boulder, CO: Persceus.

Technology and Professional Development

Allen D. Glenn

INTRODUCTION

Visit a classroom. While at first glance it may share many of the characteristics of a classroom from twenty years ago, there are interesting and significant differences. Desks, tables, and textbooks are there, and the trusty overhead projector and VCR are clearly present. But, in more and more classrooms, digital technologies are quite common and an integral part of the teaching and learning experience. There may be one computer at the teacher's desk, or there may be a variety of computers available to the students. With increasing probability, there is access to the Internet. And, in some classrooms, there are wireless laptops, digital cameras, DVD players, and Smart Boards. In these classrooms, students are engaged in a variety of technology-related activities. They are learning content, practicing skills, seeking information, and creating multimedia documents. The reality is that today's classrooms are being reshaped by emerging digital technologies.

What this means is that today and tomorrow's teachers must be able to effectively integrate digital technologies into the classroom. They must be able to not only use these technologies themselves, but also assist students in learning to use the technologies and then use them as integral components of their learning experiences. In today's classrooms, both teacher and student must *learn to use* new technologies and also *use them to learn.*

In meeting the demands to *learn to use* and *use to learn* emerging technologies, teachers have a variety of opportunities beginning with teacher preparation programs and continuing throughout their careers. At the preservice level, there is a long history of preparing teachers to use new technologies in the classroom. The old audio-visual course sought to provide the needed skills to enable the teacher to use the overhead and filmstrip and movie projectors. By the mid-1970s, it was replaced with a course designed to teach the basic skills needed to use the newest tool available to the teacher and student: the computer. Since that time, teacher education programs have sought to prepare beginning teachers to use computers and related technologies in their classrooms. Required courses, placement in classrooms where computers are used, and technology-enriched curriculum projects are examples used in teacher education.

On becoming a teacher, voluntary workshops are available to teach skills, explore software applications, learn the essentials of the Internet and Web-based instruction, and provide an overview of the district's philosophy and expectations about technology's role in the classroom. In some cases, workshops are one-day affairs, while in others, they last for several days. Follow-up sessions may or may not take place. Some teachers also choose to take additional courses from higher education institutions and to attend conferences focusing on computer applications. They also learn at home because more and more teachers have computers and access to the Internet, and they use this access to communicate with each other and seek information on the World Wide Web.

As a consequence, teachers today are more knowledgeable about emerging technologies and better prepared to use them in the classroom. But, the problem, as noted in the CEO Forum Year 2 Report, *Professional Development: A Link to Better Learning,* is that:

> *Teachers, like all professionals, need and deserve ongoing exposure to technology so it becomes a seamless component of instruction that leads to real results for students. They need professional development. (CEO Forum, 1999, p. 2)*

If emerging technologies are to become "a link to better learning," technology must become an integral part of the professional development of the teacher.

Professional development is defined here as "formal and informal activities designed to enhance career growth." For the educator, it is "an on-going, long-term commitment that begins with the decision to pursue a career in education, and continues, through a combination of formal and informal learning opportunities, for the duration of a career" (CEO Forum, 1999, p. 10). Professional development, consequently, is the commitment a teacher brings to the profession. However, the commitment is shaped by a variety of factors such as the individual's own needs, the environment in which teaching occurs, the type and quality of the providers, and the incentives to continue to develop as a professional.

This chapter addresses the issue of professional development for teachers in the area of technology, discusses the challenges of facilitating learning utilizing these new and ever-changing tools, and examines issues that will shape the continued use of digital technologies in the classroom.

TEACHERS AND PROFESSIONAL DEVELOPMENT: A BRIEF PERSPECTIVE

Reasons for Professional Development

From early in the twentieth century, teacher education has been the responsibility of four-year colleges, many of which were once normal schools. During this preparation, future teachers learn much about what it means to be a teacher. Upon entering the field, however, teachers quickly realize that continued professional development will be important for a number of reasons.

First, whether a beginning teacher or a veteran, one finds that teaching is a complex profession. What may seem like a straightforward task becomes extremely multifaceted once the teacher is placed in charge of a classroom filled with a set of diverse students. Second, curriculum content and teaching strategies continue to evolve. A beginning teacher quickly learns that he or she does not know the subject matter at the depth needed to be an effective teacher. New knowledge is continually being created, and "keeping up" with the field is a challenge. Additional content learning is critical but not sufficient as research in cognition and learning is providing important insights into the teaching/learning process. For example, an emphasis on student-centered learning based on cognitive learning research is causing educators to rethink the nature and context of learning. As a consequence, teachers are being asked to adapt pedagogical paradigms long held and practiced. To do so means to reconsider how one teaches. Because most teachers teach in isolation, professional development provides an avenue to continue to seek answers and insights into critical pedagogical questions.

Third, the tools of teaching continue to evolve and demand that the teacher have more technical skills and the ability to use these new tools as an integral part of instruction. Decades ago, the chalkboard, the overhead transparency, the filmstrip and movie projector, and a tape recorder were the essentials and did not take extensive training to learn to use. A one-day workshop or peer instruction were usually sufficient. Not so today. The computer and accompanying digital technologies can't be understood in one quick lesson.

The computer, now in its third decade in the school, has evolved from a complex tool available to a few, select teachers and as an object of study to a technology available to all. Digitalization and miniaturization have resulted in the creation of small laptops linked to wireless networks, DVD players, and handheld devices. In addition, the availability of educational software and computer tools requires learning new skills and classroom applications. Professional development is essential. New connectivity means access to the Internet and the World Wide Web. Suddenly, the teacher and student have access to information unheard of a few years before and the ability to communicate with others who have similar access. This access creates enormous opportunities and challenges for both teacher and student. These new technologies change the dynamic in the classroom. New skills and new pedagogical strategies are needed.

Fourth, state policy makers have created new technology requirements for all teachers. The State of Washington, for example, requires that, within five years after beginning one's career, the teacher must have successfully completed a professional development plan that leads to a Professional Teaching Certificate. Included in this plan are credits from a higher education institution, acceptance of work within the school district, and options to enroll in other learning programs such as online courses and workshops from private providers. States are also asking teachers, schools, and school districts to meet state learning standards and to be more accountable for how well students are meeting these standards. In responding to policies created at the national level, states have created standards for student learning across key content areas, means of assessing student knowledge (tests), reporting mechanisms, and consequences for lack of success.[1] Finally, another powerful incentive to return to school for additional education is that credits and degrees translate into higher pay. Therefore, a beginning teacher with an average salary in 2000–2001 of $43,250 (NCTAF, 2003b, p. 11) quickly realizes that additional credits or a graduate degree will mean a change in status on the district's pay scale. Although fees must be paid by the individual, the long-term financial benefits outweigh the tuition costs.

As a consequence, professional development attracts considerable resources. School districts spend somewhere between 2 percent and 8 percent of their budgets for continuing education (Killeen, Monk, & Plecki, 2002, p. 2) which amounts to over nine million dollars.[2] When other costs such as individual teacher out-of-pocket expenses and teacher and professional organization expenditures are included, it is clear that professional development is big business.

Providers of Professional Education

Chief providers of formal and informal professional education are institutions of higher education, school districts, state educational service units, regional educational laboratories, professional associations, and professional consultants. Each provides a set of opportunities for the individual teacher, for groups of teachers, or for teachers from across a district.

HIGHER EDUCATION

Historically, higher education institutions have provided significant continuing education opportunities for classroom teachers. Teachers turn to these institutions for advanced degrees to learn content and pedagogical knowledge and to earn additional credits to advance on the salary schedule. Graduate degree programs continue to draw teachers to higher education. In addition, higher education institutions offer intensive workshops often supported by funds from the United States Department of Education through the National Science Foundation (NSF) and other agencies. These intensive sessions are designed to address specific content needs. For example, for over thirty years, NSF has supported workshops for teachers to improve the teaching of mathematics and science, and thousands of teachers have participated. Higher education institutions also provide content and pedagogy consultants to individual school districts. These individuals present one-day workshops, run extended workshops, contract services over an extended period, and/or provide advice on various school district projects and learning goals.

A significant shift has taken place over the last decade among higher education institutions because of the growth of for-profit and online providers who may or may not be affiliated with an institution of higher education. Historically, local higher education institutions served the needs of teachers in the region. They provided programs that were convenient and affordable. Occasionally, teachers would be drawn from across the nation to attend summer institutes, but, generally, local teachers attended institutions within a commuting radius and completed academic degrees in either education or a content area. In doing so, teachers met the requirements of the academy.

Competition and connection to the Internet have changed this relationship. Within the last decade, there has been a marked increase in the number of institutions (private and for-profit) that offer professional development learning opportunities to teachers as an alternative to the traditional academic programs of graduate education. Characteristics of these programs include classes at convenient times and sites (business centers), a focus on practical application, use of professionals from the field as instructors, and courses that may be completed in shorter periods of time. In some cases, these programs also offer online courses to supplement on-site offerings.

Similar "brick and click" programs have been offered by higher education institutions that establish learning centers in various locations. Often, they are private institutions, such as Lesley College of Massachusetts, that have a long history of outreach. In some cases, the outreach programs are offered by institutions not located in centers of population, thus reaching out to teachers to meet enrollment and service needs. A growing number, however, exist in the form of for-profit universities created to provide an alternative to the traditional higher education institution and allow working adults to enroll in programs that meet their needs. In 2003, the market for online programs was estimated to be between $4 and $5 billion dollars with a potential growth to $15 billion by 2005 (Charp, 2002, p. 10). The University of Phoenix, one of the most well-known, has grown significantly and now offers on-site programs for educators in over twenty-five states and online programs for teachers anywhere.

Online learning opportunities consequently are growing rapidly. Some predict that e-learning (the name used for online learning) will overtake classroom-based instruction as the primary method sometime in the near future. Such offerings are portable (available on the Web at any time and from any place), modular (consisting of multiple units), and interactive (students must respond to inquiries and exchange messages/chat with peers and teachers) (Charp, 2002, p. 10).

As a result of the expansion of institutions offering degrees and other professional development opportunities, educators have a wide range of alternatives from which to choose. As a consequence of the increased competition, traditional higher education institutions are aware that existing academic programs and offerings must change.[3] Emerging communication technologies and an abundance of choice will reshape professional development offerings on campuses across the nation.

School Districts

School districts allocate increasingly fewer resources for the professional development of school personnel. What is provided varies widely across the United States, with larger, urban school districts spending more of the district's budget for professional development than small and rural districts (Killeen et al., pp. 2–3). Traditionally, all districts open the school year with teacher workshops that serve a variety of functions ranging from building district spirit to providing specific training related to curriculum and student learning. These opening workshops range from one day to five days.

Some districts with sufficient resources have professional development administrative units devoted to continuing professional education. These units determine the goals for the district, design and deliver the workshops, and evaluate the outcomes. Districts also work with outside consultants and agencies to craft specific programs to meet district needs. To provide incentives to teachers to attend and complete work, districts may pay teachers and/or provide "credit" that may be applied to continuing education requirements of both the state and district. How many professional development activities a teacher may attend is determined, in part, by the contract negotiated between the district and the teachers' representative organization.

Informal Providers

Educators also have a variety of other less formalized sources for professional development. Many teachers, for example, belong to professional organizations related to their content subject area, such as mathematics, English, social studies, and technology, and attend local, state, regional, and national meetings. These occasions provide a wide range of opportunities to learn about content, teaching strategies, and new materials. It is not unusual, for example, for the National Council of Teachers of Mathematics (NCTM) to draw 10,000 educators to its national convention. Teachers who choose to participate in these conventions benefit from the specific workshops, expert speakers, and informal interactions with colleagues from across the country and the world.

Other sources of professional development include teacher associations, such as the National Education Association and the American Federation of Teachers, museums, public television, and cable television. Within most states, there are also educational service districts supported in part by state resources and pay-for-service activities that provide a wide range of services to districts. Nationally, educational laboratories, funded in part by the federal government, are also regional providers. Currently, there are ten such labs located across the country.

A more recent resource for professional development exists in the form of online providers available on the World Wide Web. In a recent search using the key words, "professional development for teachers," almost 900,000 sites were available. Providers include those noted above as well as small organizations and individuals with specific messages. The United States Department of Education site (http://www.ed.gov/teachtech/) is a significant resource and link to professional development activities, as are the Web sites of the ten regional educational laboratories. The North Central Regional Educational Laboratory (http://www.ncrel.org), for example, has an extensive set of resources and professional development activities related to assisting teachers in integrating technology into instruction. The Eisenhower National Clearinghouse (http://www.enc.org) also identifies curriculum materials and ideas about the effective use of teaching, especially in the area of science and mathematics. And, each state educational agency has a Web site devoted to technology issues.

The International Society for Technology in Education (ISTE) (http://www.iste.org) also provides a wide range of materials for educators. Most well-known are its publications on standards for students, teachers, and administrators and its curriculum guide. In addition, its journal, *Learning & Leading with Technology*, provides information about the effective use of technology in education. Other journals such as *T.H.E. Journal* (http://www.thejournal.com), *Converge* (http://www.centerdigitaled.com/converge/), and *Access Learning* (http://www.ciconline.org/default) provide educators both print materials about integrating technologies into the classroom as well as Internet resources.

Educational foundations also provide professional development materials and resources. A well-known example is the George Lucas Educational Foundation (GLEF) (http://www.glef.org). Its Web site provides examples for teachers of how technology is being integrated into project-based learning classrooms and links to a variety of sources. GLEF's publication, *edutopia*, also provides examples that practicing teachers may use when considering how to incorporate technology into the classroom. GLEF is just one example of many foundations focusing on technology and education.

Professional development opportunities, both formal and informal, are available to the educator. These opportunities range in scope and quality, but one cannot claim, "Nothing is out there to help me integrate technology into my teaching." If that is the case, what should one look for in a professional development program and experience?

Essentials of Professional Development

One needs only to listen to professional teachers to gain insight into the numerous shortcomings regarding professional development activities. Chief among the complaints are that far too many are "one shot" workshops with no follow-up and that topics don't address a classroom problem or issue or relate to the grade level taught. In fact, in-service teachers, while eager for new knowledge, are often a most critical audience unless they see the practical application to their classroom. However, given the number of less than helpful professional activities that they are required to attend, their critical view is understandable.

There is, however, considerable knowledge about the kinds and types of professional development activities that can contribute to educator learning and the acquisition of new pedagogical skills. Figure 6.1 presents those developed by the National Staff Development Council (NSDC, 2001).

This is indeed a powerful set of criteria by which to gauge professional development activities. In fact, the essential elements condemn the vast majority of professional development activities that take place today, those that are, in the words of the National Commission on Teaching and America's Future (NCTAF), "drive-by professional development" experiences designed as "one-size-fits-all" for all teachers (NCTAF, 2003a, p. 130).

Quality professional development following the NSDC guidelines would be:

- Connected to and derived from teachers' work with their students (classroom based);
- Sustained, ongoing, and intensive, supported by peers and school leaders;

FIGURE 6.1 National Staff Development Council standards for staff development.

CONTEXT STANDARDS

Staff development that improves the learning of all students:

• Organizes adults into learning communities whose goals are aligned with those of the school and district. (Learning Communities)
• Requires skillful school and district leaders who guide continuous instructional improvement. (Leadership)
• Requires resources to support adult learning and collaboration. (Resources)

PROCESS STANDARDS

Staff development that improves the learning of all students:

• Uses disaggregated student data to determine adult learning priorities, monitor progress, and help sustain continuous improvement. (Data-Driven)
• Uses multiple sources of information to guide improvement and demonstrate its impact. (Evaluation)
• Prepares educators to apply research to decision making. (Research-Based)
• Uses learning strategies appropriate to the intended goal. (Design)
• Applies knowledge about human learning and change. (Learning)
• Provides educators with the knowledge and skills to collaborate. (Collaboration)

CONTENT STANDARDS

Staff development that improves the learning of all students:

• Prepares educators to understand and appreciate all students; create safe, orderly and supportive learning environments; and hold high expectations for their academic achievement. (Equity)
• Deepens educators' content knowledge, provides them with research-based instructional strategies to assist students in meeting rigorous academic standards, and prepares them to use various types of classroom assessments appropriately. (Quality Teaching)
• Provides educators with knowledge and skills to involve families and other stakeholders appropriately. (Family Involvement)

- Organized around collective problem solving that focuses on specific problems of practice;

- Integrated into the larger framework of teacher career regulations and incentives; and

- Responsive to social and educational priorities at the national, state, and local level.

Current and emerging digital technologies have become essential in providing teachers with access to specific resources and to collaborative communities of colleagues sharing and developing new skills and strategies. NCTAF notes that "Technology is perhaps the most important—and most underutilized—tool for providing teachers access to the targeted professional development they need, when and how they need it" (NCATF, 2003b, p. 28). The access to online resources, courses, and informal collegial support is critical to a professional who has little free time during the school day given the current structure of public schooling.

What is evident is that there is a growing body of knowledge and research related to effective professional development strategies, and technology can play an integral role. Based on this general picture of professional development, let's turn our attention to issues of technology and professional development.

TECHNOLOGY AND THE PROFESSIONAL DEVELOPMENT OF TEACHERS

Educators today are well aware that digital technologies are an integral part of American society and that these technologies "belong" to today's children and youth. They shape students' expectations about learning and how they interact with each other and with the teacher. For an overwhelming majority of today's students, microcomputers have always been a part of their lives because they were born after their invention. Jason Frand notes in *The Information-Age Mindset: Changes in Students and Implications for Higher Education* that these students are:

> more comfortable working on a keyboard than writing in a spiral notebook, and are happier reading from a computer screen than from paper in hand. For them, constant connectivity—being in touch with friends and family at any time and from any place—is of utmost importance. (2000, p. 15)

While Frand describes college students, elementary and secondary students are not far behind. Digital game devices, cell phones, home computers, and the Internet are increasingly a part of more children's worlds. There is, of course, a digital divide between socioeconomic groups; however, through the power of television, advertising, and school experiences, students across all grades know that theirs is a digital age and that they must be particpants.

Teachers in today and tomorrow's classrooms work in ever-increasingly technological environments for a number of reasons. First, school districts continue to purchase technology for the classroom and to link school buildings and individual classrooms to the Internet. Second, parents, business organizations, and policy makers continue to insist that tomorrow's students have the needed skills to use technology as part of the learning process. Therefore, today's teacher, whether new to the profession or a seasoned veteran, knows that this "fad" will not go away. Teachers may debate about when and how often these new technologies should be used, but it is clear that digital technologies are now a part of schooling.

What is also clear is that "adequate and appropriate training for teachers is crucial for computer-based technology to have an effect on student learning" (White, Ringstaff, & Kelly, 2002, p. 5). The better prepared the teacher is to use technology, the greater the probability that his/her students will use technology to engage in higher-order thinking (White et al., 2002, p. 5). Student learning can be enhanced through specific, technology-related professional development that expands the knowledge, skills, and growth of the teacher. Given the unprecedented presence and prevalence of technology, limited "technology training" is no longer sufficient (CEO Forum, 1999, p. 10). Intermittent sessions offered sporadically cannot meet the demands for improved student learning. Therefore, let us turn our attention to the issues surrounding the professional development of teachers in order to become competent professionals who are able to use effectively technologies in their classrooms and empower students to become more active learners.

A Brief History of Technology Professional Development: 1970–2000

Programs to prepare teachers to use technology as a tool and as part of instruction are in their third decade. Teachers certified in the late 1970s are ending their teaching careers as the first generation of teachers that had computers introduced into the classroom. During the tenure of these educators, computers evolved from objects of instruction focusing on hardware and programming, to tools for teacher and student to use to supplement teaching and learning, to instruments that should be infused into the learning environment. These teachers began their careers with the image of a handheld device belonging to *Star Trek*. They complete their careers with handheld calculators as common as pencils.

To assist these teachers, formal and informal professional development providers offered a wide range of courses, new degree programs, and extensive workshops. Professional development programs drew upon the current practices in professional education and modeled workshops on those designed for other content areas. Initially, courses and workshops focused on two key components, the computer, its language and hardware, and classroom software packages. It was believed that teachers needed to be able to program the computer and understand how it worked in order to be computer literate. Not all teachers were willing to learn a computer language, so, during the early years, computers were more likely found in the mathematics and vocational education content areas. The vast majority of students did not have access to computers as a part of their learning experience. But changes quickly occurred.

Computers, with the introduction of the desktop computer, evolved from complex machines to ones that began to appear in many classrooms. Accompanying these computers was educational software designed to provide practice for content and skills, to teach new content and skills, and to enable students to use tools such as word processing and graphics. This trend has been chronicled in texts such as Taylor's *The Computer in the School: Tutor, Tool, Tutee* (1980) and the report by the Office of Technology Assessment (OTA), *POWER ON! New Tools for Teaching and Learning* (1988).[4] *POWER ON!* provided the first national report of the status of technology use in schools and teacher education programs. The report included proposed actions across a wide range of topics—teacher preparation, classroom use, software, research, and the role of state and national government. It provided a yardstick against which to measure progress for the next twenty years.

With time, software began to become more abundant. An early provider, the Minnesota Education Computing Consortium (MECC) funded by the state of Minnesota, provided classroom software for use on the new microcomputers (Apple II, Commodore, Pet, Atari, and Radio Shack) that were much more user-friendly. Technology began moving from a curiosity to a useful tool to help schools provide better curriculum and instruction (Valdez, 1986). Teachers could tap into software programs for drill and practice, simulation, data analysis, and word processing as new tools in the classroom. Electronic grade books and presentation software also aided the teacher. Programming was still considered essential to understanding the computer, but the shift from unique to common tool had begun.

Being able to use the computer as a personal tool and as a part of students' learning experiences became targeted competencies for every classroom teacher and for those who were preparing to be teachers. Suddenly schools, colleges, and departments of education needed to ensure that beginning teachers were prepared to use these new tools, and school districts were confronted with the need to provide professional development activities for teachers in grades K-12 and across a wide range of content areas. Given that little was known about these rapidly evolving technologies and how teachers understood them, professional development activities followed traditional formats—for-credit courses offered by higher education institutions, workshops of varying length, and in-school activities. Most programs focused on learning to "run" the computer, manage the peripherals (printers and disk drives), and use software tools and class applications. Preparing and supporting teachers to use digital technologies became integral components of professional development. Integration into the total curriculum was yet to come.

State and accreditation agencies also took notice of the emergence of this new technology. States developed certification programs for individuals seeking to become computer specialists in their district or school and established criteria for teacher education programs for graduates. By 2000, the National Council for Accreditation of Teacher Education (NCATE) began to include technology standards as part of the accreditation of initial certification programs and became perhaps the most important driving force for technology integration (Fulton et al., 2002).

Standards for technology use for both students and teachers became the yardsticks to guide teacher development and student competencies and use in the classroom. The ISTE emerged as the voice for a set of standards to guide practitioners and policy makers. ISTE's National Educational Technology Standards (NETS) serve as the standards for the United States, and the NETS for Students (NETS*S) outline what students from preschool to grade 12 should know about and be able to do with technology. A similar document (NETS*T) outlines standards for teachers. A related publication, *NETS: Connecting Curriculum and Technology* (2000), provides standards and curricular examples of how these standards may be applied across the school curriculum. *Connecting Curriculum and Technology* has become a standard for technology-using educators.

In addition to the work of ISTE and NCATE, researchers and policy makers have made significant contributions to the growing knowledge base on technology and education. For example, research by Dwyer and others for the Apple Classroom of Tomorrow project (Dwyer, Ringstaff, & Sandholtz, 1990a,

1990b) documents the challenges associated with restructuring classrooms with technology and the resulting impact on the teacher. ACOT (Apple Classroom of Tomorrow) has documented the time needed to move from an entry level setting to one in which new learning environments are created. Teachers need time to acquire basic computer skills before they can begin to adapt, infuse, and innovate instructional strategies in the classroom. These findings support the contention that engaging teachers in the use of technology is more complex and time-consuming than can be achieved through any one-day or one-week workshop.

Additional insights into the complexity of preparing both preservice and inservice teachers was brought to the forefront by the survey conducted by Research Partnerships for a consortia of the Regional Technology in Education Consortia in 1997.[5] The findings suggest that while progress has been made in the technology education of preservice teachers, faculty development, the need for new hardware and software, and links to schools remain significant issues. Another survey conducted by ISTE with support from the Milken Exchange on Education found similar issues still in need of addressing (Moursund & Bielefeldt, 1998).

In 1999, The OTA issued its second report, *Teachers and Technology: Making the Connection*, that provided a broad assessment of technology's use in schools and teacher education. The findings were no surprise in that they demonstrate that progress had been made since the initial report in 1988 but that much work is yet needed. Of particular interest here is the recommendation "to give teachers time for lesson preparation and learning and support for continuing work" (OTA, 1999b, p. 41). Professional development is key, especially with the continued emergence of new digital technologies and the Internet.

An important response by the federal government to various calls for continued support for technology integration into schools and teacher education came in 1999 with the United States Department of Education's Preparing Tomorrow's Teachers to Use Technology (PT3) program. PT3 awarded grants to support national, state, and local initiatives to transform teacher preparation programs. Over 350 awards were made to a variety of institutions of higher education, higher education/PK-12 partnerships, and other education-related organizations. These awards supplied critically needed resources to accelerate the learning of effective practices, to build capacity, and to implement innovative program improvements. A final set of grants was awarded in 2003.

PT3 was the largest, most widespread technology-related professional development initiative funded by the United States Department of Education and reached thousands of educators in both PK-12 and higher education.

The federally funded regional education laboratories have also provided significant support for technology integration. The North Central Regional Educational Laboratory, for example, has a national reputation for its research, online support materials, and instruments to assess technology's impact on teaching, learning, and teacher preparation. Other labs are also engaged in similar work.

Computer companies, foundations, policy organizations, and state departments of education are also engaged in a variety of activities related to the infusion of technology into schools and teacher education. Foundations such as the George Lucas Educational Foundation, the Milken Exchange, and the Gates Foundation have provided and continue to provide important resources and support for technology integration. Partnerships such as the CEO Forum on Education and Technology, formed in 1996, provide important venues for business people and educators interested in technology, publishing reports, and making materials available on their Web sites.

Educators in both PK–12 education and higher education entered the twenty-first century with considerable experience in using technology, creating professional development opportunities, and examining programs in light of a commonly held set of standards. Each year, thousands of teachers attend formal and informal professional development activities and large conferences. The National Education Computer Conference (NECC) draws over 10,000 educators, for example.

But reports, such as the CEO Forum's *School Technology and Readiness Report: Year 2, Professional Development: A Link to Better Learning*, continue to suggest that considerable work needs to be completed if technology is to become an integral part of teaching and learning. Teachers still do not use technology across the curriculum. Student access is still limited. And, student achievement still does not meet standards. What is going on? Why is it so difficult to use technology effectively in an age when it permeates our lives? Let's examine the complexity of the problem.

The Challenges of Professional Development and Technology

The phrase has been used so often that it has become part of the lore of educational renewal. The original author is no longer remembered by most, including this author. The phrase goes something like this, "Remember . . . reform is steady work!" Indeed it is, and the infusion of technology, while important to many educators, is but one piece of a very complex puzzle of bringing about innovation in education. To gain a perspective on technology's role, it is important to examine at least four critical areas: (1) the numbers; (2) changing technology; (3) the educational environment; and (4) individual pedagogy. To seek a simple answer is to waste one's time. Those who advocate a simple answer do not understand the problem. Let's examine these four critical areas. But, before doing so, we must acknowledge that these issues cannot be considered as separate; they are intricately linked to one another in a complex model of change.

THE NUMBERS

There are approximately 3.5 million teachers in the United States (NCTAFa, 2003a, p. 24). They teach in large, urban districts with thousands of students and in small, rural districts with several hundred students. Some districts have considerable resources at their disposal for professional education; others have very limited resources. No matter the size of the district, involving all the teachers in a professional development program designed to enhance technology skills and prepare the individual teacher to effectively use technology to improve student learning is a challenge. Simply providing an initial experience and some follow-up for each teacher means considerable planning and resources. This planning and resource allocation is complicated by the fact that these teachers teach in grades from kindergarten to grade 12 and, at the secondary level, teach different subject matter. Therefore, a one-size-fits-all experience will not work. Specialization creates additional problems. But, they are minor when examined in the following light.

Each year hundreds of thousands of individuals enter teaching, move to another school, district, or state, or leave because of retirement or for other personal reasons. In 1999–2000, almost 540,000 entered, moved, or left the system, which meant that 15.7 percent of the teaching force was mobile (NCTAFa, 2003a, pp. 24–25). In some districts, especially urban, poor districts, the turnover is well above that figure. NCTAF states the problem in two ways. Its report, *No Dream Denied: A Pledge to America's Children*, contends that America's schools lose about the same number of teachers as they hire each year (NCTAF, 2003a, p. 29), and "The real school staffing problem is teacher retention" (NCTAF, 2003b, p. 6).

What this inflow and outflow of teachers means is that districts and institutions of higher education are continually confronted with individuals who are entering the district and/or the school. While today's beginning teachers may be better prepared to use technology more than those in the past, the challenge to prepare them to use technology effectively in their classroom remains. Each year districts face significant numbers of individuals who need to be, at a minimum, introduced to technology in their building and what can be done with it in the classroom. This constant influx and movement make it difficult to prepare a school's staff to effectively integrate technology into instruction.[6] Consequently, districts face a continual problem of renewal and readjustment. Complicating the matter is the fact that a significant number of teachers who have spent their careers as part of the technology movement and who have been exemplary teachers and leaders, are ending their thirty-year careers and retiring. When thinking about institutionalizing a program or plan, one must "do the numbers" to understand the scope of the challenge. If NCTAF is correct, the numbers suggest a significant retention and support problem.

CHANGING TECHNOLOGY

As educators entered the twenty-first century, few would have imagined the impact of the Internet on education. Nor would they have predicted the unbelievable growth in cell telephones among the populace. A significant number of educators can still remember when microcomputers appeared in the schools. During their tenure, as we noted above, they have witnessed the miniaturization of technologies that have continued to get smaller and yet more powerful. Handheld PDAs and cell phones have a thousandfold greater capacity than those early Apples, Ataris, and Radio Shack computers. Digital cameras make it possible to capture images and immediately use them in reports and presentations. The Internet and World Wide Web have opened the world to the classroom, and wireless computers even make it possible to not leave the classroom or to seek out phone lines.

While each new innovation has ushered in unique opportunities to integrate technology with the classroom in a more meaningful and powerful way, it has also meant that new skills have to be learned and mastered. It seems that as soon as one learns how to use a particular computer and a set of educational applications, an upgraded computer and software are purchased with unique features unheard of before. What worked in the past no longer works. Time and energy must be spent updating skills and materials.

Rapid innovation also means that "old" technologies no longer have the capacity to run the new software and access the Internet. Each new model increases the power and speed enabling the computer to use new software tools and to access the Internet at a faster rate. Computers purchased three years ago, for example, are now Model Ts in a world of racecars. To utilize the full capacity of technology for student learning, resources must be allocated to buy or lease new technology. This allocation must take place even though states and districts are facing difficult financial conditions.

To develop mastery, therefore, requires an outlay of time, energy, and financial resources. Or, to use ACOT terminology, a significant investment is required to move from entry-level skills to a skill and pedagogical comfort level where new learning environments can be created. It seems that no sooner does one get familiar with a digital technology then it changes, and sometimes the changes are frustrating, especially for someone whose responsibilities include the learning of all the students entrusted to his or her care in the classroom.

What this means for professional development is that renewal and support must continue for the teacher. Professional development activities that a teacher participated in several years ago are no longer sufficient for today's needs. For example, while a teacher might learn about creating Web pages on his or her own, most teachers need some initial preparation, significant support once back in the classroom, and continued updating on potential curriculum applications that will assist him or her in meeting various academic standards. The process must be ongoing.

EDUCATIONAL ENVIRONMENT

While it may appear to be heresy in a chapter on technology and professional development to say this, it is important that the following be noted. Learning how to infuse technology into the classroom is only one in a series of major issues confronting states, districts, schools, and teachers. Some would argue, in fact, that it is far down the list of priorities confronting education. As noted in the previous chapter, today's schools are facing a variety of critical issues that are asking them to meet higher academic standards and be accountable for the progress or the lack thereof. Criterion-referenced tests, increased public reporting, emphasis on performance, and compliance with standards are hallmarks. Controversy exists around these initiatives with opinions ranging widely. Whether or not an educator agrees or disagrees with the standards and accountability movement is not the issue. The reality is that it is a primary driving force in public education and teacher education today.

What this means for those interested in technology use in the classroom is that professional development activities must compete for resources that are being earmarked for increasing the proficiency of students in reading, writing, and mathematics. It also means that educators want to know how the use of technology can enhance student learning of standards and enable students to meet the standards as demonstrated by state and/or national examinations.

White and colleagues at WestEd reviewed the research in this area. Their findings, while supportive, raise interesting challenges. They found that: (1) the computer must be considered a means to an end, not the end; (2) technology is complex and expensive, and less is known about how to fully realize its potential than other pedagogical strategies; and (3) substantial planning and organization are required if computer-based technology is to enhance student learning (White et al., 2002, p. 2). They note that research does suggest that computer-based technology can have a positive effect on student learning but only under certain conditions and when used for certain purposes. They also acknowledge that "there is no magic formula that educators and policymakers can use to determine if this 'return' is actually worth the 'investment' " (White et al., 2002, p. 2). While they outline the conditions, this means that professional development in the area of technology faces a difficult task in maintaining a strong position in the overall professional development program of the state, district, and school. Cost may not be everything, but it is near the top of the list of factors to consider when making choices in a publicly funded system.

INDIVIDUAL PEDAGOGY

Over a period of extended practice, teachers develop a teaching style that merges their own philosophy of teaching and learning with that of the school and community within which they teach and in consideration of the characteristics of the students they teach. In doing so, teachers draw upon what they have learned about content, pedagogy, and learning. An element of this teaching style is knowledge about and attitude toward using technology.

Included in most educators' sets of teaching skills is a set of instructional strategies that range from expository to inquiry. Expository practices are more teacher-directed and ask students to read/listen, recall/recite, and answer questions on an assessment instrument. Inquiry practices, in contrast, have the teacher posing questions, facilitating student exploration and the gathering of data, assisting in the development of conclusions, and asking students to apply what they have learned to another problem.

Which instructional strategies should be centerpiece of a classroom? The debate is appropriately normative and as old as teaching. While current educational literature and literature related to the infusion of technology into teaching and learning favor the student-centered approach,[7] the reality is that instructional strategies vary widely and that one might contend that much of teaching today still favors a more directed-teacher model.

Whichever teaching style a teacher develops, digital technologies impact the teacher's beliefs about teaching and learning. The introduction of computers and related digital technologies creates new opportunities and problems for the teacher and the student. Initially, both need to *learn to use* the technologies before they can *use to learn* the technologies. This means the need for direct opportunities to learn, time to develop skills, support in the process, and a clarification of where these technologies fit into the curriculum.

As noted earlier, the ACOT studies suggest the existence of a developmental process for most teachers. This model has been extended by Anderson and van Weert (2002). These authors propose that the core stages of learning are emerging, applying, infusing, and transforming. *Emerging* describes the stage when teachers explore the potential of the technologies. *Applying* means teachers are using computers for tasks such as word processing, creating databases, exploring content software, and accessing the Internet. *Infusing* means that teachers are using the technologies as a part of the instructional process, and students are more directly engaged. Finally, *transforming* means that a major reconstruction of the classroom has occurred; it has become a learning-centered classroom where students explore a variety of real-world problems in an inquiry-oriented learning environment.

Modifying a teaching style is a complex endeavor, especially when the use of a particular instructional strategy conflicts with basic philosophical positions. Teachers may find that applying technology and infusing it into the classroom essentially requires the learning of new skills that, when mastered, enhance the engagement of and learning by students. A classroom characterized by teacher as a colearner with students exploring a set of problems is markedly different from a classroom that is teacher directed. Project-based learning is not the same as direct instruction. To alter that classroom may mean significant changes for *both* the teacher and the students.

Constraints to changing teaching styles are not insurmountable however. Becker and Riel (2000) suggest that teachers who interact with peers, are engaged professionally, work in collaborative settings, share their work, and participate in leadership activities are much more likely to use computers and related technologies to engage students than teachers who do not exhibit these characteristics. Collaboration, sharing, and participating in professional activities are essential.

INFUSING TECHNOLOGY: PROFESSIONAL DEVELOPMENT'S ROLE

Professional development has as a basic tenet that through continuous learning, a teacher can assist students in the achievement of higher standards of learning. And, if all students need the ability to effectively use digital technologies as an integral part of their learning, teachers must be provided with appropriate professional development opportunities and access to resources to help them develop new knowledge and skills to achieve this. In creating these opportunities for continued growth, those who design professional development activities must understand that teachers have different teaching styles, different strengths, and different needs. Essentially, teachers start and end at different places during any professional development experience. Research has also shown that teachers resist technology innovations that do not match the context in which they work and do not address problems related to their classroom. Given these issues, what are the essentials of any program of technology professional development?

Grant (1996) provides the following initial parameters. He suggests that professional development for technology must:

- Extend a vision of technology as an empowering tool for teachers and students;
- Stimulate reflective practice and be grounded in the context of teaching;
- Exemplify our deepest beliefs about learning: inquiry, collaboration, and discourse;
- Recognize the interplay in learning between activity and belief;
- Value and cultivate a culture of collegiality;
- Provide continual contexts for formal and informal learning;

- Provide opportunities for meaningful teacher leadership roles to emerge; and
- Enable teachers to shape their own learning.

From this perspective, professional development must be integrated into the core of teachers' professional learning. While short-term workshops, for example, may provide introductory level skills and possible classroom applications, they cannot assist the teacher in adapting and integrating technology into the core of activities in the classroom. If the goal is to have the teacher move beyond tool use, more than skill acquisition must occur (Orrill, 2001).

Professional development needs to be personalized, long-term, and based on individual teacher needs. When teachers personalize computer tools, for example, a sense of ownership is created and a positive attitude and sense of personal efficacy about using technology are engendered (Orrill, 2001; Charischak, 2000; Moore & Orey, 2000). And, because implementing technology does not happen quickly, continuous support and training are needed in order for the teacher not to become discouraged. Professional development activities should assist the teacher in finding her or his own way.

To use digital technologies as an integral component of the teaching and learning process, a teacher needs a variety of learning and support activities. Five are most critical.

1. *Technical learning experiences ought to be problem-based related to actual classroom situations.* Individuals learn to use new tools when those tools provide assistance in solving an important problem. Telling teachers that they must learn to use technology because technology is important may motivate some educators. But, linking the preparation to actual classroom situations and toward solving problems is a better strategy and will engage the teacher.

2. *Teachers need to set goals and reflect on their teaching continually.* Teachers need to set specific goals for what they wish to achieve with the new skills in using technology, and they need to reflect on what happens when they use technology as part of instruction. When reflecting on the classroom experience, they must ask questions that go beyond, "How did this session go?" "What management or hardware problems emerged?" or "Were the students

engaged?" Research (Orrill, 2001) suggests that the focus should be on the interaction between the teacher and the students and how the teacher promotes students' problem-solving skills. The most important issue is not whether the students enjoyed using the technology, but rather what they learned.

3. *One-on-one collaborative support should be available.* A colleague or an external coach should provide feedback, mentoring, and support. Another perspective may enable the teacher to understand more clearly the instructional issues. A mentor who asks the right question can assist the teacher in creating better goals and strategies for infusing technology.

4. *Collaboration with others engaged in using technology should be available.* Learning from others (McKay & McGrath, 2000; Becker & Reil, 2000; Cradler & Cradler, 1995) who can serve as outside experts can assist the teacher in developing new teaching methods (Hawkes, 2000). Collegial groups can provide a "safe place" to share thoughts and concerns. For example, Hawkes recommends "computer-mediated communication" as one means of collaboration where teachers exchange text, data, images, and sound via the Internet (2000, p. 268). Such exchanges may be synchronous or asynchronous. E-mail, news groups, listservs, and the Internet all provide options for teachers. In fact, many Web sites supported by a variety of groups provide opportunities for teachers to share materials, engage in chat rooms, and ask various questions related to teaching.

5. *Opportunities to read professional materials (research, theory, and application) should be available.* Readings from the literature are also important. They may be part of the online communication among teachers or read individually. Such materials can assist the individual and/or group to develop knowledge of learning theory, pedagogy, and subject matter (Orrill, 2001). These materials may be printed or, as is often the case, available on the World Wide Web where they may be read on screen or downloaded.

The ultimate goal of these five core activities is to enable to the teacher to continue to develop as a professional who is able to utilize technology to enrich the learning experiences of students and to assist them in meeting higher learning standards. What is clear from the research is that this process must be engaging, address appropriate tasks and questions, and be long-term in nature. No short-term experiences will provide the support needed.

What is also evident is that both formal and informal methods are needed. Classes, workshops, and technical support are critical, but so are opportunities to reach out to colleagues who are engaged in similar activities, to examine curricular materials, view examples from similar content and grade levels, and to read about technology and educational applications. Today's teacher who has access to the Internet and the World Wide Web has an opportunity to continue to grow professionally at his or her own pace and when time permits. The World Wide Web has done much to reduce the isolation a teacher often feels and to bring a wide array of resources to his or her doorstep. What does the future hold?

LOOKING TO THE FUTURE

As educators look to the future, they do so knowing that changes will continue to reshape school and schooling. In some instances, and for some schools, these changes may be quite radical and create new models by which to judge current offerings. For most educators, advances in technology will continue to open new doors to teaching and learning and create tensions between what was the norm and what will be. Schools, cornerstones of American society, will continue to evolve, but at a pace that does not put them too far ahead of the public they serve.

As we look to the future, we know that today's teachers are better prepared to use technology than ever before, that digital technologies are an integral part of their lives, that computers and related technology are more available in classrooms than ever before, and that Internet access continues to increase. School districts, even though facing difficult financial situations, continue to invest in new technologies and related professional development. And, the technology itself continues to increase in power while, at the same time, becoming smaller and more portable. Handhelds and writing tablets link to wireless systems and allow teachers and students opportunities to expand the classroom in ways not possible only a few short years ago.

While advocates for technology use are disappointed in the slow pace of renewal and reform, the reality is that technology continues to become a more and more integral part of teaching and learning. Both teachers and students are more comfortable using technology to produce examples of learning, to access information, and to broaden their learning experiences. The World Wide Web has opened the classroom to the world and has increased the power of the teacher to find and adapt materials to meet the learning needs of the students. In doing so, a whole new set of skills is needed for both the teacher and the students, skills to help them understand the differences, for example, between information and knowledge, and skills that will enable both teacher and student to become learners together in a connected learning environment.

Given these conditions, what are some of the issues related to technology that will shape education, educators, and professional development? Three are offered for consideration: (1) access and expectations; (2) knowledge; and (3) alternatives and competition.

Access and Expectations

In 2004, having access to a sufficient number of computers and to the Internet remains a problem for many schools. The "digital divide" between the rich and poor is real; however, differences between the "have" and "have nots" will continue to narrow as access costs are driven lower by new technologies and through support from governments and external agencies. For example, in 2004, only about a third of public schools were using wireless technology (Charp, 2002, p. 10). However, as districts continue to purchase new technologies and push toward a wireless environment, more and more students will have access to emerging technologies. As access becomes commonplace, it will create tensions within the educational community. It will raise expectations of what technologies are available and how they can be integrated into the learning experience. Teachers, who were once delighted to have one or two computers in their classrooms, now want enough computers for groups of students to use them in the classroom. In fact, the best situation would be a set of wireless laptops so that students can access the district's server for information and the Internet for additional information. The encyclopedia and the text will no longer be the major sources of information.

Students' expectations will also continue to drive technology use in education. As students utilize digital technologies to create reports, presentations, and videos, their demands for better technologies will increase. Who wants to develop film when a digital camera offers so many more options? Who wants to simply word process a report after being able to use words, graphics, and

Internet linkages to make the case? In fact, one only needs to look at the latest digital game popular among students to have an idea of what students expect from technology.

These increasing expectations will continue to place pressures on school districts and professional education providers. What it means for school districts is that the expenditures for emerging technologies will continue to be an important part of budgetary considerations. It also means that resources will be needed to prepare teachers to integrate these technologies and support the teachers once they have the technologies in the classroom. Unanswered at this point are what the costs for connectivity will be. While computing power has increased dramatically, the costs remain constant. Who is to say that once schools are connected and dependent on the connectivity to accomplish their education mission that costs will not increase?

As digital technologies become more ubiquitous, teachers will confront philosophical issues about teaching and learning. This will mean that more professional development activities will need to be focused on *using to learn* with technologies than simply *learning to use* them. It also means that, at the district level, serious considerations will need to occur about what Grant identifies as "a vision of technology as an empowering tool for teachers and students" (1996, p. 2). Creating and extending such a vision in light of competing educational issues will be a challenge for most districts.

Increased access will also raise questions about how much access and what type of information should be available to students. A significant body of information available on the World Wide Web is not appropriate for children and youth and does not have educational uses. Should access to the World Wide Web be limited? Should districts have a list of approved Web sites and control access through a central location? Who should be able to access district, building, and individual classroom Web sites? These and other questions will shape policies and practices over the next several years, and responses will impact educational practices and individual freedoms.

The increasing availability and access to digital technologies will be important drivers and shapers of educational activities. The world is a globally connected environment. The classroom cannot be isolated from that world. As access increases expectations for teachers and students, the public will continue to pressure educators to prepare students to live productive lives in a technological world. The pressure to infuse these technologies into the classroom will be constant.

Knowledge

For decades, two sources of knowledge dominated the classroom—the teacher and textbooks. Students expected their teacher to know the subject matter and to be able to help them learn what was important. It is also historically true that there has often been a difference of opinion between what the teacher thinks is important to know and what students believe to be important. No matter, the teacher has had the final say. In addition, students have relied on the textbook as a major source of information. Other sources have been available and used, but the textbook has been the cornerstone of knowledge in the field. The curriculum scope and sequence (what was taught and when) has been orderly and linear in nature based on what content experts and educators have believed is the best way to structure knowledge.

The World Wide Web and the Internet have changed the structured world of knowledge and the curriculum. Suddenly information is available from across the world and from a multitude of sources that may present a variety of answers to the same question. A student can now access the latest scientific research, political poll, or review of literature rather than rely on the teacher or a textbook published years before. In some cases, the information gathered might be contrary to what was presented in the textbook or by the teacher. Who is right?

Multimedia has also changed the nature of the curriculum. Where does the course begin? Where does it end? Accessing the Internet and reviewing materials is not like starting on page one of the textbook, and there is no "end." One simply seeks out information and decides how to do so. Also, what happens to scope and sequence when students continue to discuss and explore a topic outside of the class? For a teacher who prefers to end the lesson and begin at that point when class resumes, such discussions may create difficulties.

In today's educational environment, the answer to the question, "What is knowledge?" is being shaped by academic standards created by educators and experts in the content areas. Tests drive what students need to know. However, the issues surrounding access to information and knowledge continue to create problems for the district, school, teacher, and professional development provider. One only needs to enter a key word in a search engine to find out the amount of information available on a given topic. First, the amount of information available is overwhelming to the searcher. How can one make sense of 100,000 pieces of data? Second, one quickly realizes that anyone may place information on the World Wide Web and that some of these individuals have a particular view of the world that may not represent what scholars consider to be academically sound information. How does one judge sources? Additionally, some sources available on the World Wide Web are inappropriate for children and youth.

What is clear is that the amount of information available will continue to grow as more and more people have access to the Internet. Educators must not only teach students how to access information but also to evaluate that information against a set of standards. They must also assist students in learning that "information" is not "knowledge" and then how to use information to create knowledge about a particular topic, issue, or problem. New skills will need to be taught and learned that will once again put pressure on current teaching practices.

The access to information will also bring pressures to define intellectual property rights to resources. Educators are used to being able to reproduce materials for educational purposes and also being able to modify materials to fit specific needs. Although laws exist, the increasing ease of reproducing and accessing materials brings to the forefront questions about legal rights to the materials. The current controversy about downloading music and videos will continue and spread to other materials used in educational settings. Pressures will continue to mount as more and more providers seek to receive payment for the use of materials. Educators will be confronted with questions about their rights to free material access. Today's educators expect most Internet materials to be free or inexpensive. The future may be different.

Textbook publishers will also face new pressures. Some districts will seek to reduce costs by using sources on the World Wide Web rather than buying textbooks that quickly become outdated. While mainline publishers now are able to demonstrate how materials are correlated with standards, online providers, some of whom represent publishing companies, are also demonstrating how databases and Web-based materials can meet the same standards. Given that resources are limited, expect continued debates about textbooks and technology.

While all of the above are important issues in today's climate, the major challenge confronting advocates of technology in the schools is the question, "Does infusing technology into the classroom enable students to meet the learning standards of the district?" If not, why should districts spend scarce resources to purchase new technologies and to prepare teachers to use them in the classroom? In some ways, the question is not a fair question to ask because "a central theme of the research is that computer-based technology, like the more basic classroom tools of pencil and paper, is a means, not an end. Its power lies in how it is used" (White et al., 2002, p. 2). To be fair, educators ought to ask whether a pencil used to write notes from a lecture is an effective use of the pencil to meet high standards. The problem is that pencils cost almost nothing and have a long history in the classroom. Computer technologies have neither.

As discussed earlier in the chapter, it does appear that teachers who are known as exemplary teachers and who use technology to engage learners in project-based or problem-based learning indeed do demonstrate that technology makes a difference in the students' learning. At issue, of course, is how a district provides sufficient professional development to get all teachers to such a level of proficiency. We are back to the issue of professional development.

Alternatives and Competition

Another outcome from advances in technology and access to the World Wide Web will be the continued growth of competition among current providers of professional development for educators and the growth of the number of providers. Educators are going to continue to have choices when selecting a provider for professional development, and these providers will not be limited to those within a local community. These alternatives will increase the power of the educator to choose and adapt materials to his/her own educational needs. Competition will favor quality providers and eliminate those whose products do not meet needs. Professional development providers, especially institutions of higher education, will face a competitive environment in which quality of materials will be critical, but so, too, will be the price one pays for access to the materials.

Competition, however, may also limit choice. As witnessed in many of the mass media corporations in the United States, more and more sources are owned by a few large entities, thereby severely limiting real choice. Being able to choose from 100 television stations on a specific cable network is not necessarily choice. One's choices are limited to those provided by the cable company that chooses what to make available to the viewer. The trend toward the consolidation of publishing companies and software developers also suggests that choices among providers may be limited. Lessig's *The Future of Ideas: The Fate of the Commons in a Connected World* (2001) provides a perspective on the issues surrounding the determination of who controls what educators and others can access. What is evident as we look to the future is that competition can enhance the availability of products and programs that the educator may use to enhance his or her understanding of and ability to use technology as an integral part of teaching and learning. These choices, however, will not come without costs economically and in freedom of choice. Educators cannot have it both ways; receiving high quality without having to pay a competitive price is an unlikely proposition.

CONCLUDING REMARKS

James Burke (2002) presents a picture of professional development in 2015 that combines the features of face-to-face learning experiences with informal learning experiences utilizing images that have been downloaded to a set of eye glasses that, in turn, download these images to the retina with audio provided to an earpiece. The information is specifically designed to meet the learning needs of the individual. Later, the learner has an opportunity to sit around a table with several holograms of other participants originating from remote locations.

Under this vision, professional development in 2015 would combine the best of informal and formal learning opportunities. Individuals would choose from a range of learning communities characterized by:

- Long-term versus short-term;
- Continuous versus targeted learning;
- Lifelong versus short-term goals;
- Real community versus school;
- Virtual versus physical;
- No formal instructor versus a formal instructor;
- Sharing of virtual resources by community members versus sharing of physical resources by member organizations; and
- Unscheduled learning at the convenience of community members versus scheduled learning.

New technologies would enhance these optional learning opportunities and enrich the learning experience. They would also permit the learner to craft what best works for him or her. Flexibility would be key.

While Burke's article is written in the context of a flight to Mars, the ideas are not unrealistic. We know that emerging technologies will continue to push current thinking about teaching and learning. We need to provide high quality technology-related professional development if we want the public schools to be places where students learn the skills and knowledge and develop the attitudes needed to be effective citizens in the twenty-first century.

NOTES

1. See Chapter 7 for a more detailed discussion of legislative policy and its impact on education and teacher education.

2. The reader should be aware that it is difficult to ascertain exactly what is spent on professional development. Selected activities vary across districts, and national data are dependent upon surveys from districts.

3. For a discussion of these and related challenges facing higher education, see: Donald E. Hanna, Building a leadership vision: Eleven strategic challenges for higher education, *EDUCAUSE* July/August (2003), pp. 25–34.

4. The United State Congress and the U.S. Department of Education have played important roles in supporting the use of emerging technologies in education. Another OTA study was completed in 1995. A variety of initiatives culminating with the funding of the Preparing Tomorrow's Teachers to Use Technology (PT3) by USDOE have also advanced technology use in both public schools and institutions of higher education.

5. In the mid-1990s, Congress funded six regional consortia (that later grew to ten) to provide assistance to educators as they learn to use technology more effectively.

6. Americans, however, can gain insight into the issue of numbers by examining the challenges in China. For example, between 1999 and 2000, the Chinese government provided 190 hours of in-service training in technology to 10 million teachers! American numbers pale in comparison.

7. For an excellent summary, see: P. Resta, (Ed.), (2002), *Information and Communication Technologies in Teacher Education: A Planning Guide.* UNESCO, Paris.

BIBLIOGRAPHY

Anderson, J., & Van Weert, T. (Eds.) (2002). *Information and communication technology education: A curriculum for schools and programmes of teacher development.* Paris, UNESCO.

Becker, H. J., & Riel, M. M. (2000). *Teacher professional engagement and constructivist-compatible computer use.* University of California, Irvine, and University of Minnesota: Center for Research on Information Technology and Organizations.

Burke, J. (2002). Professional development in 2015. *Converge*, 1(3): 74–75.

CEO Forum. (1999). *CEO forum school technology and readiness report: Year 2, Professional development, A link to better learning.* Washington, DC: CEO Forum.

Charischak, I. (2000). A Look at technology's role in professional development of mathematics teachers at the middle school level. *School Science and Mathematics, 100*(7), 349–354.

Charp, S. (May 2002). Changes to traditional teaching. *T.H.E. Journal, 29*(10), 10, 12.

Cradler, J., & Cradler, R. (1995). *Prior studies for technology insertion.* San Francisco, CA: WestED.

Dwyer, D. C., Ringstaff, C., & Sandholtz, J. H. (1990a). *Teacher beliefs and practices, part I: Patterns of change.* Cuppertino, CA: Apple Computer.

Dwyer, D. C., Ringstaff, C., & Sandholtz, J. H. (1990b). *Teacher beliefs and practices, part II: Support for change.* Cuppertino, CA: Apple Computer.

Frand, J. L. (2000). The Information-age mindset: Changes in students and implications for higher education. *EDUCAUSE Review, 35*(5), 15–24.

Fulton, K., Glenn, A. D., Valdez, G., & Blomeyer, R. (2002). *Preparing technology competent teachers for urban and rural classrooms: A teacher education challenge.* Napier, IL: North Central Regional Educational Laboratory.

Glenn, A. D. (2002). *Grantee abstracts: Preparing tomorrow's teachers to use technology.* Washington, DC: U.S. Department of Education, 103.

Grant, C. M. (1996). *Professional development in a technological age: New Definitions, old challenges, new resources.* Boston, MA: TERC. Retrieved September 1, 2004, from http://fa.terc.edu/publications/terc-pubs/tech-infusion/prof_dev/prof-dev-principles.html/

Hawkes, M. (2000). Structuring computer-mediate communication for collaborative teacher development. *Journal of Research and Development in Education, 33,* 268–277.

ISTE. (2000). *National educational technology standards for students: Connecting curriculum and technology.* Washington, DC: ISTE and U.S. Department of Education.

Killeen, K. M., Monk, D. H., & Plecki, M. (2002). *What school districts spend on professional development.* Seattle: Center for the Study of Teaching and Policy, University of Washington.

Lessig, L. (2001). *The future of ideas: The fate of the commons in a connected world.* New York: Random House.

McKay, M., & McGrath, B. (2000). Creating Internet-based curriculum projects: A model for teacher professional development. *T.H.E. Journal, 27,* 114–124.

Moore, J. L., & Orey, M. A. (2000). The implementation of an electronic peformance support system for teachers: An examination of usage, performance, and attitudes. *Performance Improvement Quarterly, 14*(1), 26–56.

Moursund, D., & Bielefeldt, T. (1998). *Will new teachers be prepared to teach in a digital age?* Santa Monica, CA: Milken Foundation.

NCTAF. (2003a). *No dream denied: A pledge to America's children.* Washington, DC: National Commission on Teaching and America's Future.

NCTAF. (2003b). *Summary report: No dream denied: A pledge to America's children.* Washington, DC: National Commission on Teaching and America's Future.

NSDC. (2003). *NSDC standards for staff development*. Washington, DC: National Staff Development Council.

Orrill, C. H. (2001). Building technology-based, learner-centered, classrooms: The evolution of a professional development framework. *Educational Technology Research and Development, 49*, 15–34.

OTA. (1988). *POWER ON! New tools for teaching and learning: Summary*. Washington, DC: Congress of the United States, Office of Technology Assessment.

OTA. (1999). Teachers and technology: Making the Connection. Washington, DC: Congress of the United States, Office of Technology Assessment.

Taylor, R. P. (1980). *The computer in school: Tutor, tool, tutee*. New York: Teachers College Press.

Valdez, G. (1986). Realizing the potential of educational technology. *Educational Leadership, 43*, 4–6.

White, N., Ringstaff, C., & Kelly, L. (2002). *Knowledge brief: Getting the most from technology in schools*. San Francisco: WestEd.

"Highly Qualified" Teachers and the Teaching Profession: Policy Lessons from the Field

Barnett Berry, Mandy Hoke, and Eric Hirsch

INTRODUCTION

Over the last decade, it has become increasingly evident to policy makers and practitioners that the success of standards-based reform hinges on the quality of teachers and teaching as well as that of the system through which we develop and sustain a capable teacher force (Darling-Hammond & Sykes, 1999). It now seems that policy and business leaders have come to know what parents have always known—teachers make the greatest difference in student achievement. This recognition has emerged, in part, as a result of recent evidence mounted by different researchers that demonstrates that the lion's share of variance in student test scores is accounted for by teacher quality (Ferguson, 1991; Goldhaber & Brewer, 1996; Hanushek, 1996; Hanushek, Kain, & Rivkin, 1998; Sanders & Rivers, 1996). In particular, Hanushek (1992) found that a student with a "high-quality" teacher will likely achieve more than a student with a "low-quality" teacher.

At the same time, America's approach to school improvement still emphasizes the primacy of curriculum mandates and high-stakes testing and accountability. Along with high drop-out rates, poor performance on standardized tests and the unacceptable disparity in achievement among different student groups dominate media accounts of the quality of public education.

While our nation's current focus and reliance on tests have roots in the launch of Sputnik in the late 1950s, the movement toward a growing reliance on high-stakes testing as means to drive school improvement has been growing steadily ever since (Amrein & Berliner, 2002). Indeed, high-stakes accountability systems (those that set clear and high standards for teaching and learning, measure the results with standardized achievement tests, and grade schools based on their test performance, rewarding high performance and sanctioning low performance) have swept the nation (Henry & Opfer, 2004).

NO CHILD LEFT BEHIND AND TEACHER QUALITY

The pressure to close the achievement gap has been intensely compounded by the reauthorization of the Elementary and Secondary Education Act of 2001, or No Child Left Behind (NCLB). Indeed, with only 30 percent of the nation's fourth-grade students meeting reading "proficiency" on the 2002 National Assessment of Education Progress, NCLB poses new opportunities and challenges for educators and policy makers alike. Under NCLB, all children must learn to read by the third grade, all students must reach proficiency in core academic areas by 2014, and states must rate their schools based on whether or not they are making "adequate yearly progress" (AYP) in terms of a number of student subgroups, including those defined by ethnic minority status, lower socioeconomic class, and enrollment in special education programs. For the 2002–2003 school year, states have identified at least 23,812 schools as not making AYP and at least 5,200 as "in need of improvement," that is, missing the AYP mark for two or more consecutive years (Olsen, 2003). To be sure, NCLB mandates a more strident approach to school-level accountability, with rewards for those schools that improve and consequences for those that do not, as well as parental empowerment through regular reports of student performance data and school choice if their children's schools do not improve quickly on standardized tests.

Therefore, it is no surprise that NCLB not only requires students to make adequate yearly progress toward state standards but also mandates the assignment of "highly qualified" teachers (HQT) for students in core academic subjects by the end of the 2005–2006 school year. According to federal requirements, a HQT: (1) has a four-year college degree; (2) has a full state teaching license; and (3) demonstrates knowledge of the subject he/she is teaching, either by majoring in that subject in college or by passing a rigorous subject matter test or other state-mandated evaluation. In addition, the NCLB legislation calls for the examination and elimination of out-of-field and emergency credentialing, mandating that states ensure that poor and minority children, in particular, are not taught by inexperienced, unqualified, or out-of-field teachers at higher rates than other children. Over the last several years, evidence has been mounting that poor children and those of color are far more likely not to have qualified teachers (Esch & Shields, 2002; Darling-Hammond, 2000; Haycock, 1998). Darling-Hammond and Sykes have noted that, while our nation's teacher preparation programs actually produce sufficient numbers of new teachers, serious shortages in specific teaching fields exist, and the hiring of "unqualified teachers" is a consequence of "distributional inequities" and retention as opposed to the general shortages of qualified individuals (2003, p. 3).

NCLB requires also that all teachers have access to effective professional development, and the law calls for local needs assessments to "take into account" the knowledge and skills teachers and principals need to help students meet academic standards. To ensure the law is followed, states must now begin reporting on the extent to which teachers have access to high-quality, scientifically-based professional development.

With its high-stakes testing and accountability provisions, NCLB has been described as a dramatic new direction in federal law, providing some precedent for the nation's government to take a heavier hand in setting a higher bar for teachers. In 2003, Title II of NCLB provided states and districts with almost $3 billion to improve educator quality, along with over $50 million in special appropriations to help members of the military and midcareer professionals become teachers and new college graduates to become educators in high-need schools. The federal focus on HQTs has the potential to drive new state and local actions, prompting universities to prepare teachers more effectively, school districts to create more effective professional development programs, local administrators to implement new recruitment and retention strategies, and teachers to think and act differently with regards to their own profession.

While the sanctions for not meeting the HQT requirements are much less punitive than those for not making progress toward student achievement goals, they can be very public in nature. Districts must send letters home to parents of students in Title I schools (as identified by a high percentage of students eligible to receive free or reduced lunch) not taught by highly qualified teachers, and, under the parental right-to-know provisions, districts must provide parents with information about teacher qualifications in an accessible, user-friendly format upon request. Most importantly, the law requires specific reporting on HQT, not only in the aggregate, but also for high-poverty schools.

In the hands of highly capable and visionary leaders, the federal mandate offers unprecedented opportunities to reshape teacher preparation in ways that will produce the gains in student achievement reformers have long sought. However, NCLB has specified that a HQT must have full state certification *and/or* pass the state's licensing examination, suggesting that neither professional knowledge and skills nor completion of a teacher preparation program are necessary in and of themselves. In defining a highly qualified teacher, NCLB relies heavily on state teacher tests, assuming that they are sufficiently rigorous, aligned with what prospective teachers are taught in their college courses, and meaningful given the content they will teach in their classrooms. In fact, the federal definition of a HQT, and therefore the state definition on which it is based, is driven almost exclusively by content knowledge, virtually ignoring the need for teachers to develop and use pedagogical skills. Secretary of Education Rod Paige, in his annual report on teacher quality, focuses solely on two teacher quality principles: raising academic standards for teachers and simultaneously lowering barriers to those trying to enter the profession. In fact, the secretary's reports have been highly critical of teacher education, viewing teacher preparation and licensure requirements as part of a "broken system" and promoting that education coursework and student teaching become "optional" (U.S. Department of Education, 2003, p. 19).

THE DEVELOPMENT OF THE TEACHING PROFESSION

Since the publication of *A Nation at Risk* (1983), a document that challenged many assumptions about the effectiveness of the public schools, states have been upgrading student standards, and a number of efforts have been made to upgrade the teaching profession. State legislatures and state boards of education, the governmental bodies most notably in charge of the rules governing the teaching profession, have been on a slow march to advance teacher standards by increasing admission requirements to preparation programs, demanding more content knowledge, and extending internships. Since the release of the 1996 report, *What Matters Most: Teaching for America's Future*, some progress on the teacher professionalism front has been made. For ex-

ample, there has been increased attention paid to having all education programs meet the standards of the National Council for Accreditation of Teacher
Education (NCATE). Close to 700 of the 1200 universities preparing teachers
are now approved by NCATE, and forty-seven states are in partnership using
the NCATE teacher education standards in their own program approval process. While the previous NCATE system looked primarily at college curricula
and other inputs, the new system now requires that colleges and universities
produce hard evidence that their prospective teachers meet professional,
state, and institutional standards. To graduate from an NCATE-accredited institution, teacher candidates are expected to show mastery of the content
knowledge in their fields and demonstrate that they can teach it effectively. In
addition, most states use the new teacher standards of the Interstate New
Teacher Assessment and Support Consortium (INTASC) to outline their licensing framework. However, these states, other than that of Connecticut,
have not invested in the kinds of new teacher assessments that can capture
the wide range of content and pedagogical knowledge and skills novices need
in order to begin their careers. Eighteen states have now established professional standards boards that charge teachers themselves with the responsibility of setting and enforcing rigorous new standards for teacher
licensure—although most do not have full governing and financial control
over setting and enforcing these professional standards (Berry, Buxton,
Darling-Hammond, & Hirsch, 2001).

In addition, the creation of the National Board for Professional Teaching
Standards (NBPTS) may be the most notable development in the creation of a
true teaching profession in America. The board's mission to codify a body of
knowledge for effective teaching and identify and reward accomplished practitioners is similar to what has already been developed in more established
professions like medicine, engineering, and architecture. The NBPTS identifies accomplished teachers through a year-long assessment process, using
portfolio, video-taped lessons, and essay-type tests of content and pedagogy.
With certificates available in twenty-seven different content–and student–age
specific fields, as of late fall 2003, the NBPTS has identified over 32,000
"board certified teachers." These relatively expensive teaching assessments,
which cost $2300 per teacher, push teachers to show that they know their con-
tent and how to teach it to diverse learners[1] and, in doing so, expand the role
of teacher education and professional development and extend thinking about
how teachers may serve as leaders in school improvement. Importantly, while
the teaching profession has yet to create a uniform way to assess the knowl-

edge and skills of the over 3 million teachers nationwide, the NBPTS tests are designed to assess the skills of experienced, accomplished practitioners, and, as a result, the board's efforts have created the technological know-how and basic infrastructure to move the profession forward.

Central to recent federal efforts to improve teacher quality has been the direct challenge to the usefulness of teacher education programs themselves. Through both rhetoric and programs emphasizing shortcut, alternative routes into teaching, the secretary and the United States Department of Education have been diminishing the importance of preservice preparation. The Department of Education is now encouraging states to adopt a subject matter paper-and-pencil test in order to quickly get teachers highly qualified without any preparation in learning to teach. In particular, the department is supporting, with a recent $35 million grant, the development of a new teacher test being created by the American Board for Certification of Teacher Excellence (ABCTE). Although the focus of the ABCTE assessment is primarily on content knowledge, it may count as the sole requirement for licensure (ABCTE, 2003). At the end of 2003, two states—Pennsylvania and Idaho—had already passed policies that granted those passing the ABCTE test a provisional license.

In part, the development of ABCTE and its primary (if not sole) focus on content stands in contrast to the NBPTS. Critics of the NBPTS have spoken to its assessments that bypass the judgments of principals and focus on teachers' use of professional knowledge and how to teach different children at the expense of knowing content. Much has been made of the NBPTS not having data that directly link teachers who are certified by them with gains in student achievement (Podgursky, 2001). However, all of this has changed of late—with the release of a study, utilizing a sophisticated value-added model, showing that National Board Certified Teachers (1) are more effective at raising student achievement than teachers who pursue, but fail to obtain, this certification; (2) are more effective at raising student achievement outside of the year in which they apply than teachers who do not pursue this certification; (3) have a greater impact with younger students; and (4) have a greater impact on improving performance of low-income students (Goldhaber & Anthony, 2004).

Despite this recent report on student achievement, the federal focus on alternative routes into teaching has shined a spotlight on programs like Teach for America as a preferred way to "prepare" teachers and fill classrooms. The assumption is that teacher education just does not matter much in improving student learning, and, therefore, there is little reason to invest in it. As discussed in detail in Chapter 2, alternative programs range from graduate level teacher education programs to short-term alternative certification programs that reduce the requirements for a state license to traditional emergency hiring practices that fill vacancies in any way possible. In these truncated programs, teacher candidates tend to get four to six weeks of basic training in classroom management, instruction on how to develop lessons plans, and a general introduction to the complex world of teaching. These are the programs Secretary Paige advocates in his reports and calls for action (U.S. Department of Education, 2003).

In the fall of 2003, the United States Department of Education approved the creation of the Teacher Education Accrediting Council (TEAC), an alternative to NCATE and an organization through which colleges of education may seek approval for their professional training. Unlike NCATE, whose results-oriented approval processes hinge on a common set of professional standards, TEAC requires only that universities develop what is called an "inquiry brief," which is described as a scholarly work that lays out the evidence supporting why a college deserves accreditation and, in doing so, "allows colleges to set their own professional standards" (Galley, 2003).

Interestingly, the NCLB professional development provisions focus on ensuring that teachers and administrators gain both the content knowledge and the teaching skills to help students meet content and achievement standards. The law's provisions actually mirror the kinds of changes being advanced by the NCATE, NBPTS, and INTASC and their vision for more fully developed teacher professionalism. For example, NCLB professional development provisions focus on ensuring that teachers have understandings of effective instructional strategies, use data and assessments to inform and implement classroom practice, and know how to teach students with special needs and those who are second language learners. However, these teaching skills appear to be totally ignored by the federal definition of teacher qualification as evidenced by the recent push to offer multiple forms of professional accreditation and the alternative route programs being promoted by the federal government.

While NCLB is promoting a much needed, nationwide focus on teacher quality and equity, teachers and administrators (and eventually the public) may end up receiving mixed messages as to what needs to be done to improve teaching, and the capacity of schools to recruit and retain the teachers may be limited. This is why we undertook an in-depth investigation into the impact of the law's teacher quality provisions, focusing on schools that were most likely to face AYP sanctions and in the most need of recruiting and retaining highly qualified teachers.

We will present initial findings on how specific states are defining HQT as well as the key issues state and local officials are facing in implementing the NCLB "highly qualified" teacher mandates. Between October 2003 and February 2004, researchers at the Southeast Center for Teaching Quality conducted three-day site visits in twenty-four high needs schools (in twelve districts) in Alabama, Georgia, North Carolina, and Tennessee, where we interviewed a representative sample of teachers, principals, superintendents, and district-level administrators (particularly those in charge of human resources, Title I, and professional development programs). A group of stakeholders in each state helped us select sites that were either on the federal "needs improvement" AYP list or had received some lower performing rating from their respective state. We also wanted to study schools that had higher than state average teacher turnover rates. Because of the purpose of our policy research, and the nature of our design, most of the sites we visited were located in isolated rural areas. We also selected several urban school districts with serious teacher shortages but also a demonstrated will to recruit and retain teachers.

While we supplement our case study data with a range of other source materials (e.g., state and local documents, state-level teacher survey data, etc.), our focus is on bringing a "ground-level" view of what it takes to ensure a HQT for each student and what the NCLB law portends for the future of teaching in America. We begin by summarizing how the four states are initially meeting the HQT mandates and then how current alternative routes into teaching play into efforts to recruit and retain the teachers they need. We intend that these initial lessons from the field can be used to support the kinds of changes needed in America's teaching profession.

HOW STATES ARE MEETING THE HQT MANDATES

Initial investigation of the four states found overstressed officials in understaffed state departments of education making hurried decisions about the definition of a HQT. The new requirements went into effect for all new hires in Title I schools as of the beginning of the 2002–2003 school year, giving states a mere seven months after the passage of the law to establish and implement a working definition of a HQT. State officials repeatedly noted the lack of guidance from the United States Department of Education. In fact, very few states were able to meet the initial deadline; most states did not publish even their draft models for the highly qualified definition until the spring of 2003.

Under tight deadlines, officials have had to fit their often idiosyncratic and complex teacher licensing systems into the narrow HQT framework established by the United States Department of Education, without much opportunity to reflect on the effects of these decisions upon a decade of policies aimed at raising standards for new teachers. In our interviews, we found consistently across the four states that the HQT time frame had offered little opportunity for education leaders to consider how they might use the momentum of NCLB as a catalyst to build a standards-based teacher development system. For the most part, the four states we investigated (as well as many other states, according to their Web sites) have stuck closely to the minimum requirements of the federal government's HQT guidelines.

In the initial reporting of the HQT numbers, each of the states reported wide variations in the percentage of those labeled as HQT and the percentage of classes taught by them in high-poverty schools (see Table 7.1). For example, Georgia claimed that 94 percent of its teachers were highly qualified, while in Alabama and Tennessee, the percentages were 35 and 34, respectively. These variations were due, in large part, to the different states' capabilities to track this kind of data and to provide different options for subject matter competency. For example, Tennessee's numbers are based solely on state-level testing records; districts there had only just begun to gather more detailed information on their teachers when the baseline numbers were required. In Alabama, the numbers reflect the fact that neither a subject matter test nor a High Objective Uniform State System of Evaluation (HOUSSE) standard were available to teachers at the time state reports were required.

These "highly qualified" numbers are even more suspect given the varied complications we uncovered in our study. For example, we found states and districts struggling with matters related to data gathering and reporting, as well as using questionable teacher evaluation systems to measure subject matter knowledge.

Data Gathering and Reporting

In our four states, documenting the status of teachers and assembling the data for the federally mandated report card has been difficult. For these states, most with antiquated data-collection systems, identifying and reporting on

TABLE 7.1: Highly qualified teacher data as of December 2003.

	Percent of classes taught by "highly qualified" teachers statewide	Percent of classes taught by "highly qualified" teachers in high-poverty schools
Alabama*	35	29
Georgia*	94	95
North Carolina**	83	78
Tennessee***	34	35

Source: Education Week, 2003b
**Source: North Carolina Department of Public Instruction, 2003*
***Source: Personal communication, Debbie Gilliam, 19 December 2003*

HQTs has been no simple task. For example, in Alabama, state and district officials have been hand counting HQTs. Local officials complete a checklist for identifying HQTs, and then state department employees (six of them) verify the checklists for the state's 48,000 teachers. On one day in May 2003, a single department staffer had 1,500 teacher checklists waiting to be reviewed in addition to other responsibilities, including processing certificates and renewals.

North Carolina is using its state-level database to match each teacher's tested area with his or her assigned area, then sending the names of all teachers who cannot be verified as highly qualified to district personnel, asking them to find a means of documenting highly qualified status for those teachers. Relying on districts (that have to send letters home to parents and face some sanctions based on the status of their teaching corps) to provide this kind of information with little or no guidance is likely to produce unreliable data across and within states. Although Tennessee has yet to decide upon a process to document HQT status, it will most likely be in a situation similar to that of North Carolina, relying on districts to provide information about teachers' qualifications.

Georgia is perhaps the farthest along in this regard, using a new database that matches teachers' certification areas with the areas to which they are assigned, then notifying local constituencies when teachers have possible deficiencies. Yet, teachers in Georgia reported that data inaccuracies and timing caused some panic among veteran teachers who were told prematurely that they might not be highly qualified.

As part of NCLB, states are also required to report on the percentage of teachers receiving high quality professional development. At the time of writing, *none* of the four states studied by Southeast Center researchers had developed any concrete plans to accomplish this task. Professional development delivery and evaluation have always been issues left largely in the hands of districts, and, while states can set standards for professional development, most currently have no methods to evaluate and monitor district-level activity or compliance. In many of the districts, building-level principals were not even aware that high quality professional development is a requirement of the law. Several principals interviewed were confident that their teachers consistently participate in such professional development but had no idea how their districts were identifying which activities met the requirements or documenting which teachers were participating. District level administrators were only slightly more aware of this requirement, and, in most cases, districts were simply planning to use data from their current systems for documenting professional development for certification renewal and had few plans for implementing methods to establish any greater degree of quality control.

Using Tests to Measure Content Knowledge

North Carolina, Georgia, and Tennessee all use the Praxis teacher tests, designed by the Education Testing Service (ETS), to measure the content knowledge of its teachers. However, Tennessee previously had no requirement that middle school teachers pass subject area tests for licensure and had to quickly adopt them. The tests are now optional and necessary only to attain highly qualified status. Georgia and North Carolina have required subject tests (Praxis II) for licensure for several years now. New teachers, then, will be automatically considered highly qualified if they are teaching in field. Alabama, due to serious teacher testing problems and ensuing litigation, has not had a state-mandated test.[2]

In early 2003, only thirty-four states required teaching candidates to pass a test in at least one academic content area prior to licensure (Olsen, 2003). Across the nation, current teacher testing for licensure purposes is a patchwork of efforts, with over 600 exams in use. In Table 7.2 below, the variation in tests used in Georgia, North Carolina, and Tennessee and their respective required passing scores are shown. As a variation of a few points has signifi-

TABLE 7.2: Required Praxis tests and passing scores by state (sample math and special education).

	Elementary Content		Math Content		Special Education	
	Test	Pass Score	Test	Pass Score	Test	Pass Score
GA	EE: Content Exercise	137	Mathematics: Content Knowledge	136	Special Education: Knowledge-Based Core Principles	152
	EE: Curriculum, Instruction, and Assessment	154	Mathematics: Proofs, Models, and Problems, Part 1	159		
NC	EE: Content Exercise	Combined score of 313	Mathematics: Content Knowledge	Combined score of 281	Special Education: Knowledge-Based Core Principles	143
	EE: Curriculum, Instruction, and Assessment		Mathematics Pedagogy			
TN	EE: Content Knowledge	140	Mathematics: Content Knowledge	136	Education of Exceptional Students: Core Content Knowledge	Test required, no passing score set
	EE: Curriculum, Instruction, and Assessment	159	Mathematics Pedagogy	125		
AL	None required		None required		None required	

Source: Educational Testing Service, 2003 http://www.ets.org/praxis/prxstate.html

cant effects on the proportion of teachers passing, and therefore attaining highly qualified status, the consistency of what it means to be highly qualified across states is compromised.

Each of the current teacher tests being used to measure HQTs is relatively inexpensive to take. For example, the current Praxis II costs about seventy to eighty dollars, which is far below the expense of taking a licensure exam in other professions. In engineering, for example, a series of initial licensure tests costs well over $1,000 (National Council of Examiners for Engineering and Surveying, 2004). Yet, according to a recent National Academy of Sciences (NAS) report, even more well-developed tests are not designed to test all of the competencies relevant to beginning practice (Mitchell, Robinson, Plake, & Knowles, 2001). Furthermore, states use a variety of unclear methods to set their passing scores on the teacher tests, most of which are below the twenty-fifth percentile of national test-takers. Because these tests are designed only to assess the minimal knowledge needed to teach (as are other professional licensure exams), none can distinguish minimally qualified from highly qualified teachers.

It is important to note that North Carolina, a state that has been implementing more rigorous teacher standards of late, has taken steps to lower standards around teachers' content knowledge. The State Board of Education recently made a "change in certification policy (that will supposedly) align North Carolina teacher certification requirements with the requirements of NCLB and will allow middle school and high school teachers to be designated 'highly qualified' *without* having to take (the PRAXIS II) test" (North Carolina Department of Public Instruction, 2004).

Using Coursework to Measure Content Knowledge

Another option for teachers at the middle or secondary level to be considered highly qualified is to complete an academic major, advanced degree, or equivalent coursework in each subject area they teach. The states involved in the study, however, have had no statewide standard for what counts as an academic major, leaving the determination to institutions of higher education and making it difficult to create a common statewide standard. This is not an insignificant matter, and the federal guidance on this issue is unclear, opening the door to wide interpretations and further problems with using the data to understand the extent of a state's teacher quality problems or progress.

Alabama's solution is to use the average of the required number of hours at each of its twenty-nine bachelor's degree–granting institutions as the standard. For middle or secondary teachers, this equivalent is thirty-two total hours with at least nineteen of them in upper division courses. Alabama's HQT model also allows elementary teachers to demonstrate subject matter competency through the equivalent of an academic major (which is supposed to be prohibited under NCLB), defined as twelve hours each of reading, math, science, and social studies (Alabama State Board of Education, 2003). North Carolina and Tennessee have both set the equivalent for an academic major at twenty-four hours, while Georgia's is twenty-one hours of upper division courses (North Carolina State Board of Education, 2003; Tennessee State Board of Education, 2003).

To complicate matters further, states are redefining their licensing and endorsements within the core subjects specified in NCLB, in some cases moving from specific subfields, such as chemistry, physics, and so forth, to broad fields like science to ensure a greater number of HQTs. In Tennessee, for example, a major in one subfield, with at least nine hours in another of the fields, allows a teacher to be considered highly qualified for both. Therefore, a history major (twenty-four hours) with only nine hours in geography can be considered highly qualified in both subjects (Tennessee State Board of Education, 2003). The situation is similar in Alabama, where a teacher certified in general social science who holds an academic major or the equivalent in political science and has earned just one credit in history will be deemed highly qualified in both subjects. The same holds true for a teacher with a general science degree, where one course in biology may allow one to be deemed highly qualified to teach that subject. These state responses to the HQT mandates, apparently approved by the federal government, may end up countermanding efforts to eliminate out-of-field teaching.

A similar problem emerges with upper level elementary and sixth-grade teachers. Federal guidance on this issue has been unclear. In one state studied, an eighth-grade science teacher in a 6–8 middle school could have to demonstrate science competency, while an eighth-grade science teacher in a K–8 elementary school (as designated by the state), must pass a test in the basic elementary curriculum. What this means more than anything is that a highly qualified teacher in one school may not be a highly qualified one in another—even within the same state.

Fortunately, we have found some states that seem to be attempting to comply with the spirit of the law, erring on the side of caution and requiring more, not less, content knowledge in the upper elementary grades and middle school. Georgia provides perhaps the best example. In Georgia, teachers with early childhood certification (P–5) teaching in a departmentalized setting in grades 4 and 5 must have an endorsement in the subjects they teach in order to be considered highly qualified (Georgia Professional Standards Commission, 2003). Furthermore, Georgia mandates all middle school teachers, many of whom formerly had a "generalist" certificate, to earn an endorsement in each subject they teach in order to be highly qualified. The certification process is changing because of this. Several local administrators and teachers revealed that one of the benefits of this legislation is that it requires principals to look more closely at who is being hired and where they are placed and is helping to close some of the loopholes, like out-of-field teaching, that have plagued schools in the past.

However, facing new teacher shortages of late, the Georgia Professional Standards Commission voted 11 to 2 in February 2004 to adopt new certification rules that will soon allow candidates to get teaching certificates on the basis of solely passing the state's teacher tests and earning a college major in a field "closely related" to the subjects they want to teach. Under the new rules, candidates must pass Praxis basic skills, subject matter, and principles of teaching and learning tests. They must also already have a job offer from a district. Once in the classroom, having been granted a full five-year, nonrenewable license, the district must provide the teacher with a mentor. After five years, the teachers with this new certification will need a district recommendation for a renewable license. In essence, the state's standards board has lowered the bar for entering the profession, a bar that had been set higher in the previous year.

Using Teacher Evaluation to Measure Content Knowledge

The states have considerable discretion in developing and using a High Objective Uniform State System of Evaluation (HOUSSE) to determine a veteran teacher's content competency and highly qualified status. The HOUSSE standard must meet six criteria specified by the United States Department of Education in its nonregulatory guidance and can take into account, but not be based solely on, years of teaching experience. As such, the four states are in the process of employing some type of evaluation based on demonstration of competence through a combination of years of experience, college coursework, professional development, services to the profession, awards and publications, etc. In late fall 2003, state officials approved a model in which veteran teachers get a certain number of points for different types of professional activities. However, there is some significant variation in the ways that states are implementing these HOUSSE systems. For example, Georgia and Tennessee both allow for a maze of professional development and leadership activities in the content area to count toward the 100-point requirement in their HOUSSE systems. Georgia has a seven-year limit on activities that can count, while Tennessee has a ten-year limit. Alabama has no such limit.

The states give different weight to different professional activities as well. Whereas teachers in Tennessee can earn five points for each year of teaching in the content area, for a maximum of forty points, Alabama teachers can only earn two for a maximum of forty. Thus a Tennessee teacher can have only eight years' experience to earn forty points, while an Alabama teacher must have twenty years. Tennessee is also planning to add a content-specific piece to its teacher assessment system, the Framework for Evaluation and Professional Growth. The state will also allow teachers to volunteer their teacher effectiveness scores from the Tennessee Value Added Assessment System to prove their competence. During school visits in Tennessee, researchers found a seventh-grade math teacher whose students' value-added assessments indicate that she is consistently fostering significant academic growth each year. Yet, because she does not have a content area major, she is not considered highly qualified. Although the test scores are now part of the HOUSSE standard, the system is yet to be put in place. Hypothetically, the principal should have sent a letter home to parents letting them know that this accomplished teacher was not officially highly qualified.

Two of the states studied, North Carolina and Georgia, have done a great deal over the last several years to forge new joint teacher education-arts and sciences curriculum development at the college and university levels. These states have attempted to redefine the content that teachers need to meet the K–12 standards and determine what the entire university, not just the education school, needs to do. However, the states' HQT designations seem to ignore those efforts to create a new way of conceiving and measuring content knowledge.

At the same time, while each of these states has developed standardized teacher evaluation systems, the actual outcomes of these systems depend on technical design issues (e.g., methods, instrumentation, sources of evidence, and training and expertise of evaluators), as well as organizational ones (e.g., time, resources, and leadership). In our discussions, few teachers and administrators mentioned the utility of their respective teacher evaluation systems, especially around measuring content knowledge. Thus, it should not be surprising that, in a July 2003 report to Congress, the Government Accounting Office (GAO) recommended that "the Secretary of Education provide more information to states in order to evaluate subject area knowledge of current teachers" (U.S. General Accounting Office, 2003). Yet, even these imperfect district and state systems were preferred by school personnel to something developed at the federal level and applied uniformly to all schools across the country.

Indeed, initial findings from our case studies yielded a consistent message from the administrators and teachers we interviewed: The definition of and the current means to identify HQTs do not meet their needs. In particular, we heard that the federal government's approach to alternative routes into teaching will not begin to address their demand for truly effective teachers. We address this issue more fully next.

ALTERNATIVE ROUTES AND THE CAPACITY TO RECRUIT AND RETAIN "HIGHLY QUALIFIED" TEACHERS

As previously noted, nonregulatory guidance promulgated by the United States Department of Education allows individuals participating in an alternate route program, with just a few weeks of training, to be deemed highly qualified as long as these "teachers" are making satisfactory progress toward full certification as prescribed by the state. The initial federal guidance states that teachers in alternate routes must receive "high-quality professional development that is sustained, intensive and classroom focused," participate in a "program of intensive supervision that consists of structured guidance and regular ongoing support for teachers or a teacher mentoring program," and be the teacher of record for no longer than three years" (U.S. Department of Education, 2002, p. 12).

The federal emphasis on teacher learning after one begins teaching begs the question of the status of new teacher induction programs. Administrators in the districts we studied lamented the lack of qualified teachers available, the limited production of new teacher education graduates, and how, of late, they have been relying more and more on alternative route teachers. However, what we found was a striking lack of capacity to prepare and support teachers who had been entering the profession through alternative routes. Administrators and teachers reported the specific skills these teachers did not possess (e.g., classroom management, basic grading practices, knowledge of how to use student assessment data) as well as their own inability to induct the teachers effectively. Indeed, this latter finding turned our attention to the extent to which the four states had established new teacher induction programs.

Drawing upon the 1999–2000 School and Staffing Survey data, there was a wide range—between 43 to 75 percent—of new teachers that reported participating in some kind of new teacher induction program in the four states studied (see Table 7.3).

While these data are from 1999–2000, our tracking of induction policies in the region suggests that these trends have not changed much. Tennessee has a state board policy that requires an induction program for its beginning teachers and a long-standing requirement that beginning teachers will receive mentor support from *two* mentors, at least one of whom must be of a similar teaching assignment. However, since this mandate has never been funded, district compliance has varied greatly throughout the state. There is no statewide teacher induction program in Georgia, but the Professional Teaching Standards Commission is developing standards for induction programs and mentor certification in Georgia. The State Department of Education has developed a mentor teacher program for new teachers and has launched a mentor certification program (Teacher Support Specialist Certificate) with standardized training offered by the regional education service associations across the state, districts, and universities. Alabama does not have a formal induction program, either, but the University of Alabama, Birmingham, has de-

TABLE 7.3: New teacher* participation in induction programs.

State	Participation in induction program
Alabama	43.7%
Georgia	55.0
North Carolina	74.6
Tennessee	48.4
National	59.9

Source: Southeast Center for Teaching Quality, 2003

*Teachers with five years or less experience reporting

TABLE 7.4: New teachers and mentors: Access, subject-specific, helpful?

State	Worked closely with mentor	Mentor in same subject	Mentor helped to a great extent
Alabama	60%	84%	49%
Georgia	58	76	36
North Carolina	84	64	48
Tennessee	51	73	45
National	63	75	36

Source: Southeast Center for Teaching Quality, 2002

(New teachers of five years or less reporting, and only those who had participated in an induction program)

veloped for district use an induction and mentoring manual that offers guidance on the mentoring relationship, curriculum, and management and organization issues, as well as how to improve instruction and assessment through cognitive coaching. Also, the state's Title II Teacher Quality Enhancement grant has funded a series of induction pilots in which beginning teachers participate in training modules tied to the state's teacher evaluation instrument. The state, however, has no funds to further develop the pilots. North Carolina's performance-based licensure program requires that all Initially Licensed Teachers (ILTs) be assigned a trained mentor for the first two years. Selection of these mentors is a local decision, but mentors are required to have career status, be successful teachers, have a commitment to mentoring, and agree to twenty-four hours of mentor training, using one of the many training programs available in the state. The state also requires each local district to provide an orientation for new teachers and pay for three days of release time.

The federal guidance on alternative route programs suggests that new teachers can learn on the job with support from mentors. However, as Table 7.4 reveals, our states have yet to uniformly figure out how to ensure that novices actually have access to their mentors and that mentors teach the same subject as their novices. These data also suggest that current mentoring may not be all that helpful.

While North Carolina seems to fare better in terms of access, and Alabama helpfulness, one must remember that only 44 percent of Alabama's new teachers report that they participated in an induction program. No more than 49 percent of new teachers in our four states reported that their mentor helped them to a great extent. Without a mentoring structure in place, there is no way that schools and districts can begin to address the "quality" standard posed by United States Department of Education in their press for more alternative certification programs whereby the sole training new teachers receive will be in the context of the induction and mentoring programs. The loose state structures and inadequate or nonexistent new teacher induction funding have severely limited local administrators from creating the kinds of programs they need.

In fact, our school visits in several states revealed clearly that the mentoring function is virtually nonexistent for the teachers participating in alternative certification programs as part of their designation as "highly qualified." Some of the programs examined in the Southeast Center's initial analysis have no professional development or mentoring requirements at all. For example, the Alternative Type E license in Tennessee, which allows individuals to switch to a teaching career as long as they have either a subject major or a passing score on the appropriate Praxis II exam, does not require that these candidates participate either in intensive professional development or a mentoring program. None of the alternative routes in Alabama details any type of preservice professional development requirement or mentoring opportunity. State officials informed us that they rely on districts to provide mentoring support for new teachers, including those entering now through the alternative certification route, and have little means to monitor the quality of the district efforts. In one rural middle school we visited, 61 percent of the school's faculty reported entering the classroom on a "lateral entry" license, meaning that they had no preparation for teaching. This means the school has few experienced, prepared teachers needed to serve as mentors for the revolving door of new teachers who enter the school annually. Further, these "lateral entry" and other alternative route teachers are not seen as being highly qualified in minds of administrators and teachers.

Uniformly across the hundreds of educators we interviewed in the course of our case studies, teachers, principals, and superintendents repeatedly lamented the focus of the NCLB "highly qualified" teacher definition with its over-emphasis on content knowledge and its virtual neglect of the full range of attributes that define HQTs and effective teaching. We heard repeatedly and loudly that for teachers to be successful in the schools we visited (all under-performing in some ways), they needed to possess more than just content knowledge. As one human resources director from an Alabama school district noted:

> *I've been in this business for thirty-eight years, and to be honest I have never seen a teacher get into difficulty because they didn't have the content. It has always been they didn't have the mastery of teaching strategies, management and those kinds of skills that you hopefully learn in a teacher education program.*

Our interviewees generated extensive lists of the complex skills that teachers must possess to be successful in a real classroom setting. We heard consistently that teachers need to know how to communicate content-related concepts to a classroom full of diverse learners and that this was not easy to learn on the job. One teacher sized it up this way: "I know people that are brilliant when it comes to being able to perform certain math equations that I'll never be able to perform. But ask me if they know how to get that across to their kids in the classroom and they have not a clue."

We heard repeatedly that a truly highly qualified teacher is one who can reach students where they are, regardless of their level, and move them forward. Other HQT criteria mentioned by both administrators and teachers included knowledge of child development and how to use student assessment data to analyze, reflect upon, and revise instruction on a daily basis. Administrators informed us that new teacher education graduates are being better prepared than ever before, and, in fact, states like North Carolina and Georgia have taken a number of steps over the last decade to improve their teacher education programs. However, in a number of schools we visited, especially in the most isolated, rural areas, these new graduates are insufficient in number or unwilling to entertain offers of employment that would see them teaching in such schools.

While administrator opinions were mixed about the effectiveness of the alternatively prepared teachers in the schools we visited, the general conclusion was that the minimal preparation provided to most alternate route teachers leaves them totally unprepared for the classroom and demands they face from the students, much less highly qualified. A district administrator in Alabama declared:

> *9 out of 10 of people we have hired on alternative BAs are dismal fail-*
> *ures. We hired one person with a great science background, but he had*
> *not ever had the first education class. He had no clue. That was dis-*
> *astrous for those students, not to mention the wear and tear on all of*
> *us.*

A special education teacher who went through the Georgia Teacher Alternative Preparation Program told us:

> *I wouldn't consider myself highly qualified. On my first day, I really*
> *felt like I didn't know what I was doing. We went through a two-week*
> *training and were put in a classroom. Two weeks is not enough to pre-*
> *pare you. And thank God I did inclusion and wasn't thrown into a set-*
> *ting completely by myself, but some teachers were and I'm glad I wasn't*
> *one of them.*

When we heard positive comments about alternative route teachers, we found
that, for the most part, these teachers already had significant experience in
classroom settings as paraprofessionals or substitutes.

Indeed, in spite of the "new" Title I and II dollars for states and districts to
improve teacher quality, we found that the underperforming schools we visited uniformly did not have the capacity to recruit and retain teachers in high-
shortage areas. One rural superintendent told us:

> *There is an extreme shortage of math and science teachers. I'll use math*
> *as an example. This year we hired two math teachers, but they had just*
> *been released by another school system. I think they were both "highly*
> *qualified" (according to the letter of the law). In both cases they were*
> *virtually the only candidates. We hire and keep them for 2 to 3 years*
> *and then don't renew them. So we are passing around teachers who are*
> *not very competent.*

To be sure, very few teachers or principals were aware that their districts
had "new" federal money that could be used for teacher quality, and very few
district personnel knew that their states had funds to support a larger set of
strategies. However, what we found was that extreme state budget cuts from
the last several years (e.g., in 2003, the budget shortfalls were $2 billion in
North Carolina and $1.3 billion in Georgia) have forced states to use their
teacher quality dollars to supplement basic funding. Indeed, a recent report to
Congress by the General Accounting Office revealed that most states are planning to use Title II funds to continue already existing programs and activities

(U.S. General Accounting Office, 2003) and not implement more innovative ones that could include lower class sizes and student loads for teachers in hard-to-staff schools and the utilization of NBCTs in leading school improvement efforts and the like.

In our initial visits, we found that the technical assistance states are providing to districts varies widely both in quality and quantity, and, again, fiscal constraints make it difficult for many states to provide the necessary guidance to help districts think differently about the use of federal monies. Most state officials have been so focused on the AYP mandates and requirements that very little guidance has been offered to local officials. In fact, we found many principals and teachers in our case site schools that had heard very little of both the mandates and opportunities afforded by the NCLB "highly qualified" provisions. If they did, they saw little hope that these provisions would create more capacity to recruit and retain the teachers they need. While the law has potential to improve teacher quality, groups like the Education Trust (2003) have already noted that certain actions and inactions of the federal government are limiting the search for truly highly qualified teachers. We would argue that these actions and inactions also have grave implications for the progress that has been made in the creation of a true teaching profession in America.

THE SEARCH FOR HQTS AND THE TEACHING PROFESSION

While consensus is growing that teachers are the strongest determinant of student achievement, there is still not much more than ephemeral agreement on what teaching quality is and how every student might access a quality teacher. In large measure, much of the debate is ideological in nature and centers on whether or not teaching is a straightforward task that most reasonably smart individuals can do or a more sophisticated, complex one, requiring greater degrees of preparation, support, and professionalization (Cochran-Smith & Fries, 2001). Indeed, over the last several years, the political debate between those who are advocating deregulation of teaching (Fordham Foundation, 1999) and those who are pushing for greater teacher professionalism (Darling-Hammond, 1997) has escalated (Archer, 2002). As we have already noted, the rhetoric and actions of the United States Department of Education have clearly favored the former.

To be sure, teaching has long been noted as a *semiprofession* due to its ill-defined body of knowledge, truncated training, unenforced standards, and limited teacher autonomy (Etzioni, 1969), and many improvements in preparation, assessment, and compensation still need to be made in order for teaching to become more fully professionalized. While teaching is developing a body of knowledge, in part through the recent creation of the NBPTS, this knowledge base is still too limited, and the means for spreading it are ill-defined and ephemeral. Although the federal government has positioned itself to make a visible commitment to improving teacher quality, we have surfaced several issues that need to be addressed if NCLB will actually improve the profession.

First, in our case studies, we found that the current federal implementation strategy leaves school administrators scrambling to have teachers pass multiple-choice content tests that do little to probe a teacher's ability to teach the content to a diverse student population. Similarly, many teachers are required to take additional university-based content courses that may not address teaching strategies that have been shown to improve learning in schools with diverse student populations.

Despite the rhetoric from the United States Department of Education, the research literature, taken as a whole, sends strong signals to policymakers and practitioners that teachers need to know their content *and* how to teach. The demands of today's public schools clearly require all teachers to know a great deal about how humans learn and how to manage the complexity of the learning process (Bransford, Brown, & Cocking, 1999). Today, this means knowing how to manage classrooms, develop standards-based lessons, assess student work (and grade papers and tests fairly and appropriately), and work with growing numbers of special needs and second language learners (McDonnell & Hill, 1993; McLaughlin, 1995; Yasin, 2000).

For example, in the four states, we found educators that need more knowledge of and support in working with increasingly diverse (especially second language) learners. In North Carolina, over 46 percent of the state's teachers are estimated to be teaching students whose primary language is not English, but only 6 percent of the teachers have had a modest eight hours or more in "learning to teach" second language learners (see Table 7.5).

The federal government's focus on using limited paper-and-pencil tests to measure teacher knowledge will do little to spread the kind of knowledge needed to teach second language learners, as well as address other critical teacher knowledge areas such as literacy (American Federation of Teachers, 1999; Snow, Burns, & Griffin, 1998). The federal government is investing in

TABLE 7.5: Percent of teachers who taught Limited English Proficient students and percent with training, 1999–2000.

State	Taught	Trained*
Alabama	19.8%	2.4%
Georgia	35.2	6.2
North Carolina	46.6	5.5
Tennessee	22.3	1.4
U.S.	41.2	12.5

Source: Southeast Center for Teaching Quality, 2003

*Teachers teaching LEP students who had eight or more hours of training in the last three years on how to teach LEP students

the ABCTE examination, which, if adopted by states, promises to create a more unified approach to teacher testing across states. However, the focus of the ABCTE exam, much like the current tests in use, will again be on content knowledge and could actually limit the spread of the growing teacher knowledge base on how to work with our nation's most disadvantaged learners who are supposed to be focus of the law's intent.

Currently, only seven states nationwide assess teaching performance of any kind, and only four require a portfolio or other authentic measure of performance (Education Week, 2003a). Performance assessments, like the more expensive one used in Connecticut, can test for how well teachers apply knowledge and make appropriate decisions, as well as work with diverse learners in more authentic ways. North Carolina launched a similar new teacher assessment model in the late 1990s, but, due to its poor implementation (lack of training and mentors to support novices), it was quickly abandoned (Berry, Hopkins-Thompson, & Hoke, 2002). None of the other three states we studied had any plans to expand its teacher assessments; they were struggling financially and technically on how to just meet the letter of the NCLB law.

Second, the federal approach to calling a teacher highly qualified once he or she passes one of these rather singularly-minded exams or completes an alternative preparation program while already teaching students is worthy of

George Orwell's concept of "doublespeak" in *1984* where "highly qualified" actually means, at best, "minimally qualified." We have already seen from state to state widely reported percentages of teachers who are considered highly qualified. These numbers have surfaced in newspapers and are used in policy deliberations and public conversations about the quality of schools and teachers. We are concerned that educators and the range of stakeholders that need to know the real facts will not get them.

The lack of guidance from the federal government, and its bias against ensuring that teachers have sufficient teaching knowledge before they begin teaching, has allowed states to find all kinds of ways to game the system of identifying HQTs. In some cases, states are able to get away with not requiring a test of content (and content-specific pedagogy as measured by the Praxis), like in North Carolina. In other cases, like in Georgia, states are able to bypass any form of preparation whatsoever.

The heart of a profession is not just what a practitioner knows and how that knowledge is applied, but also in how the public can come to trust that the profession is actually enforcing the standards that it sets for itself. With varied definitions of what constitutes a "HQT" and loose use of the label itself, the policy makers, practitioners, and public are bound to be confused. Indeed, we have already found administrators baffled over how to explain to parents that a twenty-year award-winning NBCT who leads the school's reading program is not labeled "highly qualified," but a twenty-two-year-old Teach for America novice with no pedagogical knowledge at all is.

Part of the problem is definitional, but the fact is that the states, districts, and schools we are studying have very little capacity to collect and report on the kind of teacher quality data the policy makers, practitioners, and public need and deserve. In some states, like Alabama, teacher quality numbers are derived from the examination of individual academic transcripts which still cannot surface what teachers really need to know and do in order to truly be highly qualified. We found understaffed state agencies and school systems struggling to deal with the HQT mandates, often hindered by limited technological capacity to generate relevant numbers in timely way. None of the states had collected any useful data on high quality professional development, a major component of the law, primarily because states do not have the time or money or know how to do so. The federal government has placed very little, if any, emphasis on helping state and local agencies build their teacher quality data infrastructures that could yield valid and reliable data needed to identify HQTs and develop a stronger teacher profession.

The other part of the problem is political will. Too many stakeholders are not willing to argue for changes in teacher education and teacher testing that may require new dollars or a reallocation of the ones already in play. Politicians, looking for a short-term fix, are apt to go for the solutions that can fill a classroom with at least a warm body and use the right rhetoric to convince the public, by any means necessary, that the teachers who are in the classroom are highly qualified.

Finally, the hallmark of a profession also includes the provision that practitioners have developed a body of specialized knowledge and have accumulated and transmitted it through professional education, most importantly through clinical and mentored practice. Indeed, NCLB places a premium on teachers' learning through the support of induction programs and mentoring that novices receive from expert veterans. At the same time, "a distinguishing characteristic of a profession is that it clearly distinguishes between novices, who must be supervised, and full members of the profession" (Wise, Darling-Hammond, Berry, & Klein, 1987, p. 16.)

A recent analysis by Smith and Ingersoll (2003) revealed that if new teachers have "helpful mentors," the chance of their leaving teaching after their first year is greatly diminished. Common planning time and collaboration with other teachers are also strong predictors of novices staying in the school and the profession. New teachers need a great deal of support in understanding how to implement curriculum, teach and assess standards-based lessons, address specific student needs, and learn from expert peers who are teaching in their subject areas (Feiman-Nemser, 2003). However, in our school visits, we found very few new teachers who had access to such "high-end" learning opportunities (common planning time, access to helpful mentors, and so forth) in their induction programs. In fact, we found little focus on this important dimension of implementing the law and building a profession. Local administrators who we interviewed had neither the technical know-how nor the resources to put together the kinds of programs they needed. Some of the sites we visited were in isolated rural areas and thus had no nearby universities that could assist them in building stronger partnerships. Further, we found no funding mechanism or governing structure that could facilitate such school-university partnerships in building more robust new teacher induction and mentoring programs.

However, sound induction programs that raise retention rates will provide novices: (1) opportunities to observe and analyze good teaching in real situations; (2) guidance and assessment by highly trained, content-specific mentors; (3) reduced workloads to provide more learning time; and (4) assistance in meeting licensure standards through performance-based assessments. High-quality induction programs range from $2000 to $7000 per teacher per year, depending how well state and district funding and other professional development programs are aligned (Berry et al., 2002).[3]

A recent study found that, within the first three years of teaching, the attrition rate for new teachers who had participated in an induction program was only 15 percent, compared with 26 percent for teachers who had not received any induction support. The difference in the two figures represents thousands of teachers and millions of (wasted) dollars invested in teacher recruitment and preparation. A Texas study found that the state's annual 15.5 percent teacher turnover rate (40 percent for new teachers within their first three years) costs the state a minimum of $330 million per year (Berry et al., 2002). Data like these should get the attention of policy makers, and the NCLB "highly qualified" teacher provisions could be a catalyst for action. However, based upon our initial work in these four states, we found little, if any, evidence to suggest that the limited kind of teacher quality data being generated for NCLB will propel much positive political action to create and sustain high quality induction programs.

CONCLUDING REMARKS

We would suggest that, under the present conditions, NCLB will not be the impetus needed to improve the teaching profession. While the profession-building work of NCATE and NBPTS has been substantial of late, the law's provisions and the Department's implementation strategy appear to be undermining those efforts, and the result will not be the kinds of teachers needed in our hard-to-staff schools. In the four states of Alabama, Georgia, North Carolina, and Tennessee, recent state policies in the areas of teacher recruitment, education, and induction appear to be having a limited effect on the needs of schools that have the most difficult time recruiting and retaining teachers. From the perspective of educators we interviewed, the search for HQTs extends well beyond the federal definition, and the means to find them appears to be outside their grasp. The rhetoric surrounding the teacher quality debates falls on the deaf ears of teachers and administrators who struggle to meet the letter of the law—without adequate information, resources, and tools to ensure a caring, competent, and qualified teacher for each child.

NOTES

1. The National Board for Professional Teaching Standards is built upon five core propositions, including (1) Teachers are committed to students and their learning; (2) Teachers know the subjects they teach and how to teach those subjects to students; (3) Teachers are responsible for managing and monitoring student learning; (4) Teachers think systematically about their practice and learn from experience; (5) Teachers are members of learning communities.

2. While an agreement was finally reached with ETS to begin administering the Praxis II in January 2004, the state has asked for a waiver on the parental notification requirement related to highly qualified teachers (Meyer, 2003).

3. Connecticut's Beginning Educator Support and Training (BEST) program comes closest to fitting this bill. BEST has made the most progress in the nation in connecting assessment and support components through a well-institutionalized, performance-based licensing (PBL) system. There, the traditional "teaching observation" process has been supplemented with an ambitious subject-specific portfolio system framed by an elaborate support structure that includes content-specific seminars and highly trained mentors. These new teacher induction structures not only provide a means to better prepare new teachers on the job, but also a means to more precisely identify them as qualified teachers. We found no such mechanisms in our four states and no evidence that any of the available Title I and II funding could or would be used for such purposes. The lack of such support programs for novices was clearly one of several Achilles heels of the states' and districts' efforts to use alternative routes as a means to attracting and placing HQTs.

BIBLIOGRAPHY

Alabama State Board of Education. (2003, June 26). *The Alabama model for identifying highly qualified teachers*. Retrieved August 14, 2003, from ftp://ftp.alsde.edu/documents/66/SBE_Alabama_Model_for_Highly_Qualified_Teachers.pdf

American Board for Certification of Teacher Excellence. (2003). *Passport to teaching certification*. Retrieved August 6, 2003, from http://www.abcte.org/passport.html

American Federation of Teachers. (1999). *Teaching reading is rocket science: What expert teachers of reading should know and be able to do*. Washington, DC: AFT.

Amrein, A. L., & Berliner, D. C. (2002, March 28). High-stakes testing, uncertainty, and student learning. *Education Policy Analysis Archives, 10*(18). Retrieved December 1, 2002, from http://epaa.asu.edu/epaa/v10n18/

Archer, J. (2002, April 3). Research: Focusing in on teachers. *Education Week,* 36–39.

Berry, B., Buxton, J. B., Darling-Hammond, L., & Hirsch E. (2001). *Cross-state analysis of NCTAF partner state Status of Teaching Reports 1997–1999*. Chapel Hill, NC: Southeast Center for Teaching Quality.

Berry, B., Hoke, M., & Hirsch, E. (2003). Unpublished data, Southeast Center for Teaching Quality.

Berry, B., Hopkins-Thompson, P., & Hoke, M. (2002, December). *Assessing and supporting new teachers: Lessons from the Southeast.* Chapel Hill, NC: Southeast Center for Teaching Quality.

Bransford, J. D., Brown, A. L., & Cocking, R. R. (Eds.). 1999. *How people learn: Brain, mind, experience and school.* Washington, DC: National Academy Press.

Cochran-Smith, M., & Fries, M. K. (2001). Sticks, stones, and ideology: The discourse of reform in teacher education. *Educational Researcher, 30*(8), 3–15.

Darling-Hammond, L. (1997). *Doing what matters most: Investing in quality teaching.* New York: National Commission on Teaching and America's Future.

Darling-Hammond, L. (2000). Teacher quality and student achievement: A review of state policy evidence. *Education Policy Analysis Archives, 8*(1). Retrieved October 15, 2002, from http://epaa.asu.edu/epaa/v8n1

Darling-Hammond, L., & Sykes, G. (Eds.). (1999). *The Heart of the matter: Teaching as a learning profession.* San Francisco: Jossey-Bass.

Darling-Hammond, L., & Sykes., G. (2003). Wanted: A national teacher supply policy for education, The right way to meet the "Highly Qualified Teacher" challenge? *Education Policy Analysis Archives, 11*(33). Retrieved September 20, 2003, from http://epaa.asu.edu/epaa/v11n33

Darling-Hammond, L., & Youngs, P. (2002). Defining "highly qualified teachers:" What does "scientifically-based research" tell us? *Education Researcher, 31*(9), 13–25.

Educational Testing Service. (2003). *State requirements.* Retrieved December 22, 2003, from http://www.ets.org/praxis/prxstate.html

Education Trust. (2003). *In need of improvement. Ten ways the U.S. Department of Education has failed to live up to its teacher quality commitments.* Washington, DC: Author.

Education Week. (2003). *Quality counts 2003: If I can't learn from you.* Washington, DC: Author.

Education Week. (2003a, October 29). *Tracking teacher quality.* Retrieved December 22, 2003, from http://www.edweek.org/ew/ewstory.cfm?slug=09Qualified -b1.h23

Esch, C., & Shields, P. (2002). *Who is teaching California's children?* Santa Cruz, CA: The Center for the Future of Teaching and Learning.

Etzioni, A. (1969). *The semi-professions and their organization: Teachers, nurses, social workers.* New York, London: The Free Press.

Feiman-Nemser, S. (2003). What new teachers need to learn. *Educational Leadership, 60*(8), 25–29.

Ferguson, R. F. (1991, Summer). Paying for public education: New evidence on how and why money matters. *Harvard Journal on Legislation, 28*(2), 465–498.

Fordham Foundation. (1999). *The Teachers we want and how to get more of them: A manifesto.* Washington, DC: Author.

Galley, M. (2003). Alternative accrediting body gets recognition. *Education Week,* October 8.

Georgia Professional Standards Commission. (2003, September). *Draft Georgia implementation guidelines: Criteria for highly qualified teachers.* Retrieved December 22, 2003, from http://www.gapsc.com/nclb/Admin/Files/ImpPolicy.pdf

Goldhaber, D., & Anthony, E. (2004). *Can teacher quality be effectively assessed?* Seattle: Center for Reinventing Education. Retrieved April 27, 2004, from http://www.crpe.org/workingpapers/pdf/NBPTSquality_report.pdf

Goldhaber, D. D., & Brewer, D. (1996). Evaluating the effect of teacher degree level on educational performance. In W. J. Fowler (Ed.), *Developments in school finance, 1996* (pp. 197–210). Washington, DC: The Thomas B. Fordham Foundation.

Goldrick, L. (2002). *Improving teacher evaluation to improve teaching quality.* Washington, DC: National Governors Association, Center for Best Practices.

Hanushek, E. A. (1992). The trade-off between child quantity and quality. *Journal of Political Economy, 100*(1): 84–117.

Hanushek, E. A. (1996). *School resources and achievement in Maryland.* Baltimore: Maryland State Department of Education.

Hanushek, E. A., Kain, J. F., & Rivkin, S. J. (1998). Teachers, schools, and academic achievement. National Bureau of Economic Research Working Paper 6691.

Haycock, K. (1998). Good teaching matters: How well-qualified teachers can close the gap. *The Education Trust, Thinking K-16, 3*(2), 1–14.

Henry, G. T., & Opfer, D. (2004). *Responses to high stakes accountability in the South: Final report to the Spencer Foundation.* Atlanta: Andrew Young School of Policy Studies, Georgia State University.

King Rice, J. (2003). *Teacher quality: Understanding the effectiveness of teacher attributes.* Washington, DC: Economic Policy Institute.

McDonnell, L. M., & Hill, P. T. (1993). *Newcomers in American schools: Meeting the educational needs of immigrant youth.* Santa Monica, CA: RAND.

McLaughlin, B. (1995). *Fostering second language development in young children: Principles and practices.* Washington, DC: National Center for Research on Cultural Diversity and Second Language Learning.

Meyer, L. (2002, January 10). The State of States. Retrieved August 14, 2003, from http://counts.edweek.org

Mitchell, K. J., Robinson, D. Z., Plake, B. S., & Knowles, K. T. (Eds.). (2001). *Testing teacher candidates: The role of licensure tests in improving teacher quality.* Washington, DC: National Academy Press.

National Commission on Excellence in Education. (1983). *A nation at risk: The imperative for educational reform.* Washington, DC: U.S. Government Printing Office.

National Commission on Teaching and America's Future. (1996). *What matters most: Teaching for America's Future.* Washington, DC: U.S. Government Printing Office.

National Council of Examiners for Engineering and Surveying. (2004). *What are the fees and deadlines for examinations in South Carolina?* Retrieved March 9, 2004, from http://www.ncees.org/exams/fundamentals/

National Research Council. (1998). *Preventing reading difficulties in young children.* Washington, DC: NRC.

North Carolina Department of Public Instruction. (2003, November 25). *Baseline information on federal teacher quality measures completed.* Retrieved December 22, 2003, from http://www.ncpublicschools.org/news/03-04/112503.html

North Carolina State Board of Education. (2003, February 6). *Changes in licensure policies to comply with NCLB.* Retrieved August 14, 2003, from http://www.ncpublicschools.org/SBE_meetings/0302/0302_QP.pdf

North Carolina State Board of Education. (2004, January 6). *Report and recommendations from the Special Committee on Teacher Reciprocity.* Retrieved March 9, 2004, from http://www.ncpublicschools.org/SBE_meetings/0401/0401_QP.pdf

Olsen, L. (2003). In ESEA wake, school data flowing forth. *Education Week, 23*(15), 1, 16–18.

Podgursky, M. (2001). Should states subsidize national certification? *Education Week, 20*(30), 38, 40–41.

Sanders, W. L., & Rivers, J. C. (1996). *Cumulative and residual effects of teachers on future academic achievement.* Knoxville: University of Tennessee Value-Added Research and Assessment Center.

Smith, T. M., & Ingersoll, R. M. (2003). Reducing teacher turnover: Do induction and mentoring programs help? Paper presented at the annual meeting of the American Association of Educational Research. Chicago, IL, April 21–25.

Snow, C., Burns, S., & Griffin, P. (Eds.). (1998). Preventing reading difficulties in young children. Washington, DC: National Academy Press.

Sykes, G., & Millman, J. (1995). The assessment of teaching based on evidence of student learning. In S. Bacharach and B. Mundell (Eds.), *Images of schools: Structures and roles in organizational behavior.* Thousand Oaks, CA: Corwin Press.

Tennessee State Board of Education. (2003, August). *Tennessee plan for implementing the teacher and paraprofessional quality provisions of the No Child Left Behind Act Of 2001.* Retrieved December 22, 2003, from http://www.state.tn.us/education/fpnclbtchqltyimplplan.pdf

United States Department of Education. (2002). *Improving teacher quality state grants: Title II, Part A non-regulatory guidance.* Washington, DC: U.S. Department of Education.

United States Department of Education. (2003). *Meeting the highly qualified teachers challenge: The secretary's second annual report on teacher quality.* Washington, DC: U.S. Department of Education, Office of Postsecondary Education.

United States General Accounting Office. (2003). *No Child Left Behind Act: More information would help states determine which teachers are highly qualified* (No. GAO-03-631). Washington, DC: USGAO.

Wilson. S., Floden, B., & Ferrini-Mundy, J. (2001). *Teacher preparation research: Current knowledge, gaps, and recommendations.* Seattle: Center for Teaching Policy, University of Washington.

Wise, A. E., Darling-Hammond, L., Berry B., & Klein, S. (1987). *Licensing teachers: Design for a teaching profession.* Santa Monica, CA: RAND Corporation.

Yasin, S. (2000). More attention to language diversity needed in teacher preparation. *American Association of Colleges for Teacher Education Briefs, 21*(11), 1.

What's Next?
Challenges and Opportunities Facing
Teachers and the Teaching Profession

David M. Moss and Wendy J. Glenn

We find ourselves once again at a critical juncture in education. Our profession is characterized by a continuous series of these pivotal moments in which much hangs in the balance with regard to the education of our children. Long periods of stability seem elusive, as new challenges compound old ones, and the complexity of America's classrooms deepens with each passing decade. During these first few years of the new millennium, we find ourselves navigating a world dominated by concerns regarding national security. As a nation, we appear still to be merely reacting to ongoing events rather than proactively positioning ourselves to deal with the substantial issues underpinning our current reality. How well will we be prepared to deal effectively with the emotional, financial, and logistical responsibilities of what is to come? The question concerning the role and value of education in society has never been more pressing.

The questions facing our society are certainly complex, whether they deal with our economy, environment, social policies, or national security. To view these as unrelated is to ignore the multifaceted whole in favor of the individual parts. In an era dominated by six-second news clips and rapid-fire images, in conjunction with what seems at times an overwhelming volume of issues, it certainly is tempting to boil down the many challenges we face into palatable, uncomplicated segments. Yet, we must avoid the temptation to oversimplify. Issues are inherently complicated, and to problematize them is to embrace their complexity and recognize that we must deal with them at a core level and over the long term. Our youngest citizens cannot afford to be a passive generation influenced by weak arguments designed to obfuscate the specifics and make them afraid of change. Ready or not, this next generation will be comprised of the first truly global citizens living in a world in which notions of interconnectedness and diversity must replace those of segregation and homogeneity. Equality and social justice must be paramount in the minds of our future citizens and policy makers.

This transition to a more holistic and equitable perspective will not be an easy one. Our public schools must play *the* pivotal role if we are to succeed in progressing out of an age of fear and stagnation. Teachers will be the agents of change. Although at first blush this may seem a tremendous burden to place on individuals working in the profession, as we have argued throughout this book, teaching is a normative endeavor, and value-laden decisions are commonplace. Given their experience in making these complicated decisions, teachers are prepared for the challenge.

The road will be neither easy nor linear, and there is no single path that takes us to our desired destination. As we bring closure to this book, we have asked our contributors to build upon their earlier writings by addressing the following two questions:

> What forces will shape the teaching profession over the next decade?
>
> What qualities will teachers need to possess to meet the demands of the profession in the twenty-first century?

Their responses are as eclectic as the experiences of the individuals themselves. Together they form what we believe to be a most appropriate conclusion to this book, providing both a summative dimension, as well offering an insightful, and sometimes provocative, perspective on the future of our profession.

WHAT FORCES WILL SHAPE THE TEACHING PROFESSION OVER THE NEXT DECADE?

I have been a part of the teaching profession for the past three decades. During these years, I have witnessed myriad reforms, and reformers come and go. The one constant in all these years is the dedication of teachers and their commitment to children. As I look ahead to the next decade, one force that I feel will impact the profession is the retirement of the Baby Boomer generation, of which I am included. There will be a need to recruit and keep qualified teachers to fill this great void while maintaining high standards for teacher certification. Our children deserve nothing less.

Another force on the profession will be state and federal mandates that overemphasize assessment. I am yet to be convinced that a student is educated just because she can pass a test. Isn't it equally important for students to develop creatively, emotionally, and socially? Testing is becoming the sole measure of a student's worth. I struggle to find a workable balance, and so will the teachers of the next decade.

Shirley Reilly

Politics will make the biggest impact on the teaching profession over the next decade. If the forces that wish to deregulate entry into teaching prevail, preservice preparation will be severely impacted. Programs that clearly produce better teachers will prosper only if they can prove their efficacy to the populations they serve. At the same time, the overall quality of teaching will decline because of the entry of individuals who should not be teaching and who are ill-prepared for the task. Teacher retention will become a greater problem.

If the No Child Left Behind legislation, and the testing mania that accompanies, it continue unabated, then the limitation of teachers' autonomy over both curriculum and pedagogy will drive some of the very best teachers from the profession. This, too, will lessen the quality of teaching in the United States and have a negative impact on teacher retention.

Michael Andrew

If you were to talk to anyone who is successful in life, I would guarantee that he/she would report that a great teacher has in some way influenced him/her. Whether it was the result of simply spending a little extra time listening after class or serving as a mentor over an extended period, a common catalyst for success is the teacher. However, today there is little incentive to become a teacher or, for those who are already teaching, to remain a teacher. Teachers today are underpaid, overworked, and rarely supported by those outside the educational field. It seems little is understood about the profession.

The way teachers are viewed and treated in this society must evolve in order for our educational system to serve a global society.

Chris Burdman

Tomorrow's classrooms will be markedly different for two fundamental reasons. First, more of the students who attend school will come from diverse backgrounds in which English may not be the primary language spoken in the home. Schools have always been places of socialization into the American culture, but tomorrow's schools—urban, suburban, and rural—will be challenged to meet the social *and* academic needs of these students and to resolve the tensions among these diverse cultures.

Second, access to information will continue to explode. Schools may seek ways to control access, but they will fail. The reality of tomorrow is that communication with others and access to information will be at the fingertips of students. This access will create tensions between the learner and the school. The school must respond, adapt, and enable students to become critical consumers and knowledge builders.

Allen Glenn

In the near future, we will move out from under standardized testing's shadow. The general public will begin to realize what classroom teachers have long suspected—for all the information standardized tests provide, the data are not very useful in making instructional decisions. Once people recognize that testing is an industry in which textbook publishers and test developers are one and the same, the "accountability" agenda will be exposed as a political movement that was never genuinely concerned about providing educational opportunities for all students.

John Settlage

School finance issues will affect all aspects of public education, most particularly, the profession of teaching. This issue is much broader than improving teachers' salaries, upgrading their working conditions, and providing sufficient resources for effective instruction, although certainly, the causal link between adequate resources and effective teaching needs to be asserted in public policy. For effective instruction, like effective work of any kind, money matters. But beyond simply increasing public funding for education, what is needed is a change in the American ethic about public support for public services. Our contemporary national culture promotes mistrust between citizens and their publicly funded agencies, and our political leaders uphold tax resistance as a civic right. Teachers' work will be valued work only when American citizens recognize that their support of public education is a responsibility and privilege of citizenship. Adequate and equitable school financing is a collective investment in the future that empowers teachers' work, improves the profession, and ensures an American democracy.

Kate Rousmaniere

For the first time in my thirty plus years as a teacher educator, I am witnessing teacher education programs taking student performance assessment seriously and building databases that can be used for systematic study. In the next five years, we will also begin to see results from the longitudinal research that is currently being funded. One example is evidenced by the Teachers for a New Era grants funded by the Carnegie Corporation and the Ford and Annenberg Foundations that encourage eleven major universities to conduct longitudinal, systematic follow-up of graduates and their influence on student achievement. Teacher preparation programs that maintain high placement and retention rates in the profession and can show how graduates affect student learning will thrive. On the flip side, I see a bleak future for college- and university-based programs that cannot distinguish themselves from alternative, quick-fix programs that have grown exponentially in the last decade.

Richard Schwab

Governmental policy will no doubt contribute to shaping the teaching profession over the next decade. I don't think it is possible to be in a public school right now without feeling some impact from No Child Left Behind, highlighting the frightening swiftness with which top-down policy making permeates an entire country. Policy that continues to rely primarily upon a standardized test as the determining factor of student achievement will undermine the sense of professionalism toward which we are diligently working. I hope that in the next decade, we will acknowledge our educational missteps and reverse our direction. Our educational system needs to be responsive to each child and not merely some limited measure of the whole. Meeting each student's learning needs should be left to each individual teacher. We must embrace project-based learning and authentic assessments, such as portfolios, as our primary means of serving a diverse population.

Sayward Parsons

Fear will continue to play a central role in teaching—with fear about students' future competitiveness in the global economy continuing to provide support for oppressive and profoundly ill-advised accountability policies. These fears will continue trickling down through the education system. Politicians and CEOs worried about profits and the status of the United States will continue to pressure school systems, and educators afraid of threatened sanctions will continue pressuring students and parents. The profound materialism of American culture will empower these fears. Meanwhile, growing dissatisfaction with test-driven, high-stakes accountability systems will lead to the slow erosion of such systems, but will leave the nation deeply divided about educational goals, content, methods, assessment, and accountability. Caught between profoundly divergent views of education and reform, educators, students, and parents will be extraordinarily frustrated and confused. However, this environment may create "teachable moments" in which the public is open to learning more about meaningful, effective education.

Karl Wheatley

Over the next decade, the teaching profession will be shaped by whether or not school reform and teaching policies will focus primarily on prescriptive, narrow school curriculum delivered by an underprepared, inexpensive, cadre of "alternative route" teachers who have limited teaching knowledge OR on more ambitious school curriculum developed and led by well-prepared, well-paid, and well-supported teachers who know a great deal about content, teaching, the specific students they teach, and new technologies that can revolutionize teaching and learning. Movement down one path or the other will depend on how well the teaching profession itself can communicate to the larger public the choices we face in our public education system and our larger democratic society as well as the kinds of schools and teachers each one of our students deserves. Public opinion polls have revealed that most Americans want highly prepared teachers for all children, but the public is largely uninformed about the policies being promoted that undermine the development of a true profession in this country.

Barnett Berry

The accountability movement will continue to be a dominant force in shaping the profession. The obsession with high-stakes standardized testing will continue to distract teachers, administrators, and students from more meaningful, productive educational endeavors. As has been the case with so many fads that have played out in education, it will eventually be recognized that high-stakes standardized testing has been ineffective in promoting effective educational reform. Hopefully, the advances in learning and assessment theory will lead to more authentic forms of instruction and assessment. These authentic strategies will be based on the recognition that skilled teachers, working in concert with students, administrators, and parents, can provide the most productive learning environments and reliable and valid assessments of student performance.

Rob Lonning

The testing movement as a way to improve education. The population found in American public schools will continue to become more culturally and linguistically diverse. As such, the current testing movement is destined to fail, as it does not respond to these factors and hinders the differentiation of curriculum and instruction.

Kay Norlunder-Case

Multiple forces will shape our profession, so any list I give here will be incomplete, but I offer a few. On the negative side, federal educational initiatives that result in the standardization and sterilization of school curricula may weaken our public schools. These initiatives are not only dangerous because they contain unfunded mandates; the mandates themselves will result in a radical dumbing-down of curricula. The criteria used to measure success are severely limited, preventing educators from recognizing both the untapped *potential* of students and the wider range of essential skills and talents for which wide-scale test formats cannot account. Another potentially negative force is the increasing willingness of states to embrace alternative route certification programs that offer insufficient teacher preparation. This is akin to allowing doctors to seek a quick route to their certification because politicians perceive that there are "high-need" medical areas.

On the positive side, I think that the political pendulum may be swinging back. People who do not understand the complexities of education have held the bully pulpit for a long time; they have done their best to devalue the work of teachers and deprofessionalize their jobs. Teachers, and even members of state legislatures, are beginning to respond. I sense that we are at the dawn of a new grassroots movement in which teachers will demand the resources, autonomy, and respect that will help them to make real school change.

Doug Kaufman

WHAT QUALITIES WILL TEACHERS NEED TO POSSESS TO MEET THE DEMANDS OF THE PROFESSION IN THE TWENTY-FIRST CENTURY?

Immigration is now a defining characteristic of our nation, and the implications for schools are profound. Mainstream Americans may only recognize this by changes in the complexion of those in entry-level positions. Schools, however, are already facing a student population that speaks a variety of languages; has suffered the terrors of political persecution, civil unrest, and involuntary displacement; and have cultural traditions that may not be as readily discarded as was true for immigrants in previous generations. Teachers will need to teach an increasingly diverse population of students, administrators will need to become skilled as cross-cultural negotiators, and many colleges will need to dramatically revise the ways in which they prepare and support classroom teachers.

John Settlage

Teachers must be better prepared academically, have the disposition to care for each and every child, and work to help all children develop to their fullest potential. Teachers for the twenty-first century must also be prepared to work collaboratively and take active leadership roles in improving schooling at the local level. They must also seek a unified voice in shaping educational policy at the state and national levels.

If the majority of teachers in the twenty-first century does not rise to this challenge, then it is better that new teachers be obedient servants of the state and be satisfied with jobs as technicians. Those who are filled with the desire to serve children, improve schools, and improve our democracy should seek other lines of work.

Michael Andrew

America needs teachers that are prepared to teach all students in their classrooms the knowledge, skills, and democratic values essential to be effective citizens. That's not going to change. We need teachers who have an understanding of the academic content and what it means to have students learn this content. We need teachers who want to spend their days working with children and young adults and who find personal satisfaction in doing so. We need teachers who can thrive in an educational system that is constantly buffeted by political and social forces. We need teachers who understand that, no matter what the rhetoric, they will never have the same social and economic status of some other professions and can live with that reality.

Teachers of the twenty-first century, however, must also be comfortable with emerging technologies and sharing power with students and other educational providers. Emerging technologies will impact *what* they teach and *how* they teach; therefore, teachers of the twenty-first century need to be agile and fearless as they negotiate the path to the future.

Allen Glenn

Teachers will need the same qualities that have made them successful throughout history. First, they will need a moral compass that drives the decisions they make in classrooms and life in general. Second, they will need an undying sense of enthusiasm for the profession and a desire to help all students succeed. Third, they will need to understand the subjects they teach as well as the best ways to assist students in mastering that subject. Fourth, they will need to know how to utilize various forms of assessment to inform their teaching. Finally, they will need to understand how to use all the tools at their disposal to help enhance the student learning experience. These tools include a wide range of emerging technologies that holds great promise for enhancing student achievement.

Richard Schwab

One of the major problems in education, especially at the secondary level, has been the overemphasis on subject area content at the expense of student understanding. Secondary teachers tend to see themselves as teachers of disciplines (science, mathematics, social studies) rather than teachers of students. This overemphasis on content has created a system in which students are rewarded for memorizing and regurgitating facts rather than developing meaningful understanding. Over time, as disciplinary knowledge has grown, the problem has become worse as teachers have felt obligated to cover more and more content. Overcoming this culture of coverage will require teachers with the courage and stamina to challenge the "teaching as content coverage" paradigm. In addition, teachers will need strong collaborative skills to mount an effective grassroots campaign if we are to overcome the culture of coverage and begin to teach for student understanding.

Rob Lonning

The two main qualities that teachers will need to possess are passion for their profession and compassion for their students. These are the qualities I try to model for the next generation of teachers. They can't learn this from a textbook. Nothing in the world is better than making a child smile, gain confidence, and grow intellectually. For some of our students, school is the happiest, healthiest, and safest part of their day. We must never take that away from them.

Teachers will also need to become even more technologically literate. The students they will teach have never known a world without computers. They will be forced to motivate students who have grown up on sound bytes, Game Boys, and Play Stations. This will not be an easy task.

Teachers in the twenty-first century must also be leaders, collaborators, and facilitators. They will be members of a professional learning community and, as such, will need to possess the skills of diplomacy and initiation. They must also prepare students for life in a global society by living and teaching global awareness and cultural diversity.

Shirley Reilly

Organization, flexibility, and management! Certainly teachers need content knowledge and pedagogy, but, without the skills necessary to respond to a dynamic classroom environment, teaching will be an impossible task. Teaching in a challenging setting, I have found that the clear difference between successful teachers and those who go home frustrated and emotionally beaten down is how one is able to manage the classroom climate and respond to a fluid series of challenges. Due to the high number of students in my school, confrontations among students are commonplace and often lead to physical altercations. This poses a significant challenge when you are attempting to implement a hands-on, activities-centered curriculum consistent with best practices. One of the most difficult aspects of a new teacher's first year of teaching is establishing a style of leadership within the classroom. Learn to be strict but fair, calm and always in control, as difficult decisions are made from moment to moment.

Chris Burdman

Obviously, as our nation becomes more pluralistic, one quality that teachers will need to have is a broader and deeper understanding of the children who populate their classrooms. They must know and respect them as individuals, but must also understand the societal and cultural practices and values that shape their students' lives. Teachers as a group must also understand acutely that their profession is inherently political. It is no longer enough to simply say that a teacher's job is to teach children, because too many forces outside the classroom influence a teacher's ability to do that well. Part of the job of teaching has to be seen as advocating for professional rights and the ability to use personal expertise to shape educational agendas. Fighting to professionalize the profession may seem removed from actual classroom teaching, but the two are intimately connected.

In this century, the rapid growth of new technologies, new discoveries, ever-evolving lexica, and the easy accessibility of massive amounts of information make it virtually impossible for school curricula, textbooks, and courses to focus on the learning of "subject matter" as their primary aim. Instead, educators must focus even more on the processes of learning—on "learning how to learn." Only by helping students develop the outlooks and complex sets of skills that allow them to seek out, find, and use new information successfully will we be achieving our broader mission.

Doug Kaufman

The willingness to work collaboratively will be the essential quality a teacher will need to possess in the twenty-first century. I am lucky to work in an extremely collaborative department and, even more specifically, with a close-knit team of early career teachers. I realize that my experiences over the last two years do not necessarily reflect the experiences of all teachers, but I feel strongly that we, as members of the profession, support the concept of a learning community as a precursor to success.

Meeting the needs of a diverse learning population will also demand an increased amount of time and consideration. Teachers are expected to serve an enormous range of student abilities and needs; therefore, flexibility and creativity will be two important qualities for teachers to have. I also feel a rich background in a teacher's subject area is extremely important. The more comfortable a teacher is with her subject, the more she will be able to devote time and energy to thriving in the dynamic environment of a classroom.

Sayward Parsons

Teachers need to be ready, willing, and able to engage in civil disobedience, to end the well-intentioned, but staggeringly misguided, accountability movements that have grown into No Child Left Behind. This will require courage, as in saying to one's principal, "No, I've talked with my colleagues, and none of us will administer the state proficiency tests this year. The tests, and the way they are used, are simply educational malpractice." Perhaps mass teacher walkouts will be needed, which will require teachers to possess a strong belief in their political efficacy. Imagine a nationwide walkout by all teachers who believe that current accountability efforts have harmed education, children, and families. Stalling the nation's economy for days or weeks would be a small price to pay if it raised public understanding that education is undermined, not improved, by enormous dependence on standardized tests and punitive approaches to motivating students and educators. Teachers will need a passion for continuing to learn about all aspects of education, and this learning will leave them equipped with powerful reasons for their strong opposition to regressive and oppressive education policies.

Karl Wheatley

Teachers of the twenty-first century will have to become better educated and prepared to teach new content, as the knowledge bases in the disciplines expand astronomically. But equally so, teachers will have to develop a wider repertoire of pedagogical or teaching skills. In particular, all teachers will need to know more about what cognitive scientists are learning about how humans learn. All teachers will have to know a great deal more about learning disabilities and differences and second language learners and how to make curricular accommodations in their classrooms. They will also have to know more about formative assessment. New research is showing that the teacher qualities that may make the most difference for student achievement are whether or not teachers can design standards-based classroom assessments; grade student work in far more reliable, valid, and consistent ways; detect student learning differences; and adapt their lessons. They must be able to use new technologies to assemble and analyze student data and enable students to manage their own learning. And they must do all of this with their colleagues and, therefore, must learn new teacher leadership skills. Finally, given the many ill-informed education policies that continue to be enacted, teachers of tomorrow must have the knowledge and skills to communicate what they know about teaching and learning to policy makers and the public alike.

Barnett Berry

Tolerance for and understanding of individual difference. Fifty years have passed since the landmark *Brown* case. Yet, we have many miles left to travel before we come to a place of parity and equity in our public schools. Before this can happen, it is essential that teachers, as part of the larger community, be both tolerant and knowledgeable of individual difference in their students, their backgrounds, and their learning characteristics.

We have yet to fulfill Dewey's philosophy and practice of education in a democratic society. Teachers in the twenty-first century must clearly understand that it is their moral obligation to prepare their students to be citizens in a social and political democracy. And further, as professional educators, teachers must be able to act as leaders, researchers, and caring individuals.

Kay Norlander-Case

Teachers need to become educational activists. They need to become public advocates for education by describing the complexity and importance of their work. They need to develop communication skills so as to explain to the public that teaching is not simply classroom instruction in academic skills but also the social and civic education of America's youth, and they need to develop strategies of engaging the public and ensuring public support. Accordingly, teachers need to develop the skills and temperament of civic watchdogs, constantly monitoring and fighting for the protection and improvement of public education. They need to develop practices of civic engagement, economic consciousness, and political acuity, both inside and outside of the classroom. Such skills should be taught in teacher education institutions and supported by educational agencies for whom such advocacy will further the professional stature of education.

Kate Rousmaniere

EPILOGUE

Teaching our children is a shared responsibility. The portrait of the profession captured in this book demonstrates clearly that there is much work to be done by each and every one of us. Whether you are considering teaching as your career, have children who attend school, are a voting taxpayer, work as a teacher, directly influence policy, work as a leader in business, or perhaps some combination of these roles, we hope this book serves as an urgent call to action. Teaching remains a semi-profession, and too long have we all suffered from the neglect of this most fundamental privilege of an open and free society. To be sure, there are many aspects of our educational system that are outstanding, yet, with each passing decade, our challenges mount, and the likelihood of achieving our full potential as a global community characterized by peace, equality, justice, and prosperity for each and every person becomes more elusive.

We are at an exciting moment in human history. There is much promise for the future. Things unimagined a mere generation ago have become commonplace—both magnificent and terrible. How will our sons and daughters view these early years of the twenty-first century? Will we have squandered our opportunities, or perhaps taken strides toward meaningful and lasting change? What role will you play?

Index

About the Contributors

Michael D. Andrew received his B.S. in science from Cornell University and both an M.A.T. and Ed.D. from Harvard University. Dr. Andrew has spent forty years working to prepare better teachers. He is Director of Teacher Education at the University of New Hampshire where he initiated, in 1973–1974, the first integrated, five-year teacher education program at a state university. Outside of his university life, Dr. Andrew works as a blacksmith and raises purebred Hampshire sheep and standard bred horses on his farm in Gorham, Maine.

Barnett Berry is the founder and president of the Southeast Center for Teaching Quality, Inc., an organization dedicated to shaping policies through teacher leadership, building coalitions, and conducting research. Dr. Berry's career includes teaching in an urban high school, working as a social scientist at the RAND Corporation, serving as a senior executive with the South Carolina State Department of Education, and directing an education policy center while he was a professor at the University of South Carolina. Dr. Berry played a major role in developing the blue ribbon report of the National Commission on Teaching and America's Future and then later leading its state policy and partnership efforts. He is author of over eighty journal articles, book chapters, and commissioned reports on school reform, accountability, and the teaching profession.

Christopher Burdman holds a master's degree in elementary education from the University of Connecticut's Neag School of Education. He went to teach for the Boston Public Schools following the completion of his teacher preparation program several years ago and currently serves as the sixth-grade cluster leader as well as a sixth-grade science teacher at the Mildred Avenue Middle School in Mattapan, Massachusetts. Chris is involved with many professional programs, including the Boston Public Schools Science Initiative supported by a grant from the National Science Foundation Urban Systemic Program and the Watershed Integrated Science Partnership (WISP) between the University of Massachusetts and science teachers from Boston and surrounding areas.

Charles W. Case is a retired professor of educational leadership and former dean of the Neag School of Education at the University of Connecticut. Dr. Case was instrumental in the creation and implementation of the innovative bachelor's/master's program at UConn and continues to advocate for equity and diversity in urban school settings.

Allen D. Glenn is a professor of curriculum and instruction and dean emeritus of the College of Education at the University of Washington, Seattle. His areas of expertise include educational technology, teacher education, and social studies education. He has coauthored six textbooks, published a wide-range of monographs and journal articles, and served as a consultant author to an elementary school social studies series. Dr. Glenn was a recipient of the American Association of Colleges for Teacher Education (AACTE) Edward L. Pomeroy Award for Outstanding Contributions to Teacher Education in February 1996 and served as AACTE president from 1997–1998.

Wendy J. Glenn is an assistant professor in curriculum and instruction in the Neag School of Education at the University of Connecticut. Dr. Glenn specializes in the preparation of secondary school English teachers. She began her career as a junior and senior high school English/Language Arts educator in the Mesa Public Schools system in Mesa, Arizona. She writes extensively on issues of adolescent literature and censorship in schools. Her work has been published in *English Journal* and *Thinking Classroom/Peremena*. She is also completing a critical biography on author Sarah Dessen as a volume in the Scarecrow Studies in Young Adult Literature series.

Eric Hirsch is vice president of policy and partnerships at the Southeast Center for Teaching Quality, Inc. Prior to working at the Center, Eric served as the executive director of the Alliance for Quality Teaching and as education program manager at the National Conference of State Legislatures. He has worked with and testified to legislatures and policy makers across the country and presented at numerous conferences about issues of teaching quality, school choice, and leadership. He has authored more than thirty articles, reports, book chapters, and policy briefs.

Mandy Hoke is a policy associate at the Southeast Center for Teaching Quality, Inc. where she leads a multistate case study project to examine the implementation of the highly qualified teacher mandates of No Child Left Behind. Prior to joining the Center, she taught at a high-poverty middle school in Durham, North Carolina. In 1998, she earned a BA in Afro-American Studies as a Morehead Scholar at the University of North Carolina at Chapel Hill and is an alumnus of the North Carolina Education Policy Fellowship Program. She has been selected as a Chancellor's Scholar to attend law school at UNC-Chapel Hill.

Douglas Kaufman is an assistant professor of curriculum and instruction with a specialization in Literacy Education at the University of Connecticut's Neag School of Education. Dr. Kaufman is the author of *Conferences and Conversations: Listening to the Literate Classroom* (Heineman). His work has appeared in *Language Arts*, *English Journal*, and *Thinking Classroom/Peremena*. He has coedited *Beyond the Boundaries: A Transdisciplinary Approach to Learning and Teaching* (Praeger). He currently teaches graduate and undergraduate courses in literacy education and writing.

Robert A. Lonning was a secondary science teacher for nearly twenty years in Minnesota before becoming a teacher educator at the University of Connecticut's Neag School of Education. Dr. Lonning was very active in science teacher education throughout Connecticut, serving on numerous boards and committees. Since his retirement from the faculty of the Neag School, he has been researching and developing alternative instructional models for secondary science teaching.

David M. Moss is an associate professor in the department of curriculum and instruction at the University of Connecticut's Neag School of Education. His current research interests are in the areas of science education reform and teacher education. As both a science educator and scientist, Dr. Moss has published widely in the areas of environmental science and science education on such diverse topics as student understandings of the nature of science, technology and education, curriculum reform, and forest health monitoring utilizing satellite capabilities. He has co-edited *Beyond the Boundaries: A Transdisciplinary Approach to Learning and Teaching*, published by Praeger. He currently teaches graduate and undergraduate courses in science education for preservice teachers.

Kay Norlander-Case is a retired professor of special education in the Neag School of Education at the University of Connecticut. Dr. Norlander-Case was instrumental in designing a conceptual model for the creation and nurturing of the reflective practitioner. She has spent countless hours working in urban settings advocating for underrepresented populations.

Sayward Parsons graduated with a master's degree from the University of Connecticut's Neag School of Education in 2002. She currently teaches ninth- and eleventh-grade English at New Canaan High School in New Canaan, Connecticut, where she also helps staff the Academic Center, a program providing reading and writing support for high school students. Sayward recently researched the effects of gender on reading and writing achievement and is working on a districtwide committee that is revamping New Canaan's K-12 Language Arts curriculum. She also collaborates with elementary and middle school English teachers to instruct a summer writing enrichment program in New Canaan for students of all ages. Ms. Parsons has been awarded a National Endowment for the Humanities fellowship to study Mark Twain at the Mark Twain House and Museum in Hartford, Connecticut.

Shirley Reilly is a veteran third-grade teacher at Dorothy C. Goodwin Elementary School in Storrs, Connecticut. She is a respected facilitator, collaborator, and leader for her grade-level team, school, and district. She is also a vital link in the University of Connecticut's Neag School of Education, serving as a member of its professional development committee and as a cooperating teacher for both undergraduate and graduate students. She is currently involved with two external grant initiatives to enhance instruction in mathematics and science. For her work in the field of science education, she was recently a corecipient of an award presented by the Neag School. Additionally, she was selected by the university to attend an educational leadership program with only fifteen other educators from across the United States and Canada.

Kate Rousmaniere is professor and chair of the department of educational leadership at Miami University, Ohio. A former high school teacher, her research centers on the history and politics of American teachers and methodological questions in the social history of education. Her publications include *City Teachers: Teaching and School Reform in Historical Perspective* (1997) and two coedited international volumes, *Discipline, Moral Regulation, and Schooling: A Social History* (1997) and *Silences and Images: A Social History of the Classroom* (1999). Dr. Rousmaniere is currently completing a biography (to be published by SUNY Press in 2005) of Margaret Haley, the turn-of-the-century leader of the Chicago Teachers' Federation.

Richard L. Schwab has been the dean of the Neag School of Education at the University of Connecticut since 1997. He began his academic career at the University of New Hampshire. He is active in the American Association of Colleges of Teacher Education. He has served on several state and national commissions on issues related to superintendent preparation, educational technology, and teacher education reform. In 2001, Dean Schwab was appointed to the National Commission for Teaching and America's Future. He has published extensively on issues related to teacher education, occupational stress and health in educational organizations, and educational technology.

John Settlage is an associate professor in the University of Connecticut's Neag School of Education. He began his career as a high school science teacher in Illinois and was also an elementary school science specialist in Missouri. Dr. Settlage has been involved in teacher education in Cleveland, Ohio, and Salt Lake City, Utah, and is known for his school-based research as well as his affinity to teach his university courses in urban and multicultural school settings. He was honored by the Association for the Education of Teachers of Science in 2001 as the Science Educator of the Year.

Karl F. Wheatley is an associate professor of early childhood education at Cleveland State University, where he teaches courses in early childhood education (PK-3), child development, and motivation. His main areas of expertise and interest are student and teacher motivation, early childhood curriculum, and education reform. His most recent work has focused on teacher efficacy beliefs and content standards. Dr. Wheatley received his B.A. in psychology from the University of Michigan, his M.A.T. in early childhood education from Oakland University, and his Ph.D. in educational psychology from Michigan State University.